# THE
# HITLER YOUTH

# THE HITLER YOUTH

A history of the Hitler Youth both in Germany and abroad and of the non-German youth movements which collaborated with it. Organization, structure, uniforms, flags, insignia.

By
DAVID LITTLEJOHN
(Assisted by Harry Hinds)

Library of Congress Catalog
Card Number 87073304

International Standard
Book Number (ISBN) 0-934870-21-7

Copyright © 1988 by

*Agincourt Publishers*

All rights reserved. No portion of this book may be reproduced or duplicated in any fashion without the express written permission from the copyright holder, Agincourt Publishers, except for brief quotations used in articles or books.

Printed in the United States of America by
THE R. L. BRYAN COMPANY
Columbia, South Carolina

# Contents

|  | PAGE |
|---|---|
| Introduction | vii |
| History of the Hitler Youth | 1 |
| Organizational Structure | 17 |
| Hitler Youth Ranks | 25 |
| Uniforms of the Hitler Youth | 27 |
| Flags and Pennants | 75 |
| Specialist Sections of the Hitler Youth | 81 |
| League of National-Socialist School Students NSS and NSSi | 113 |
| NS Factory Cell Organization | 117 |
| National-Socialist German Students Union | 119 |
| NSDSt.B Langemarck Scholarship | 127 |
| National Political Educational Institutes | 129 |
| NPEA Reichsschulen | 141 |
| Adolf Hitler Schools | 143 |
| NS Deutsche Oberschule Starnbergersee | 147 |
| Leadership Courses | 149 |
| Shooting Courses | 151 |
| Aeronautical Preparatory Tech. Schools | 153 |
| Deutsche Jungvolk | 155 |
| Bund Deutscher Mädel & Jungmädel | 177 |
| Sport | 195 |
| Camps and Foreign Visits | 205 |
| National Vocational Contest | 209 |
| Honour Badges & Awards | 215 |

# Contents

"Day" and Donation Badges .............................. 231
Daggers & Knives ........................................ 237
Hitler Youth at War ..................................... 245
Miscellaneous Facts & Figures ........................... 277
Documents & Posters ..................................... 281
Youth Resistance & Punishment ........................... 285
Unidentified or Partially Identified Items .............. 287
The Swastika Abroad ..................................... 289
The Germanic Landdienst ................................. 339
Central & Eastern Europe ................................ 341
Other Countries ......................................... 361
Bibliography ............................................ 375

# Introduction

"Prussia," said Mirabeau, the eighteenth-century French statesman, "is not so much a country with an army as an army with a country." Such a comment could be dismissed as merely facetious when applied to the domain of Frederick the Great, but which was close to literal truth with regard to that of Adolf Hitler. The National Socialists sought to convert the whole of Germany into a vast military camp where all were subject to strict discipline and supervision; a place where the will of only one man — Adolf Hitler — prevailed.

The groundwork for this intended conversion was the education of the very young. To be precise, the instruction of Germany's sons and daughters began at the impressionable age of ten. It was at that age that the Hitler Youth laid its hands on the children of the nation.

Nazi aspirations in this, as in so much else, outran their actual achievements. Nonetheless, the Hitler Youth and its associated bodies were to play a vital role in the master plan to conquer, in the words of one of their own songs, "... Today Germany, tomorrow the world...." Despite the attempts of some post-war German apologists to represent the Hitler Youth as some sort of ultra-patriotic boy scout movement, the inescapable fact remains that *all* its activities were geared towards only one end — war. As the stepping-stone into the SS (Schutzstaffel), the Hitler Youth was an integral and essential part of the Nazi apparatus of conquest and is, therefore, worthy of study.

This work is intended to provide both a general history and a detailed study of its structure, organization, uniforms and insignia. It also deals with a previously neglected aspect of its activity: its influence *outside* the German Reich.

Except where otherwise stated, the photographic illustrations of insignia were furnished by Harry Hinds, from a personal collection of outstanding merit. The author's thanks are also due to the following individuals for additional photographic input and/or information: Ver-Kulen Ager, Brian Ambrose, Klaus D. Benseler, Sony Berton, Lt. J. R. Cone, Brian L. Davis, Adrian Forman, Peter Groch, Indulis Kazocins, Dr. K-G Klietmann, Vaclav Mericka, Andrew Mollo, Karl Ortmann, Daniel Rose, Henry Rüütel, Wim Saris, Otto Spronk, Peter D. Stachura, Ian Staveley, Fred J. Stephens, Hugh P. Taylor, Jan Vincx, Heinz D. Weese and C. van Wiele. Thanks must also go to John Coy, Kurt Barickman, Ron Manion, Roger S. Steffen, Helga Sichermann-Spielhagen, F. Patt Anthony, Francis Catella, Keith Hynds, and Glenna Blevins.

# 1

## History of the Hitler Youth

The National Socialist German Workers Party (NSDAP) was founded in Munich, Bavaria, on August 8, 1920. Its first preoccupation was, naturally enough, the winning of adult support. It turned its attention to youth only later and, at this stage, without any great degree of enthusiasm. In August 1921 it appealed "to our German youth" to form athletic and sports groups within the NSDAP. It was not until February 1922 that Hitler, in response to numerous enquiries as to why, unlike other political parties, the NSDAP embodied no youth branch, decided that the time had come for one to be formed.

In its issue of March 18, 1922 the Party's official mouthpiece, the *Völkischer Beobachter* announced the creation of the *Jugendbund der NSDAP* (Youth Union of the NSDAP). The inaugural meeting of this new body took place in the well-known beer cellar in Munich (scene of much frenzied Nazi activity) on May 13th, but could hardly be described as an overwhelming success. Only seventeen youth enrolled! Adolf Lenk, an unemployed nineteen-year-old, was named Leader of the *Jugendbund*, a post directly subordinate to the chief of the SA (Storm Troops). The *Jugendbund* was divided into two age groups, both for males only, there being no girls section at this time:

(i) *Jungmannschaften* (14- to 16-year-olds);
(ii) *Jungsturm Adolf Hitler* (16- to 18-year-olds).

The latter was, in effect, a junior section of the SA. It made its first public appearance at Hitler's celebrated sally into Communist-dominated Coburg in October 1922. A number of right-wing groups planned to hold a "German Day" in that city on the 14th and 15th of that month. They invited Hitler to attend, and to "bring along a few friends." He arrived with an 800-man SA contingent (which included a section of the *Jungsturm Adolf Hitler*) — and a military band! A street battle ensued which the Nazis claimed as a famous victory. It was the first "blooding" of the NSDAP's youthful followers.

The "Battle of Coburg," if it did nothing else, did at least achieve widespread publicity for Hitler's cause. The *Jugendbund*, initially only Bavarian-based, expanded under Lenk's energetic direction to form branches throughout the Reich. It held its first "National Congress" in May 1923 in Munich.

In November of that year Hitler made a move that very nearly proved to be his undoing. He attempted to seize power in Munich and overthrow the State government of Bavaria by force. The *Putsch* of November 9th was a dismal failure. The authorities showed far greater resolution in the face of his threats than he had anticipated. The police opened fire on the marchers (who included Germany's illustrious Great War leader, General Erich Ludendorff) killing sixteen of them. Hitler, along with those leaders not fortunate enough to escape to the safety of neighbouring Austria, was arrested. He was sentenced to five years penal servitude, but in fact was released (under amnesty) after rather less than one year.

In Nazi history, 1924 remains the "missing year." The NSDAP did not actually disappear from the political scene during this time but, bereft of Hitler's dynamic leadership, it floundered and fragmented. For his part, Hitler did nothing to rectify this situation. The ineffectual Alfred Rosenberg was, theoretically, acting leader in Hitler's absence. In practice the Party simply drifted out of control.

The *Jungsturm Adolf Hitler* had been intended to participate in the November *Putsch* but, due to an error in communication, failed to do so. Hence Lenk and his associates were not among those arrested in the wake of its failure. The NSDAP was declared illegal. This, of course, included its youth section. Lenk tried to resurrect the *Jugendbund* under the name *Väterlandischer Jugendverband Grossdeutschlands* (Patriot Youth Association of Greater Germany), but the police were not taken in by this transparent artifice and Lenk was arrested. Released after a brief sojourn in custody, Lenk again tried to revive the *Jugenbund*, this time with the title *Grossdeutsche Jugendbewegung* (Greater German Youth Movement), but was again arrested and imprisoned. He was released on December 20, 1924 under the same amnesty that freed Hitler (and from the same prison).

Lenk's had not been the only attempt to keep a National Socialist youth functioning during Hitler's absence. The former *Jugenbund* leader in Saxony, Kurt Gruber, also formed a *Grossdeutsche Jungendbewegung* (GDJB). Gruber, a 20-year-old law student was, however, more successful than Lenk in this venture. In the first place, the State government of Saxony, unlike that of Bavaria, did not declare the GDJB illegal and Gruber was also successful in enlisting the support of other rightwing bodies such as Ludendorff's *Tannenbergbund*. Gruber renamed the GDJB the *Frontjugend* and it was accorded the status of youth branch of the SA, which at this time was operating under the name *Frontbann*.\*

The NSDAP was officially refounded on February 27, 1925 with Hitler as its unchallenged Leader. He was, however, in no great haste to re-establish its youth section preferring to weigh first the claims of the various rival aspirants. Apart from Lenk and Gruber, there was a serious contender in the person of the former *Freikorps* leader, Gerhard

---

\* *Bann* has, in German as in English, the punning double meaning of Band/Banned. Thus the name could be taken as Front Band or Banned Front.

Rossbach, who in 1924 had formed in Salzburg, Austria, his own youth group, known as the *Schilljugend*. Rossbach had taken part in the November *Putsch* but fled to Austria to avoid arrest. A close friend of influential Nazis such as Captain Röhm (whose homosexual proclivities he shared), Rossbach turned to Germany in 1926 after the declaration of a general amnesty for political offenders.

The *Schilljugend* professed a well-nigh identical philosophy to that of the erstwhile *Jugenbund*. During Rossbach's enforced exile, the German branch of the *Schilljugend*, under the provisional leadership of *SA-Gruppenführer* Edmund Heines, had acted as a sort of semi-official Nazi youth movement. It might indeed have achieved official status had not Rossbach, in the course of a stormy interview with Hitler in February 1926, refused to allow his youth group to be submerged within the NSDAP. Hitler demanded absolute obedience from his followers. Rossbach, although sympathetic with the main Nazi tenets, was not prepared to place himself under Hitler's total and unquestionable authority.

Disillusioned with Hitler's vacillation, the Party's general lack of interest in youth matters, and personal intrigues against himself, Lenk dropped out of the running. Gruber suffered from none of Rossbach's reluctance to accept Hitler's absolute dominance. His GDJB (it had reverted to this, its original designation, after severing its connection with the youth of the *Tannenbergbund)* was now granted recognition as the official youth movement of the NSDAP.

At the second *Reichsparteitag* (National Party Rally) at Weimar on July 3rd/4th, 1926, the GDJB was re-christened the *Hitler-Jugend*. Just as there is often controversy over who was first with any new concept or invention, so there is some question as to whose idea it was to adopt this title for the young persons section of the NSDAP. Credit is often given to Julius Streicher, the notorious Jew-baiting *Gauleiter* of Franconia, but in fact, a *Hitler-Jugend* group had been created some twelve months previously by Hans Ziegler, the Deputy *Gauleiter* of Thuringia. Whether Streicher had heard of this group or whether his choice was pure coincidence, is impossible to say. Certainly Streicher thereafter always claimed it was *his* invention! The full title adopted was *Hitler-Jugend, Bund deutscher Arbeiterjugend* (Hitler Youth, Union of German Worker Youth).

Kurt Gruber was confirmed as its leader under the high-sounding title of *Reichsführer der HJ* (National Leader of the HJ); membership at this time was hardly more than seven hundred in the whole of Germany! Gruber preferred to retain his headquarters at Plauen (Saxony) rather than move to Munich, the self-styled "Capital of the Movement," in an attempt to preserve the independence of the youth branch. Nonetheless its subordination to both the SA and the Party was confirmed by orders of October 27th (which made Gruber answerable to the Chief of Staff of the SA) and December 5th which ordained that all HJ personnel, on reaching the age of eighteen, must automatically enroll as members of the NSDAP.

Rossbach's *Schilljugend* continued to soldier on, but soon disintegrated amid the personal squabbles of its leaders. Gruber's task now was to bring within the orbit of the Hilter Youth as many as possible of the National Socialist youth associations in Germany and Austria.

---

In the annals of German youth a prominent, indeed, a preeminent place must be accorded to the *Wandervogel* movement. First conceived in Steglitz (near Berlin) in 1896, the *Wandervogel* (roughly, "Birds of Passage") was intended to organize what today would be termed "nature rambles" and hiking excursions for school children. At first, such outings were confined to boys, although later extended to girls, the sexes being strictly segregated in accordance with the *mores* of the time. There was little that was novel in this concept — German children had been taken on nature study trips by their teachers for years. What *was* unique was the fact that the leaders of the *Wandervogel* were not adults, but other young persons. The notion that "youth must be led by youth," so eagerly adopted later by the HJ, was born in the *Wandervogel*.

The great success of the *Wandervogel* in Germany and the phenomenal success of the Boy Scout Movement worldwide would seem to indicate that there was a vast youth "market" only waiting to be tapped. Both organizations developed at roughly the same time, the early years of the twentieth century. The *Wandervogel* adopted an individual style, or styles of dress, and greeted one another with the word, *"Heil."* "Ranks," using such terms as *Bursche, Bachant,* and *Oberbachant,* derived from the wandering scholars of medaeval Germany. Promotion depended on the number of trips undertaken and manifestations of interest or leadership. Apart from studying nature, a great deal of time was devoted to German folk history, folk songs, folk tales and accounts of Germany's legendary heros, such as those featured in Richard Wagner's *Ring* cycle of musical dramas.

There was about the *Wandervogel* more than a hint of youthful rebellion against the materialistic values of Wilhelmine Germany, a society even more repressive and stifling than that of Victorian England. Before the outbreak of the First World War, the *Wandervogel* movement had spread throughout Germany and Austro-Hungary. War destroyed the element of youthful idealism and romanticism of the part that had characterized the *Wandervogel*.

Bitterness entered the soul of German youth. New types of youth associations sprang up all over the defeated Reich. These may be divided into roughly two main groups — the *völkisch* (a word which, in this context, translates somewhere between "folksy" and "racist"), and the *bündische*, which is even more difficult to render in English, but indicates groups "brought together in leagues or fraternities," in the non-academic sense of the latter word.

The *völkisch* groups drew on the same folk sources as the *Wandervogel*, but the "national folk community" which they envisaged was xenophobic. Of all "foreign" elements, the Jews were the most detested. There was a great deal of praise for the virtues of peasant life. The Weimar Republic was denounced as corrupt and its early demise confidently predicted.

The *bündische Jugend* shared this loathing of, and contempt for, the new Republic, and almost all groups were, to a greater or lesser degree, anti-Semitic. There was, however, no consensus on the subject of what political system should replace the Republic. Every political party, every religions denomination, every sectional interest group — even every war veterans association — had its youthful affiliate. Few had any reverence for democracy. There was a marked inclination towards élitism and a belief in the role of the inspirational leader. Some able, if eccentric, characters did emerge. None could convince the others to accept his particular brand of leadership. Whereas, the *völkisch* groups espoused the values of "blood and soil," the *bündische*, at least those on the right, preferred "blood and iron." They drew their inspiration from German military history. It is not hard to judge the qualities most admired by groups who assumed names such as *Bismarck, York von Wartenburg, Tannenberg, Hindenburg*, or *Scharnhorst*.

There was a growing tendency among the various *Bünde*, right or left wing, to adopt a uniform, usually taking the form of shorts, a particular colour of shirt (white, blue, brown, or grey), and some special type of headgear, such as the beret. Each group had its own emblem and banner.

Longer excursions lasting not a day, as in the pre-war *Wandervogel*, but several days, became customary. Hostels sprang up all over Germany to meet the requirement. The guitar of the *Wandervogel* was replaced by the drum or trumpet; military songs supplanted the folksy ballads.

Into this world the Hitler Youth emerged, drawing on the tradition of both the *völkisch* and *bündisch* groups. From the former it took the concept of the folk community with its faith in the character-forming qualities of agricultural labour (the Nazi *Landjahr* was a typical *völkisch* precept). Borrowings from the *bündische* youth were many. There was indeed little that differentiated the Hitler Youth from the host of other *Bünde*, with their coloured shirts, flags, drums, marching songs, "war games," and celebration of pagan rituals, such as the summer or winter solstice. (In the more religious *Bünde* these festivities, essentially pre-Christian, were camouflaged as traditional church rights and accompanied by prayers led by clergymen. No such hypocrisy was, of course, practiced in their observance of the rituals by the Nazis.) Much HJ nomenclature derived from *bündische* sources — words as *Bann, Stamm, Schar, Ortsgruppe*, and *Gau*, for example. Even that extremely non-German form of headcovering, the beret, popular in *Wandervogel* and *bündische* circles was adopted, even if only briefly, by the Hitler Youth. The short blue blouse of the Nazi *Jungvolk* was modelled on one designed by Eberhard Köbel, leader of a non-Nazi *Bund*. Even the swastika, an ancient Aryan symbol, was not exclusive to the Nazis.

The youth of the NSDAP could so easily have become only one among a host of *bündische* groups, noteworthy for nothing except perhaps its greater propensity towards physical violence, just as the NSDAP itself could equally easily have been just another to add to the already existing twenty-six political parties in Germany, had it not been for one single factor — in Adolf Hitler they possessed a leader of genius, evil genius, no doubt, but one who stood head and shoulders above the pigmy politicians of the Weimar Republic.

A minor example of Hitler's political acumen was his refusal to accept any form of youthful alliance, a so-called Youth Front of right-wing *bündische* groups eager to join him, such as *Adler und Falken, Freischar Schill* (a breakaway section of Rossbach's *Schilljugend*, led by Werner Lass), *Geusen, Freischar Junger Nation, Jungwolf, Scharnhorstjugend,* and the *Bund der Artamenen.* Hitler appreciated that alliances involve policy compromises and joint leadership decisions — two things to which he was implacably opposed. Also, he did not fail to perceive that some of the groups preferred talking to action, something which he despised. He adopted the same attitude toward supplicants as that of the Catholic church toward would-be converts; accept completely our authority or remain outside.

Friendly relations were maintained with these and other right-wing *Bünde* (Hitler was not above "borrowing" some of their emblems for HJ use, e.g., the crossed hammer and sword of the *Geusen* was taken over for an early HJ flag), but a "Youth Front" as such he would never countenance.

The temptation to augment its youthful following by accepting a right-wing alliance must have been real enough. HJ membership increased painfully slowly; worse, there were isolated cases of defection. In some districts the term *Hitlerjugend* was dropped and only the subtitle, *Bund deutscher Arbeiterjugend* (BDAJ), was used in an effort to enhance its proletarian image and attract uncommitted young workers away from the Communist *Jugend-Internationale* or the Socialist *Jugendverband.* The BDAJ also challenged Gruber's authority. Fortunately for him, it failed in its purpose of winning over large numbers of working class lads and quickly faded from the picture.

Between 1926 and 1929, HJ enrollment rose from around 700 to 1,300 members, but this compared very unfavorably with the growth of NSDAP membership and was infinitesimal when seen against a background of total youth association enrollments in Germany at this time, which stood at a remarkable 4,338,850 members.**

In January 1926 Wilhelm Tempel founded a Nazi group among university students (NSDSt.B). In July 1928 its leadership was assumed by a twenty-one-year-old student at the University of Munich: His name was Baldur von Schirach.

---

\*\* Such a precise computation is possible since all youth associations had to be officially registered with the National Committee of German Youth Associations in Berlin and membership figures reported.

In view of the prominent part that this young man was destined to play in the history of the Hitler Youth, his background is not without interest, especially since it differed so markedly from that of the average Nazi leader.

The von Schirachs were an aristocratic family (ennobled by the Empress Maria Theresa in 1776, hence *von* Schirach) which had strong connections with the United States. Baldur's paternal great-grandfather emigrated to America in 1855 and his son, Friedrich Karl, served as a Major in the Union Army during the Civil War, subsequently marrying into one of America's patrician families. In 1871 he returned to Germany with his American wife, where Baldur's father, Karl Baily Norris von Schirach, was born. Von Schirach *père* remained in Germany, pursuing the career of an army officer, but reinforced the United States family connection by marrying an American girl, a Miss Emma Middleton Tillou of Philadelphia, in 1896. Baldur, the offspring of this union, was born on March 9, 1907. The following year his father resigned his commission to become director of the theater at Weimar.

Brought up the pampered child of well-to-do parents with artistic leanings, young Baldur was dispatched to Munich University to study art history and German folklore.

In Munich, the epicenter of the Nazi movement, Baldur became a member of the inner circle of its leadership, through his friendship with Hitler's personal photographer, Heinrich Hoffmann, whose daughter he later married. He enrolled in the NSDAP on May 9, 1925 (Party number 17,251) and at the same time, he joined the ranks of the SA (among the burly stalwarts of the Storm Troops, young Baldur's epicene features and podgy build were the cause of some caustic humor!). Less interested in study than in politics, Baldur was an active and successful organizer of the NSDSt.B,*** whose *Reichsführer* he became on the resignation of Tempel. The BDAJ had manifestly failed to proselytise the young of the working class. The NSDSt.B, on the other hand, had made notable strides in winning over the sons of the wealthy. Adrian von Renteln's League of National Socialist School Students (NSS), founded in 1929 to spread the word among pupils at secondary schools (almost exclusively the children of middle- or upper-class parents), had also done well.

The significance of these facts was not lost on Hitler. The NSDAP was winning greater support among the middle classes than among the workers. The time was right for a change in tone. Fortune smiled on von Schirach. Gruber, well aware of von Schirach's ambition to succeed him as HJ Leader, had cause for concern. His fears could hardly have been eased when, in May 1931, he was ordered to remove his headquarters from Plauen and relocated them in Munich. Clearly Hitler wanted to place a tighter rein on HJ activities.

At the Nürnberg Rally of 1929, the HJ had been able to muster 2,000 youths, almost half of them from Austria. Now Gruber began a frantic effort to increase numbers. He delivered himself of the wildly optimistic

---

*** Schirach did not fare as well at the university; he never graduated.

assertion that he would shortly push membership up to 50,000, "... with an HJ unit in every German town, village, and hamlet...." His inability to translate his claim into anything approaching reality, coupled with his failure to exercise firm control over unruly subordinates, resulted in his peremptory dismissal by Hitler in 1931. The organization of the NSDAP youth was restructured by Hitler who, on October 30th, issued the following decree:

(1) Within the framework of the Supreme Command of the SA a new office of *Reichsjugendführer* (RJF) has been established;
(2) The *Reichsjugendführer* is directly responsible to the Chief of Staff of the SA. I appoint Party Comrade von Schirach to the post of *Reichsjugendführer;*
*(3) The administrative competence of the Reichsjugendführer* comprises the following:
(a) NSDSt.B (under von Schirach)
(b) Hitler-Jugend (under Adrian von Renteln)
(c) NSS (under Adrian von Renteln)
(4) The RJF is advisor to the Staff of the Supreme Command of the SA on all youth matters ... his rank is that of *Gruppenführer,* his uniform has yet to be determined.

At twenty-four years of age von Schirach now occupied what was soon to prove one of the key posts in the Nazi hierarchy.

The new HJ Leader, von Renteln set about cleaning up the administrative chaos bequeathed him by Gruber whose lax control had allowed to slip by unchecked profligate conduct on the part of subordinates bordering, in a few instances, on criminality. For example, Robert Gadewoltz, leader of the Berlin HJ (total membership less than 500) had rented a nine-room office and paid himself a monthly salary of RM 400. The net result was a deficit of HJ funds to the tune of some RM 4000.

Numerous incompetent HJ bosses were dismissed or downgraded, their places being taken in the main by former NSS and NSDSt.B leaders. The class composition of the HJ had been radically altered by the time von Renteln resigned in June 1932. Von Schirach now assumed personal control of both the HJ and the NSS (which the latter was shortly thereafter obliged to merge with the HJ). Thus in July 1932 von Schirach had become the indisputable *supremo* of the NSDAP's youth, and within a year of all Germany's youth.

Gruber's dream of a membership of 50,000 was achieved and surpassed before the end of 1932, although this was due less to von Schirach's leadership than to the economic devastation of the Great Depression. Extremists on both left and right gained as a result of public despair and resentment. The Weimar Republic was visibly tottering. In its justifiable alarm at the escalation of street violence, the authorities tried to ban all political militias. Hitler foresaw this possibility, and, fearing that the HJ might be banned along with its SA "parent," decided to sever the formal link between the two. On May 13, 1932 he issued a decree which released the HJ from its subordination to the Chief of Staff of the SA. Von Schirach was elevated to the status of a Department Head *(Amtsleiter)* at NSDAP headquarters answerable only to Hitler. The Hilter Youths' independence was now absolute.

The decree came too late, however, to save the HJ from the ban which was nationwide and in force from April 13th until it was repealed on June 17th.

In the General Election of July 31, 1932 the NSDAP won 230 seats in the *Reichstag*, making it the largest single party, although without an overall majority. Among the new *Reichstag* deputies was Baldur von Schirach.

By way of celebrating his success, von Schirach arranged for a National Youth Day to be held at Potsdam that October. The RJF anticipated a possible turnout of around 20,000. The reality surpassed his wildest expectations. Some 100,000 young persons (15,000 of them girls) took part in a giant rally on October 1st/2nd. It was a triumph for Hitler and von Schirach. Only three years previously the HJ contingent at Nürnberg had numbered a mere 2,000.

A second general election was held on November 6, 1932. In it the Nazis lost some of the ground they had won in July but still remained the largest single party in the *Reichstag*. After a series of backstairs deals and intrigues which need not concern us here, President Hindenburg appointed Hitler Chancellor (Prime Minister) of Germany on January 30, 1933.

That once in power the Nazis should have sought to eliminate their enemies and rivals is in no way surprising; what *is* remarkable is the speed and apparent ease with which this was achieved. The burning of the *Reichstag* building in February was blamed on the Communists and was quickly followed by an enabling law which virtually eliminated all political opposition and gave Hitler a free hand. By that July the NSDAP was the sole permitted political party in Germany.

The annual enrollment in the HJ and BDM, which took place each April 20th, was significantly greater in the April of 1933 as many hastened to jump on the Nazi bandwagon. These young opportunists were sarcastically referred to by the regulars as "the April violets."

Certain of the *bündische* groups voluntarily aligned themselves with the Hitler Youth by adding its brassard to their existing uniform. The first to do so was the *Scharnhorst Jugend*. Its alacrity in this respect won it the right to wear its badge on the left breast pocket when later it was ordered to adopt a full HJ uniform. Other *bündische* groups which followed the example of the *Scharnhorst Jugend*, were *Bismarck Jugend, Jungwolf, Jungdeutscher Orden, Hindenburg Jugend, Adler und Falken* (and its breakaway, *Deutsche Falkenschaft)*, and Werner Lass' *Freischar Schill*.

The youth sections of the outlawed left-wing political parties vanished, of course, with the parties themselves. This still left in existence a number of right-wing, or politically uncommitted, youth groups. From these a vain attempt was made to organize not so much a rival, as an alternative, nationalist youth movement. The author of this foolhardy venture was a distinguished naval officer, Vice Admiral Adolf Trotha (former Chief of Staff of the Imperial Navy). His *Grossdeutsche Bund* brought to *Deutsche Freischar*, the *Freischar Junger Nation* (formerly called the *Jungnationaler Bund)*, the *Jungsturm Kolberg*, the *Deutsche Kolberg*, the *Deutsche Pfadfinderbund* (The German Boy Scouts[†]) and the *Geusen* in a confederation whose aims and outlook differed little from those of the Nazis. The project was doomed from the start. That Hitler would tolerate *any* alternative youth movement to that which bore his name was inconceivable. An Easter rally (1933) of the *Bund* was broken up by the police. A month later the Nazi-controlled press announced that the *Grossdeutsche Bund* had "voluntarily dissolved itself." Trotha protested but was placated by being named "Honorary Commander-in-Chief of the Marine HJ" (a mainly ceremonial post, since it involved little more than inspection duties).

The records of the Reichs Committee of German Youth Associations were seized by the Hitler Youth and the Committee replaced by a von Schirach invention, "The German Youth Leaders Council." Since all other youth groups had been ousted by this time the Council was left with no function whatsoever!

On June 17, 1933 a significant alteration was announced to the title borne by von Schirach. He became *Jugendführer des deutschen Reiches* (Youth Leader of the German Reich). Now *all* German youth came within the sphere of his authority. Before the end of 1933 all *bündische* groups had been absorbed into the Hitler Youth; with the sole exception of the *Bund der Artamenen* (shortly to be transformed into the HJ *Landjahr)*. Non-political youth bodies such as the European Youth Exchange and the German Youth Hostels Association were also swallowed up by the HJ. Only religious youth bodies remained outside its jurisdiction. It would be a misconception to suppose that the churches were unanimous in their opposition to the Nazis. What religious opposition there was emerged only later when the true nature of the Hitler regime became apparent. Certainly the Nazis encountered resistance from the Catholic youth leadership, but this was, perhaps, less due to hostility towards Nazism as such than to the normal reluctance of the Roman church to permit *any* outside interference in the education of its young.

The Protestants proved less intractable. Even a group with such an apparently devotional title as the *Bibelkreis* (Bible Circle) counted some 70% Nazi support among its members!

The concordat concluded with the Vatican in July 1933 provided for mutual non-intervention in church/state matters. If, as was agreed, the Church did not intrude in the political scene, the State for its part, Hitler promised, would not interfere with the right of Catholics to bring up their young as they saw fit. Like all Hilter's promises, this one did not long remain unbroken.

---

[†] The Boy Scout movement in Germany was, by this time, sadly fragmented. It had lost popularity after the war due to its British origin. The *Pfadfinderbund* was only one of several factions.

The death of President Hindenburg in August 1934 finally consolidated Hilter's power. He now combined in his own person the offices of President and Reichs Chancellor.

Likewise the year 1934 saw the consolidation of the power of the Hitler Youth. One dramatic event in the course of that year greatly strengthened its position. In June, on the pretext that the SA was planning a revolt against his authority, Hitler had most of its leaders shot, including his one-time closest associate, Captain Röhm. The instrument of the execution was Himmler's SS. It was a significant and symbolic act. Once the Hitler Youth had been a little-regarded adjunct to the powerful SA, while the SS had been no more than a handful of devoted personal bodyguards of the Führer. Unfortunately for itself, the SA had become redundant. It was no longer needed to clear the streets and terrorize political opponents; these were by now exiled, dead, or in concentration camps. Worse, the SA had become an embarrassment. Captain Röhm talked rashly about transforming it into a "people's army." Since Hitler was already planning to rebuild the German army (he re-introduced conscription in March 1935) this ran directly counter to his wishes.

As the power and prestige of the SA declined, that of the SS and HJ increased. The SS had proven its loyalty by its unhesitating readiness to murder its SA colleagues. It could now be entrusted with greater responsibilities. The HJ represented the Nazi élite of tomorrow; from its ranks would come the future leaders of the Reich. Cooperation between the SS and the HJ became closer, and before the end of the war the two had merged their interests almost completely.

Von Schirach's star was in the ascendant. SA leaders could no longer afford to mock the plump, boyish HJ Leader behind his back. The year 1934 saw the compulsory incorporation into the Hitler Youth of all boys under eighteen years of age who were members of sport and athletic clubs. It also witnessed the demise of the last of the *bündische* groups, with the transformation of the *Bund der Artamenen* into the *Landjahr der HJ*. Membership continued to grow, but this was not an unmixed blessing, since it brought with it the problem of finding suitable leaders. The HJ might have been willing to accept *en masse* the rank and file of the disbanded *bündische* groups, but it was far from ready to grant their former leaders corresponding positions within its own organizational framework. Indeed erstwhile *bündische* leaders were looked upon with suspicion and mistrust. Those who had remained aloof during the HJ's years of struggle could not expect to find a welcome within its *Führerschaft*.

There was no alternative but to train new leaders. Even with the institution of crash training programmes and the accelerated promotion of "old fighters," the HJ found it hard to meet the demands made upon it. For this reason obligatory HJ service, even as a theoretical possibility, was delayed for nearly four years. On December 1, 1936, *The Law for the Hitler Youth* was promulgated. It stated:

>The future of the German nation depends upon its youth. The whole of the German youth must therefore be prepared for its future duties. The government of the Reich has accordingly decided on the following law which is published herewith:
>
>(i) The whole of German youth within the frontiers of the Reich is organized in the Hitler Youth;
>
>(ii) The whole of German youth is to be educated, outside the parental home and school, in the Hitler Youth physically, intellectually and morally, in the spirit of National Socialism, for service to the nation and community;
>
>(iii) The task of educating the whole of German youth in the Hitler Youth is being entrusted to the *Reichsjugendführer* of the NSDAP. He is, therefore, Youth Leader of the German Reich and has the status of a Supreme Reich Authority, with headquarters in Berlin and is directly responsible to the *Führer und Reichskanzler*.
>
>(iv) The requisite legal decrees and general administrative orders for the carrying-out and implementation of this law will be issued by the *Führer und Reichskanzler*."

The above decree was published in the *Reichsgesetzblatt* (official gazette) on December 3, 1936. Its wording was, perhaps, deliberately vague. What did "... organized in the Hitler Youth ..." mean? It gave legal status to the *possibility* of obligatory HJ service without actually introducing it. In practice, compulsion was not applied until some three years later and then only to boys in the upper age categories.

Voluntary enlistment, whether out of conviction or opportunism (many careers now depended on evidence of HJ service), continued, exacerbating the twin shortages of leaders and accommodation. An additional problem now arose: It is easy enough to excite the enthusiasm of youth; much harder to sustain it. During the *Kampfzeit*, HJ service had been novel, often illegal, sometimes physically dangerous, always improvisatory and exciting. Now there was a risk that it could degenerate into a dull weekly routine, devoid of any purpose, since the political "enemy" no longer existed. To counteract this, new branches, such as the *Motor-*, *Flieger-*, and *Reiter-HJ* were brought into being, which catered to a wider range of interests than previously. In addition, there were constant rallies, sports competitions and camping excursions. These latter were soon extended to visits abroad to communities of racial Germans (the so-called *Volksdeutsche)* beyond the frontiers of the Reich, thus providing a useful expansion of Nazi propaganda.

Von Schirach embraced with enthusiasm all the current idiocies of the time: neo-paganism, anti-intellectualism, anti-Semitism and, of course, Hitler-idolatry; passions he tried to communicate to his youthful followers through the medium of poetry (or doggerel!), which it was his wont to compose. It has to be said that later he seems to have come to regret these follies of his youth, possibly under the influence of his wife who, on one occasion, angered Hitler by telling him to his face that Germany's treatment of Jews was "brutal."

In March 1935 Hitler reintroduced compulsory military service, something expressly forbidden by the Treaty of Versailles. The following year he again defied the Treaty by reoccupying the Rhineland. From then on it could be said that he kept Europe in a state of continuous crisis. Despite the efforts of well-intentioned persons in the West to convince themselves and others that after the horrors of 1914-1918, a new war was unthinkable, it should have been clear from the outset that it was Hilter's intention, as soon as Germany was militarily strong enough, to embark upon a war of conquest. In this grand design the Hilter Youth was intended to play an important role.

Compulsory HJ service was finally introduced on March 25, 1939, but even then it was applied only to males in the "class" of 1923 (seventeen-year-olds). It was not until September 12, 1941 that service became obligatory for both sexes from the age of ten onward.

Prior to the first introduction of obligatory service, the HJ had in 1939 a membership of around eight million. This might seem like a triumph for the voluntary principle, but since the total number of young persons in the ten- to eighteen-year-old age group was at this time in the region of twelve million; it meant that roughly one third of Germany's youth had refused to join.

*The history of the Hitler Youth during the war years is chronicled in a later chapter.*

# NOTES ON SOME OF THE BÜNDISCHE GROUPS OF THE GERMAN RIGHT

(a) *Adler und Falken* (Eagle and Falcon): founded at Bad Salzbrunn (Lower Silesia) in 1920. By 1932 it had 3,300 members.

(b) *Deutsche Falkenschaft:* A breakaway from the above, established in 1929.

(c) *Geusen:* Founded in 1919, it had about 1,500 members by the early '30s. The name, literally "Beggars" (French *Gueux*) derived from the resistance movement in the Netherlands at the time of the Spanish occupation. Of all the *Bünde*, the *Geusen* was the most pro-Hitler and was, in fact the *only* one to which Hitler Youth members were allowed simultaneously to belong. It was only its distaste for the personality of von Schirach that made it choose to join the *Grossdeutsche Jugendbewegung* of Admiral Trotha in 1933 instead of opting for union with the HJ.

(d) *Schilljugend* (full title: *Wehrjugendverband Schill):* Founded by Gerhard Rossbach in Salzburg (Austria) in 1924 with only 250 members.

(e) *Freischar Schill:* A breakaway from the above, formed in 1927 by Werner Lass. By 1932 it had a membership of about 1,500. The name derived from Ferdinand von Schill (1776-1809), a hero of Germany's "War of Liberation" against Napoleon.

(f) *Scharnhorstjugend:* This was the junior branch of the *Jungstahlhelm*, which was in its turn for younger (non-war veteran) members of the massive *Stahlhelm* (Steel Helmet) organization. By 1930 it had over 5,000 members. Named after Gerhard von Scharnhorst (1755-1813), co-founder with Gneisenau of the German General Staff.

(g) *Hindenburgjugend:* This was the youth branch of the DVP *(Deutsche Volkspartei)*, the German People's Party. It had a membership of some 12,000 by the early '30s.

(h) *Bismarckjugend:* The youth of the DNVP *(Deutsche-Nationale Volkspartei)*, the German National People's Party. By 1930 it had around 40,000 members.

(i) *Jungsturm Kolberg:* The oldest of the right-wing *bündische* groups, dating back to 1897, and taking its name from a celebrated defensive battle in 1807 during the "War of Liberation." By 1930 it had a membership of about 25,000. It must not be confused with either the Nazis' *Jungsturm Adolf Hitler*, the Communists' *Rote Jungsturm*, or the *Jungsturm* of the Social Democratic Reichsbanner Black, Red, Gold.

(j) *Jungwolf:* The youth section of the semi-clandestine war veterans association known by the intentionally punning name of *Wehrwolf*. The adults were very closely associated with the SA.

Adler und Falken

Geusen
(a) First design (b) Second design

Schilljugend

Scharnhorst Jugend

Hindenburg Jugend

Bismarck Jugend

Jugendbund Graf York von Wartenburg*

Jungwolf

Jungdeutscher Orden
(a) Boys (b) Girls

Freischar Junger Nation

Freischar Schill

Deutsche Freischar

* An example of a non-Nazi *Bund* which employed the swastika as an emblem.

## ORGANIZATIONAL STRUCTURE OF THE HITLER YOUTH

The Main Districts (*Gebiete*) of the Hitler Youth as they existed at the start of the Second World War.

# 2

# *Organizational Structure*

Due to the lack of importance that Hitler at first attached to youth participation in his movement, the structural organization of the HJ remained for several years loose and ill-organized. In 1926 the age subdivision was as follows:

| | |
|---|---|
| *Knabenmannschaften:* | Boys 10-14 years old; |
| *Jungmannschaften:* | Boys 14-16 years old; |
| *Wanderabteilungen:* | Boys 16-18 years old. |

Only the last mentioned group was held to be of any real value and was organized into:

| | |
|---|---|
| *Gruppen* | (the smallest unit); |
| *Scharen* | (squads) |
| *Abteilungen* | (detachments) |

(The term *Wanderabteilungen* would appear to have been derived from the *Wandervogel* movement.)

A number of *Wanderabteilungen* linked to form an *Ortsgruppe* under the command of an *Ortsgruppenführer*. In turn, a collection of *Ortsgruppen* comprised a *Bezirk* under a *Bezirksführer*. Finally, several *Berzirke* went to make up a *Gau* under a *Gauführer*, the second most senior rank in the HJ. At the head of the whole organization was the *Reichsführer der HJ* (Kurt Gruber) who, as noted in the previous chapter, was made subordinate to the Supreme Command of the SA as from November 1, 1926.

In 1930 the term *Wanderabteilungen* for the sixteen- to eighteen-year-old group was changed to *Scharjungen*. Each of its *Gruppen* comprised eight lads, and two or three *Gruppen* each went to make up a *Schar*. The inelegantly named *Knabenmannschaften* (literally, "boys crews") became the *Deutsche Jungvolk*, although its exact relationship to the HJ remained tenuous until the following year (1931), when it was formally linked to that organization as its junior branch.

In 1931 the organizational structure of the HJ was brought much more closely into line with that of its SA parent. Within the SA the word *Gruppe* indicated the (then) largest formation. The HJ command was now nationwide (even extraterritorial, since it included both Austria and the Free City of Danzig): To be like the SA the Hitler Youth was now restructured in ten *Gruppen*. These were:

1. Ostland      (Danzig-East Prussia)
2. Ost          (East)
3. Nord         (North)
4. Nordwest     (Northwest)
5. West
6. Südwest      (Southwest)
7. Süd          (South)
8. Mitte        (Central)
9. Schlesien    (Silesia)
10. Oesterreich (Austria)

Each of the above was subdivided into a number of *Gaue*, two of which, Munich and Berlin, were independent and enjoyed a status roughly equal to that of a *Gruppe*. The HJ *Gruppenführer* and *Gauführer* were directly responsible to their SA counterparts within the *Gruppe*; but below these grades, HJ leaders were not subject to orders from equivalent SA leaders; they were merely admonished to "... work with the SA in the best interests of the Party...."

Since the term *Gruppe* now indicated the largest formation, it was obvious that it could no longer be applied to the smallest! A change in nomenclature was required. In the HJ, a *Gruppe* became a *Kameradschaft* (circle of comrades). By 1931 the HJ structure became:

Kameradschaft
Schar
Gefolgschaft
Ortsgruppe
Bezirk
Gau
Gruppe

In June 1932 this was further amended to become:

Kameradschaft
Schar
Gefolgschaft
Unterbann (the former *Bezirk*)
Bann (the former *Gau*)
Gebiet (the former *Gruppe*)

The ten former *Gruppen* and two independent *Gaue* had, by this time, become eleven *Gebiete* and seven independent *Banne*. The eleven *Gebiete* were:

1. Nord
2. West
3. Ost
4. Gross Berlin
5. Südwest

6. Mitte
7. Nordmark
8. Nordsee
9. Berlin-Brandenburg
10. Ostsee

In 1933 a higher classification, the *Obergebiet*, was added. There were five of these:

Ost
Mitte
West
Süd
Nord

Each *Obergebiet* was subdivided into a number of *Gebiete;* there were twenty-seven by 1937:

Ost
    Berlin
    Kurmark (Brandenburg)
    Pommern (Pomerania)
    Schlesien (Silesia)
    Ostland (Danzig and East Prussia)
Mitte
    Thüringen (Thuringia)
    Sachsen (Saxony)
    Mittelelbe (Central Elbe)
    Mittelland (Midlands)
West
    Kurhessen (Grand Hesse)
    Hessen-Nassau
    Mittelrhein (Central Rhein)
    Ruhr-Niederrhein (Ruhr-Lower Rhine)
    Westmark
    Saarpfalz (Saar-Palatinate)
    Westfalen (Westphalia)
Süd
    Franken (Franconia)
    Baden
    Württemburg
    Hochland (Central Bavaria)
    Bayrische Ostmark (Eastern Bavaria)
Nord
    Ostsee (Baltic)
    Nordmark (Schleswig-Holstein)
    Hamburg
    Nordsee (North Sea)
    Mecklenberg
    Niedersachsen (Lower Saxony, *north*, not south, of Saxony proper)

In March 1938 Austria was incorporated into the Greater German Reich, with the result that seven new *Gebiete* were added:

1. Oberdonau (Upper Danube)
2. Niederdonau (Lower Danube)
3. Tirol
4. Karten (Carinthia)
5. Steiermark (Styria)
6. Salzburg
7. Wien (Vienna)

This resulted in the creation of a new Main District, *Obergebiete Südost* (Southeast), to which all the above were allotted with the exception of Tirol, which was linked with *Bayrische Ostmark*, under the new name of *Tirol Voralberg* (this was given to *Obergebiete Süd*).

Other changes introduced at this time were the disbandment of *Gebiete Ostsee* and *Gebiete Mittelrhein*. The former was added to Pommern (Pomerania), the latter divided to form two new *Gebiete*, under the names *Köln-Aachen* (Cologne-Aachen) and Düsseldorf (both of which were heavily populated areas).

In January 1939 the Sudetenland, seized from Czechoslovakia the previous October, was formally incorporated into the Reich and added to *Obergebiete Ost*.

The coming of war further expanded the frontiers of the Reich: New HJ *Obergebiete* had to be created. The final structure, as existed in 1943, was as follows:

Ost
- Ostpreussen (East Prussia)
- Mark Brandenburg (formerly Kurmark)
- Niederschlesien (Lower Silesia)
- Sudetenland
- Danzig-Westpreussen (Danzig-Prussia)
- Wartheland (part of Poland which had been incorporated into the Reich)
- Oberschlesien (Upper Silesia)

Mitte
- Kurhessen (Grand Hesse)
- Mittelland (Halle District)
- Sachsen (Saxony)
- Thüringen (Thuringia)
- Mittelelbe (Central Elbe)
- Mainfranken (Upper Franconia)

West
- Westfalen-Nord (North Westphalia)
- Rühr-Niederrhein (Ruhr-Lower Rhine)
- Köln-Aachen (Cologne-Aachen)
- Düsseldorf
- Moselland

    Westfalen-Süd (South Westphalia)
    Oldenburg
Süd
    Mitte Franken (Central Franconia)
    Hochland (Bavarian Alps)
    Württemberg
    Baden
    Schwaben (Schwabia)
    Bayreuth
    Tirol-Vorarlberg
Nord
    Berlin
    Pommern (Pomerania)
    Schleswig-Holstein (formerly Nordmark)
    Nordsee (North Sea)
    Niedersachsen (Lower Saxony)
    Mecklenburg
    Hamburg
    Osthannover (East Hanover)
Südost
    Wien (Vienna)
    Niederdonau (Lower Danube)
    Oberdonau (Upper Danube)
    Steiermark (Styria)
    Kärten (Carinthia)
    Salzburg

Six new HJ *Gebiete* were established in areas allied to, but not formally incorporated into, the Reich. These were:

    (i) *Böhmen und Mähren* (Bohemia and Moravia). The so-called "Protectorate." This was added to *Obergebiet Süd.*

    (ii) *Generalgouvernement* (The general Government, i.e., what was left of Poland after parts had been incorporated into the Reich). This was added to *Obergebiet Ost.*

    (iii) *Ostland.* The term *Ostland* (East Land) had formerly been employed to denote East Prussia and the German dominated Free City of Danzig, but with these now part of the Reich the word was applied to the Baltic states — Lithuania, Latvia and Estonia.

    (iv) Osten (the East). All other parts of the German conquered East came under this generic term. It was added to *Obergebiet Ost.*

    (v) Flandern (Flanders)

    (vi) Niederland (Netherlands)

Both the above were added to *Obergebiet West* which seem to indicate that Hitler intended these areas to become part of the Reich after final victory!

    When Arthur Axmann succeeded von Schirach as head of the Hitler Youth he slightly readjusted the bounds of some of the *Banne* in order to bring them into line with those of the *Kreise* of the NSDAP. The overall number of *Banne* was increased to 223. Further wartime modifications was the dropping of the word *Untergau* for the BDM and replacing it with the HJ term *Bann* (thus a BDM *Untergauführerin* became a *Bannmädelführerin*).

In the larger cities three or more *Banne* could be linked together to form a *Standorte der HJ* (literally: a station of the HJ) which ranked above a *Bann* but below a *Gebiet*.

| HJ | DJ | B.DM. | J.M. | Approx. numbers |
|---|---|---|---|---|
| Kameradschaft | Jungenschaft | Mädelschaft | Jungmädelschaft | 15 |
| Schar | Jungzug | Mädelschar | Jungmädelschar | 50 |
| Gefolgschaft | Fahnlein | Mädelgruppe | Jungmädelgruppe | 150 |
| Unterbann | Stamm | Mädelring | Jungmädelring | 600 |
| Bann | Jungbann | Untergau | Jungmädelundergau | 3,000 |
| Oberbann | Oberbann | Gau | Gau | 15,000 |
| Gebiet | — | Obergau | — | 75,000 |
| Obergebiet | — | Gauverband | — | 375,000 |

The above "approximate numbers" are from a wartime publication. A pre-war booklet *(Die Organization der* Hitler-*Jugend)* gives a *Gebiet* as 100,000 and an *Obergebiet* as 500,000. Probably both sets of figures represented the ideal rather than the actual. Indeed all the above have to be regarded as only approximate.

Within the *Gefolgschaft* the *Scharen* were grouped by age as follows:

Schar 4 : 14 year olds
Schar 3 : 15 year olds
Schar 2 : 16 year olds
Schar 1 : 17 year olds.

The same arrangement applied to a BDM *Mädelschar*. Similarly a DJ *Fähnlein* comprised:

Jungzug 4 : 10 year olds
Jungzug 3 : 11 year olds
Jungzug 2 : 12 year olds
Jungzug 1 : 13 year olds.

The JM *Gruppe* was likewise age divided into *Jungmädelscharen*.

The highest HJ formation was the *Obergebiet* each of which comprised not less than six, nor more than eight, *Gebiete*. In the Reich there were finally 42 *Gebiete* and 223 *Banne*. It may be remarked that the *Bann* numeral which appeared on the shoulder strap bore no relationship to this total (many *Banne* had numbers well above this figure). The choice of number was arbitrary and often related to the number of a local army regiment whose "tradition" the HJ had adopted as it own.

Immediately superior to Axmann as *Reichsjugendführer* (after August 1940) was von Schirach as head of all youth education within the framework of the NSDAP, but von Schirach's authority was by now a chimera. Apart from sponsoring various cultural events such as the Rally of European Youth in Vienna in 1942, his control over youth matters was almost entirely notional. Above von Schirach was the Ministry of the Interior and the Ministry of Justice, above them, Adolf

Hitler. But the structure of authority was not, as is often imagined, pyramidical; it was rather a series of overlapping circles of competency with no clear demarcation line between where one leader's authority ended and another's began. The inevitable result was, of course, incessant interdepartmental feuding and intrigue with consequent appeals to Hitler to settle disputes. It was a situation which the Führer did nothing to discourage since, by keeping his subordinates at one another's throats, he prevented them from "ganging up" against him and left him supreme arbiter in all matters.

The RJF was subdivided into a number of Offices *(Amter)* later redesignated departments *(Abteilungen)* which covered all aspects of HJ activity. In 1939 these were as follows:

Amt L : Basic physical training, athletics and sport;
Amt KE : "Bodily toughening-up" *(Koperliche Ertüchtigung)*.

This covered, as well as the *WE Lager*, the work of the *Flieger-, Motor-,* and *Marine-HJ.*

Amt HBA: This was concerned with hostel building
Amt O: Organization, clothing and equipment
Amt S: Social work, law, community work and *Landdienst*
Amt G: Health
Amt Pr: Press and Propaganda
Amt WS: "World outlook education" *(Weltanschauliche Schulung)* i.e., Nazi racial theory and other dogma
Amt K: Cultural work, music, choirs, etc.
Amt A: Foreign Dept. Work of the HJ outside the Reich
Amt GV: Seemingly overlapping with the above this was concerned with German communities on the periphery *(Grenz)* of the Reich and with "folksy" activities of those persons of German descent who resided outside Germany (the *Volksdeutsche*)
Amt JHF: Responsible for travel arrangements when the HJ made official visits abroad
Amt V: Administration
Amt P: Personnel.

A later reorganization into thirteen *Abteilungen* linked the related functions of the above in a more logical pattern although it still left overlapping competencies — a feature which, as mentioned above, was common to all administrative structures in Hitler's Germany.

# Hitler Youth Ranks

### (1933, 1937 and 1938)

| 1933 | 1937 | 1938 |
|---|---|---|
| 1 — Hitlerjunge | Hitlerjunge | Hitlerjunge |
| 2 — Hitlerjunge | Rottenführer | Rottenführer |
| 3 — Hitlerjunge | Rottenführer | Oberrottenführer |
| 4 — Kameradschaftsführer | Kameradschaftsführer | Kameradschaftsführer |
| 5 — Kameradschaftsführer | Kameradschaftsführer | Oberkameradschaftsfürer |
| 6 — Scharführer | Scharführer | Scharführer |
| 7 — Kameradschaftsführer | Oberscharführer | Oberscharführer |
| 8 — Gefolgschaftsführer | Gefolgschaftsführer | Gefolgschaftsführer |
| 9 — Gefolgschaftsführer | Gefolgschaftsführer | Obergefolgschaftsführer |
| 10 — Gefolgschaftsführer | Gefolgschaftsführer | Hauptgefolgschaftsführer |
| 11 — Gefolgschaftsführer | Unterbannführer | Stammführer |
| 12 — Gefolgschaftsführer | Unterbannführer | Oberstammführer |
| 13 — Bannführer | Bannführer | Bannführer |
| 14 — Oberbannführer | Oberbannführer | Oberbannführer |
| 15 — Oberbannführer | Hauptbannführer | Hauptbannführer |
| 16 — Gebietsführer | Gebietsführer | Gebietsführer |
| 17 — Obergebietsführer | Obergebietsführer | Obergebietsführer |
| 18 — Stabsführer | Stabsführer | Stabsführer |

From this list it can be seen that the HJ exactly *doubled* the number of its ranks between 1933 and 1939.

## COMPARISON OF HJ AND DJ RANKS

| HJ | DJ |
|---|---|
| 1 — Hitlerjunge | Pimpf |
| 2 — Rottenführer | Hordenführer |
| 3 — Oberrottenführer | Oberhordenführer |
| 4 — Kameradschaftsführer | Jungschaftsführer |
| 5 — Oberkammeradschaftsführer | Oberjungschaftsführer |
| 6 — Scharführer | Jungzugführer |
| 7 — Oberscharführer | Oberjungzugführer |
| 8 — Gefolgschaftsführer | Fahnleinführer |
| 9 — Obergefolgschaftsführer | Oberfahnleinführer |
| 10 — Hauptgefolgschaftsführer | Hauptfahnleinführer |
| 11 — Stammführer | Jungstammführer |
| 12 — Oberstammführer | Oberjungstammführer |
| 13 — Bannführer | Jungbannführer |
| 14 — Oberbannführer | Oberjungbannführer |

15 — Hauptbannführer                Hauptjungbannführer
16 — Gebietsführer                  Gebietsjungvolkführer
17 — Obergebietsführer              Obergebietsjungvolkführer
18 — Stabsführer
19 — Reichsjugendführer

Ranks 2-4 might be regarded as junior NCOs;
Ranks 5-6 might be regarded as senior NCOs;
Ranks 8-10 might be regarded as warrant officers;
Ranks 11-13 might be regarded as Subalterns (in the HJ these were referred to as the (*Führerkorps*);
Ranks 14-19 were called the *Hoehre Führerschaft* (the "Higher Leadership").

## COMPARISON OF HJ AND BDM RANKS

| | HJ<br>(1938-1945) | BDM<br>(1938-1945) | BDM<br>(1943-1945) |
|---|---|---|---|
| 1 — | Hitlerjunge | Mädel | Mädel |
| 2 — | Rottenführer | Mädel | Mädel |
| 3 — | Oberrottenführer | Mädel | Mädel |
| 4 — | Kameradschaftsführer | Mädelschasftsführerin | BDM Schaftsführerin |
| 5 — | Oberkameradschaftsführer | Mädelschasftsführerin | BDM Schaftsführerin |
| 6 — | Scharführer | Mädelscharführerin | BDM Scharführerin |
| 7 — | Oberscharführer | Mädelscharführerin | BDM Scharführerin |
| 8 — | Gefolgschaftsführer | Mädelgruppenführerin | BDM Gruppenführerin |
| 9 — | Obergefolgschaftsführer | Mädelgruppenführerin | BDM Gruppenführerin |
| 10 — | Hauptgefolgschaftsführer | Mädelgruppenführerin | BDM Hauptgruppenführerin |
| 11 — | Stammführer | Mädelringführerin | BDM Ringführerin |
| 12 — | Oberstammführer | Mädelringführerin | BDM Ringführerin |
| 13 — | Bannführer | Untergruppenführerin | Bannmädelführerin |
| 14 — | Oberbannführer | Gauführerin | Oberbannführerin |
| 15 — | Hauptbannführer | Gauführerin | Hauptmädelführerin |
| 16 — | Gebietsführer | Obergauführerin | Gebietsmädelführerin |
| 17 — | Obergebietsführer | Bauverbandsführerin | Gebietsmädelführerin |
| 18 — | Stabsführer | Reichsreferentin | Reichsreferentin† |
| 19 — | Reichsjugendführer<br>(Axmann) | Reichsreferentin | Reichsreferentin† |

† The title of the BDM chief was changed several times. In 1931 it was *Mädelreferentin in der Reichsleitung der HJ*. In March 1932 this became *Referentin für Mädelfragen in der Reichsleitung der HJ*. In June of the same year it was altered to *Bundesführerin des DBM*. After 1933 it became *BDM Hauptreferentin*. The final change to *BDM Reichsreferentin* was made in 1938.

26

# Uniforms of the Hitler Youth

## GENERAL REVIEW

THE EARLY DAYS: 1923-1925

The pre-Hitler Youth, the *Jugendbund* (comprising the *Jungmannschaft* and the *Jungsturm Adolf Hitler*) was garbed in white shirt and brown wind jacket. Perhaps as an indication of its affinity with the working class, the *Jugendbund* adopted the characteristic dark blue soft-peaked "sailor" cap of the German manual labourer (their equivalent of the British working man's "cloth cap," with, on the peak, a small silver swastika and, on the band, the black/white/red* cockade of the German army. Breeches and top boots could be worn to complete the uniform, but this was optional. The arm band was at this stage black/white/red (horizontally) in equal proportions with a black swastika on a white square. Like all the "uniforms" of the period, diversity rather than uniformity was the order of the day.

DER KAMPFZEIT: 1925-1932

When, after the "missing year" of 1924, the Hitler Youth was formed in 1925 it was at first conceived as a sort of "prep school" for the Storm Troopers. All its members were expected to enroll as SA men on reaching the age of 18.

The former *Jugendbund* white shirt now gave place to the brown shirt, that distinctive vestment of the NSDAP the origin of which is somewhat obscure. It is said that there existed in Austria a large consignment of khaki shirts destined for Germany's colonial troops in Africa, but the loss of the war also involved the loss of the colonies. Thus the brown shirts became "surplus to requirement." Seizing the opportunity to furnish its militia with habiliments at knock down prices, the NSDAP bought the lot. Whatever the truth, the brown shirt became, and remained, the outward and visible mark of the Nazi Party.

On the collar of the shirt the HJ boys wore SA type collar patches; even the SA *Kepi* was (briefly) worn. The too-ready confusion between HJ youths and SA adults had, in these days of recurrent street violence,

---

* The Weimar government had reverted to the more "traditional" German colours, black, *gold*, and red for the army cockade. This minor alteration aroused a quite inordinate degree of hostility. Some officers refused to wear the new colours. Significantly, Hitler restored the white after he came to power.

unfortunate results. Parents, naturally enough, protested at their sons becoming involved in the frequently bloody and sometimes lethal encounters with the Red Front. A clear visual differentiation between boys and adults was insisted upon. Thus in December 1926 we have Gruber issuing an order that, "all SA emblems are forbidden on HJ uniforms. The carrying of the Party flag and the wearing of the Party brassard is also prohibited." The regulation goes on to state that, "... the uniform of the HJ is a brown shirt, open at the neck, worn without a tie or neckerchief. It is piped in green around the collar, cuffs, and breast pocket flaps...."

The "Party brassard" referred to above which was worn by the SA was red with a black swastika on a round white field. The HJ introduced its own distinctive version with a broad white central stripe with the background to the swastika being "square" (at a 45-degree tilt to conform with the tilt of the black swastika). During the "years of struggle" (*Kampfzeit*) perhaps the only constant and consistent features of HJ uniform were this brassard and the brown shirt — although even the style and shade of this latter was the subject of some variation.

As the HJ grew in size, attempts were made to regularize its uniform. Brown trousers with lace-up top boots were authorized for the older lads. The younger boys still wore brown or black shorts (and shoes). Officers were allowed to wear breeches and black leather riding boots. The belt buckle was, at first, a junior edition of the SA type. A wide variety of privately produced buckles were also worn, and a cross-strap was added to the belt. A black neckerchief was later introduced, although often not worn. As headgear a military style soft peaked brown cap was authorized. Shoulder straps were piped in two colours. Officers could wear a short brown blouse with four pockets. This, judging from photographs of the period, appears to have been made in a velveteen material.

Ranks in the form of stars on the shoulder straps were introduced. Senior leaders wore collar patches which may have been equivalent to those of the NSDAP's Corps of Political Leaders (i.e. an HJ *Gauführer* may have worn a collar patch similar to that of an NSDAP *Gauleiter*, an HJ *Kreisführer* one similar to an NSDAP *Kreisleiter*, etc.), but no published regulations on this matter have come to light.

Due to the fact that the Hitler Youth, as a voluntary organization, was in no position to *enforce* dress regulations, a multiplicity of costumes was worn and tolerated. It has also to be remembered that all items of uniform had to be found at the boy's own expense. In a decade of economic hardship (these were the Depression years) this placed another impediment in the path of conformity of dress. Where lads were too poor to provide themselves with even the basic uniform, their better off brethren would often donate money for them to do so.

Between April 13 and June 13, 1932 there was a nationwide ban on the wearing of political uniforms — a futile attempt to curb the violence between the militias of extreme right and left. Similar bans had previously been applied from time to time in the (then) semi-autonomous

German *Länder*. The Hitler Youth, temporarily renamed the National-Socialist Youth Movement, simply countered by adopting a "civilian uniform" of white shirt and black tie — a stratagem employed in Austria (and elsewhere) to circumvent similar proscriptions on para-military apparel.

IN POWER: 1933-1939

After the Nazi accession to power in January 1933 the RJF laid down more elaborate dress regulations. In place of the former round badge, a rhombus, or diamond-shaped, device was introduced early in 1933. The older version was worn as a "traditions" badge on the left breast pocket (until replaced by the Golden Badge as the token of an "old fighter"). An all-khaki uniform was made standard. This comprised a shirt, shorts (for summer) or breeches (for winter) and soft peaked cap. In winter a brown greatcoat (of a darker shade than the rest of the attire) with four pockets was added. Boys wore a black neckerchief, officers a black tie. A belt with cross strap completed the ensemble. The same type of belt buckle was worn by all ranks until a special officers version was introduced in 1936.

Normally breeches were khaki like the rest of the uniform, but the *Motor-, Flieger-, Reiter-* and *Pioneer-HJ*, wore black. Later alterations were the substitution of a dark blue "ski" outfit for the winter khaki, the replacement of the peaked cap (seldom in fact worn except for formal parades and marches) by a khaki side cap and the change from khaki to black shorts for summer wear.

The various colours of officers cap band and shoulder straps are dealt with elsewhere. The whole character of officers dress became more formal and distinctive — reflecting, perhaps, the fact that military discipline had replaced the egalitarian spirit and camaraderie of the *Kampfzeit*. Only officers now were allowed breeches (worn with top boots — both black). After noncommissioned ranks got dark blue as their winter dress, only officer grades wore the khaki tunic formerly worn by all ranks. The officers' greatcoat had a black collar and lapels (in 1940 this was changed to black lapels only), and a more formal and rigid type of peaked cap was introduced.

Despite a profusion of regulations, it took a considerable time to achieve standardization in matters of dress. What *was* rapidly eliminated was the wearing of *unofficial* items. With the creation in 1934 of a National Quartermaster Department (*Reichszeugmeisterei*, or *RZM*), only officially approved firms were permitted to manufacture Party insignia, uniforms, flags, daggers, etc. Their *imprimatur* being the RZM stamp or tab on the said article. The punishment for unauthorized manufacture of such items was a two-year prison sentence. Thus all HJ insignia finally became standardized and the former privately produced daggers, belt buckles, etc. vanished from the scene.

AT WAR: 1939-1945

War brought clothes rationing. Coupons had to be surrendered even for Party uniforms, although these were rated at only half the coupon value of corresponding items of civilian apparel. HJ uniforms were purchased at the so-called *Braune Laden* ("Brown shops" which supplied NSDAP clothing and insignia). As a minor concession the *Beitragsgelder* (the obligatory weekly contribution to HJ funds) was abolished in 1940.

The strict dichotomy between HJ and DJ uniform was abandoned as was the division between summer and winter dress. The dark blue "ski" ensemble previously reserved for winter wear (October 15 to April 14) could now be worn at any time, especially when performing war duties.

The following sets of illustration were taken from the book, *Die Uniformen der HJ*, by Herbert Knötel and others, which was published in 1933 (there were also subsequent updated later editions). This was arguably the best illustrated book on the Hitler Youth produced during the time of the Third Reich.

Hitler Youth summer dress (1933). On the left Undress uniform (*Kleiner Dienst*) Centre and right Full dress (*Grosser Dienst*) marching order with pack, blanket (ground sheet) canteen, water bottle and entrenching tool.

H.J. Winter uniform (1933). On right: Undress uniform (*Kleiner Dienst*); on left "with tunic" (*mit Rock*) Centre: Full Dress (*Grosser Dienst*) marching order. Below with greatcoat.

The above illustrations are from the 1937 edition of the *Organisationsbuch der NSDAP*.

An officially posed photo to illustrate different types of HJ uniforms (ca. 1936). Left to right: *Flieger-HJ* (note *Luftsportscharen* emblem on right upper arm). General HJ with rain Mantle, General HJ in summer uniform, Marine-HJ in dress uniform.

NATIONAL ARCHIVES

Khaki HJ rain cape (*Regenumhang*).

ROGER S. STEFFEN

Tailor's label.

ROGER S. STEFFEN

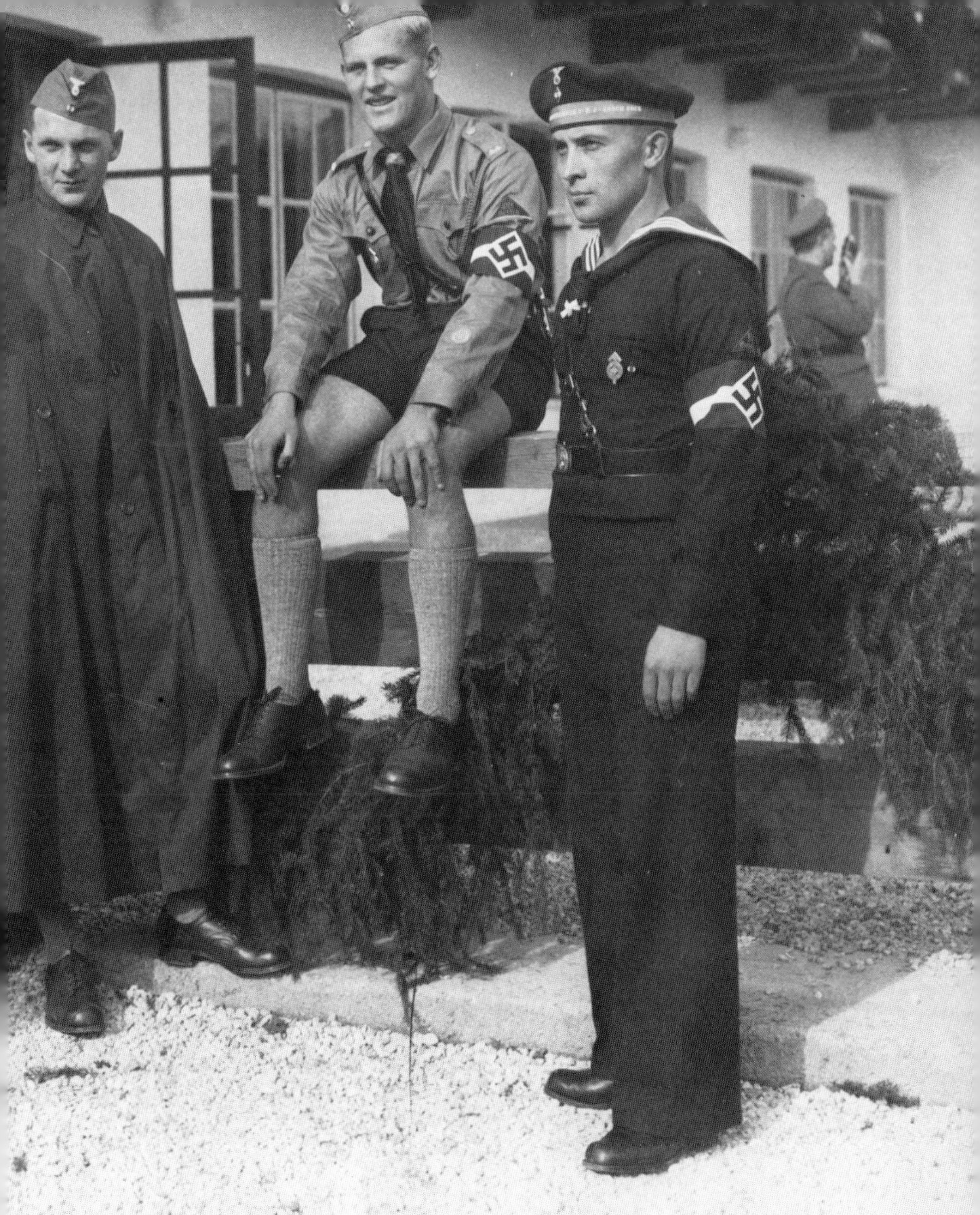

(a) *Hitlerjunge* in winter greatcoat and full marching kit
(b) HJ *Bannführer* in Undress Uniform (*Kleiner Dienstanzug*)
(c) HJ *Scharführer* in summer dress with full marching kit.

Normally HJ boys wore black shorts but those in the districts: Franconia, Hochland and German-Austria (*Deutsch-Oesterreich*) were permitted to wear the traditional leather shorts (*Lederhosen*) of those regions.

(a)       (b)       (c)

(1)       (2)       (3)

(1) HJ boys summer uniform. Khaki shirt, black shorts, black neckerchief, white stockings, black shoes. Red piped black shoulder straps and red piped khaki forage cap.
(2) HJ boys winter uniform. Dark blue ski suit and ski cap worn with khaki shirt and black tie or black neckerchief.
(3) HJ boys winter uniform with rain cape. Dark blue cape (The above are from the 1943 edition of the *Organisationsbuch der NSDAP*).

34

(1) (2) (3)

(1) Officers winter greatcoat. Mid-brown with black lapel facings. Senior officers have gold piping around collar and cap and a gold chin strap; others silver. (Pre-war the great coat also had a black collar);

(2) Full winter service dress (*Grosser Winterdienstanzug*) for Warrant Officer grades (*Gefolgschaftsführer* to *Hauptgefolgschaftsführer*). When this type of short jacket was introduced (in June 1939) for the HJ, a similar one in dark blue was brought in for DJ leaders of corresponding rank. (Note that the cap does not have a black band);

(3) Full summer service dress for subalterns (*Stammführer* to *Bannführer*) of the HJ or, in dark blue for *Jungstammführer* to *Jungbannführer* of the DJ.

(The above illustrations are from the 1943 edition of the *Organizationsbuch der NSDAP*).

Artur Axmann as *Reichsjugendführer*. His collar patches are similar to those of Himmler as *Reichsführer-SS*.

35

VK AGER

A group of RJF leaders. The two on the left wear, above their right breast pocket, the "bar" of a graduate of the Reichs Leadership School at Potsdam. Note rather unusual slant to lower tunic pocket of officer on extreme left. As an alternative to breeches and top boots, officers could wear (as here) black trousers. These have a 2 mm silver stripe down the outer seams. Higher ranking officers have a 2 mm *gold* stripe.

Insigne for a graduate of the RFS Potsdam.

Baldur von Schirach in pre-war type HJ officer's greatcoat which has a black collar and lapels. The type of greatcoat issued to HJ officers during the war had only the lapels black.

*Reichsjugendführer* Axmann wearing the greatcoat with collar tabs.

Cuff-title *Hitlerjugend*. This version in *Sütterlin* (German hand-writing script) is sometimes wrongly described as a variant of the cuff-title awarded to the 12. SS Panzer Division "Hitlerjugend." It was, in fact, worn by members of the RJF (although by no means consistently!). It can be discerned being worn in photos on the left cuff of the HJ officer guarding the podium from which Hitler addresses a rally of the HJ at Nürnberg in September 1937. Even as late as 1944 Axmann was photographed wearing an example of this cuff-title. It is in the style of those worn by the SS.

Left: collar patch as worn by Von Schirach in photograph (below) as *Reichsjugendführer*. It is gold wire upon a red velvet patch with gold piping. It is interesting to note the narrowness of the white stripe in Von Schirach's HJ brassard, also his double-breasted tunic which is that of an *NSDAP* "Political Leader" ("Walking Out" dress).

A rather chubby Baldur von Schirach wears an informal (and unofficial) version of HJ leader's uniform (c. 1934)! On his left breast pocket he has the Potsdam 1932 commemorative badge. He has no rank insignia.

Cuff-title for an HJ guard detachment assigned to a *Gauleiter*, gold chain stitching on black; narrow gold borders.

P. BAKER

## SHOULDER STRAPS

HJ rank was indicated on the shoulder straps by a scheme which bore only a vague resemblance to that of the German army but, in its final devising, a very close similarity to that of the *Waffen-SS*. To illustrate this latter point one has only to imagine the shoulder insignia of the wartime HJ transferred to the collar patch and the parallel is complete. One important concession, however, was made to the tradidions of the army. The *Bann* number adopted was often that of an army regiment associated with the area in which the HJ unit had been raised. The result is a rather arbitrary numbering of *Banne*. This numeral was woven into the shoulder strap in the army manner (occasionally metal numerals were used instead). A further military concept taken up by the HJ was the use of *Waffenfarben*. This was different colours of piping to indicate the branch of the service to which the wearer belonged. HJ *Waffenfarben* did not, in all cases, correspond to that of the army. The use of a numeral on the shoulder strap button to indicate the *Gefolgschaft* was copied from the army practice of having the company or cavalry squadron number on the shoulder button.

Between 1933 and 1938 the HJ expanded its ranks a number of times to keep pace with the enlargement of the service during this period. Between 1933-1935 the patterns were:

1 — Hitlerjunge: Khaki strap piped in the *Oberbann* colour,
2 — Kameradschaftsführer: as above, but plus one silver star,
3 — Scharführer: as above, but with two silver stars,
4 — Gefolgschaftsführer: as above, but with three silver stars,
5 — Unterbannführer: as above, but with four silver stars.
6 — Bannführer: White strap with 2mm wide piping in the *Oberbann* color, plus one silver oak leaf and acorn.
7 — Oberbannführer: Yellow strap with 2.5cm wide silver piping. Two oakleaves with a large acorn between them, smaller acorns on the stalk.
8 — Gebietsführer: Bright red strap with 2.5mm silver piping. Three silver oakleaves with two small acorns — one on either side of the stalk.
9 — Obergebietsführer: crimson[†] strap with 2.5cm gold piping. Three gold oakleaves with two small acorns, positioned as above, with one gold star below. Gold button.
10 — Stabsführer: As in number 9, but with two gold stars. Originally the stars were placed above and below the oak leaf cluster, but later this changed to both stars being positioned side by side, below the oakleaves.

In October 1934 there was a modification with regard to the use of coloured shoulder straps. These now denoted function, rather than rank. Thus an *Oberbannführer*, if acting as the leader of a *Bann*, wore a white

---

[†] The terms carmine [*karminsrot*] and crimson [*karmesin*] may be regarded as interchangeable. Carmine was the *Waffenfarbe* of the General Staff of the German army.

40

(1) (2) (3) (4) (5)

(6) (7) (8) (9) (10)

shoulder strap with the two silver oakleaves of his grade, whereas if he functioned as leader of a *Gebiete* he was entitled to wear a bright red shoulder strap with the twin silver oakleaves of his actual status. There was, at the same time, a slight alteration to the shoulder straps of the most senior grades. Departmental Chiefs (*Abteilungsleiter*) at the RJF, the *Stabsführer* and the *Reichsjugendführer's* personal adjutant now had bright red, instead of carmine, strap (with gold insignia and piping). *Bannführer* and *Oberbannführer* serving on staffs other than that of the RJF wore carmine straps with silver insignia and piping.

Between April 1935 and May 1937 new grades were introduced, making the ranking as follows:

    1 — Hitlerjunge: As before,
    2 — Rottenführer (new rank): Silver bar at the end of the strap,
    3 — Kameradschaftsführer: As before,
    4 — Scharführer: As before,
    5 — Oberscharführer (new rank): Two silver stars, worn either on or above the silver bar,
    6 — Gefolgschaftsführer: As before.

41

# H.J. SHOULDER STRAPS 1936-38

Hitlerjunge
Bann 198
Gefolgschaft 3

Rottenführer
Bann 26
(indicated by button)
Rank introduced in April 1935

Kameradschaftsführer
Bann 250

Scharführer on Staff of Gebiet 4
Rank introduced in May 1937

Oberscharführer
Bann 93

Gefolgschaftsführer
(Flieger H.J.)

In November 1936 commissioned grades were given black shoulder straps that were narrower than the previous brown type. Two new grades were also added, making the officer ranks as follows:

7 — Unterbannführer (upgraded, roughly, from Company Sergeant-Major level to Second Lieutenant status),
8 — Bannführer: As before, but on black.
9 — Oberbannführer: As before, but on black.
10 — Hauptbannführer (new rank): as in 9, but with one silver star added below the oakleaves,
11 — Gebietsführer: Three oakleaves, as before, but now in gold,
12 — Obergebietsführer: As before, but on black,
13 — Stabsführer: As before, but now on black.

In 1938 a second complete revision took place. Now *all* ranks wore black shoulder straps and five new grades were added to accommodate the enormous expansion of the service which had taken place during that year. Ranks now were as follows:

1 — Hitlerjunge,
2 — Rottenführer,
3 — Oberrottenführer (new rank): Two silver bars,
4 — Kameradschaftsführer,
5 — Oberkameradschaftsführer (new rank): One star, one bar,
6 — Scharführer,
7 — Oberscharführer,
8 — Gefolgschaftsführer,
9 — Obergefolgschaftsführer (new rank): Three stars, one bar,
10 — Hauptgefolgschatsführer (new rank): Three stars, two bars,
11 — Stammführer (replacing *Unterbannführer*),
12 — Oberstammführer (new rank): Four stars and one bar,
13 — Bannführer,
14 — Oberbannführer,
15 — Hauptbannführer,
16 — Gebietsführer,
17 — Obergebietsführer,
18 — Stabsführer.

During the 1933-1934 period, the *Unterbann* number was featured on the shoulder strap. This appeared in 10mm high Roman numerals below the *Bann* number (18mm high Arabic numerals). This practice ceased in 1934 and thereafter only the *Bann* number was used.

Special coloured straps were introduced for medical and finance department personnel — blue for the former, green for the latter. With the introduction of black shoulder straps for leaders, a finance, or paymaster officer, was distinguished by having green inner piping to the silver piping on the black shoulder strap.

Various letters and symbols appeared on the shoulder strap — the Aesculapius staff (later replaced by a "Life Rune") for medical personnel, a Gothic *W* for *Wachtgefolgsschaft Baldur von Schirach* (which formation also had its own unique shoulder strap rank insignia). Staff of an *Oberbann* had a crimson Gothic *OB*, staff of an *Obergebiete*, a Gothic *OG*, but these were dropped after 1936 although *G* was retained for *Gebiete* staff.

## H.J. SHOULDER STRAPS

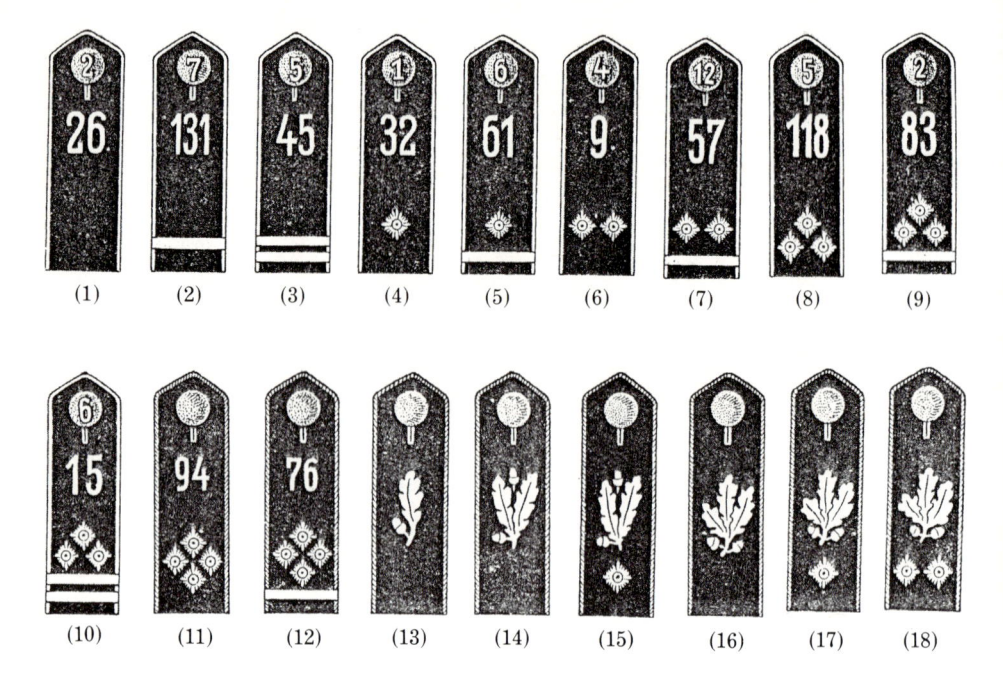

(1) (2) (3) (4) (5) (6) (7) (8) (9)

(10) (11) (12) (13) (14) (15) (16) (17) (18)

### SS COLLAR RANKS FOR COMPARISON WITH HJ SHOULDER RANKS

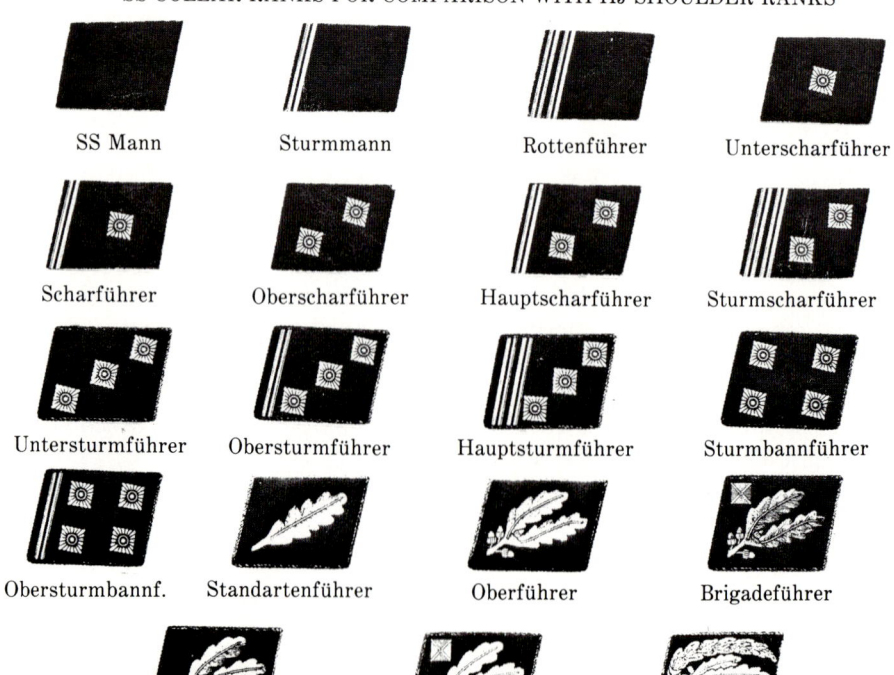

| SS Mann | Sturmmann | Rottenführer | Unterscharführer |

| Scharführer | Oberscharführer | Hauptscharführer | Sturmscharführer |

| Untersturmführer | Obersturmführer | Hauptsturmführer | Sturmbannführer |

| Obersturmbannf. | Standartenführer | Oberführer | Brigadeführer |

| Gruppenführer | Obergruppenführer | Reichsführer SS |

(The above are as in 1941. There were some later slight modifications to the form, and nomenclature, of the highest ranks.)

(a)

(b)

a) *Bannführer* in Finance or Paymaster Department of the HJ Period: 1933-1936
b) As above but after November 1936 with the introduction of black shoulder straps for senior officers. Lower grades wore the shoulder straps of the unit to which they were attached but with the special triangular shaped rank stars.

    The size of the ranks stars varied. Originally they were of the same dimensions as those of military noncommissioned officers, but in September 1935 smaller stars (of the kind worn on the collar patches of the SS) were introduced. In July 1937 administrative personnel received special triangular star (an idea apparently borrowed from the SA whose administrative officers wore stars of this sort). HJ leaders who were no longer on the active list but still held reserve commissions wore a silver bar behind the lower end of their shoulder straps (a traditional military practice). Before the war rank bars were of a special type; silver with a black central stripe, and were sewn onto the strap. Later, especially during the war when such luxuries were not readily available, army NCO braid was frequently used in its stead, this being simply slipped on in the form of a loop at the end of the strap. Another wartime innovation was a red bar (the width of which varied), worn on the end of the strap to indicate a volunteer war helper.

    Shoulder strap piping during the early period was in the colour of the *Oberbann*:

Oberbann 1: red
Oberbann 2: yellow
Oberbann 3: green

Oberbann 4: blue
Obermann 5: black
Obermann 6: white

c) *Kameradschaftsführer* on Staff of *Oberbann* 1. Crimson OB and piping. Period: 1933-1936

d) *Hitlerjunge* in *Bann* 9 (Würzburg in Franconia). A Latin B was used for *Gebiete* Franken, Hochland, Bay Ostmark Pfalz-Saar, until 1937 when 300 number were allocated instead, thus B9 became Bann 309.

e) *Kameradschaftsführer* of *Gefolgschaft* 1 (indicated by numeral on buttton) of *Unterbann* 4 of *Bann* 124 of *Oberbann* 5 (this latter being indicated by the black piping and numerals.) Period: 1933-1936 after which time the use of *Oberbann* colours ceased.

This arrangement was discontinued after 1936 when the concept of an *Oberbann* ceased to exist. For the General HJ, piping was light red (vermillion) until 1938, when a darker shade of red was introduced and made standard for all members except the specialist sections which had the following colours of piping:

| | |
|---|---|
| Motor HJ: | pink |
| Flieger HJ: | light blue |
| Signals HJ: | yellow |
| Streifendienst: | white |
| NPEA: | white (white *NPEA*) |
| Landjahr: | green |
| Marine HJ: | yellow/gold |
| Akademie für Jugendführung: | silver |
| Staff of a Gebiet: | crimson |
| Staff of the RJF: | crimson |
| Special Blind and Hard-of-Hearing/*Banne*: | black[†] |

[†] Black piping was used with the khaki shoulder straps but when black shoulder straps became standard for the HJ, this was altered to red piping.

For HJ units outside the Reichs the piping was:

Europe:    red
America:   yellow
Asia:      green
Africa:    blue
Australia: white

In all instances the unit numeral or letter on the shoulder strap was in the same colour as the piping. Officers had silver piping, the most senior ranks gold.

(a) (b) (c) (d)

(a) Hitlerjunge, *Bann 26*. Piping is vermillion (1934-38) for General HJ. Bann numeral is unusual in being in metal. (b) Rottenführer, *Bann 208*. Red piping (post-1938) for General HJ. The red "bar" at the base of the strap indicates volunteer war helper. (c) Stammführer on Staff of R.J.F. Silver bullion RJF. Large white metal stars. (d) Oberscharführer on Staff of *Gebiet 34* (Düsseldorf). Rank bar is the war-time type as distinct from that on (b). Crimson piping, "G" and numeral.

Shoulder straps of Wachgefolgschaft "Baldur von Schirach"
(i) Wachtmitglied
(ii) Unterzugführer
(iii) Zugführer
(iv) Oberzugführer
All are black with carmine piping and silver emblems.

In addition to these special shoulder ranks, the Wachgefolgschaft (Guard Company) also had a special form of headgear. In place of the normal HJ ski cap they wore a brown peaked cap with a black visor and black chin strap. On the cap band was the metal HJ diamond and on the peak a metal eagle-and-swastika. The top of the cap was piped in carmine.

47

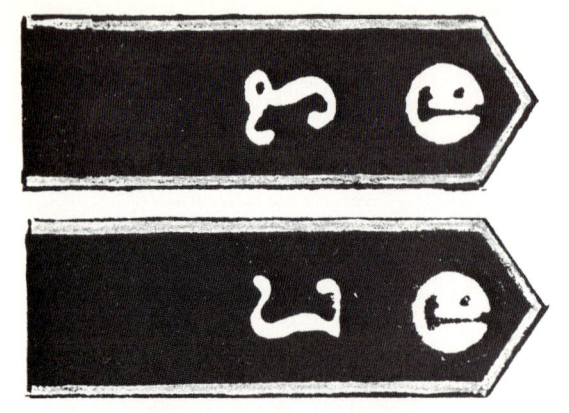

Shoulder straps of *Bann* L (Munich City) and *Bann* J (Nuremberg City). *Bann* J stood for *Bann Jungsturm* and it may have been the "tradition bearer" of the former *Jungsturm Adolf Hitler*. *Bann* L may have carried the tradition of the *Leibstandarte Adolf Hitler* (or of the former) Bavarian *Leib Regiment (München)*.

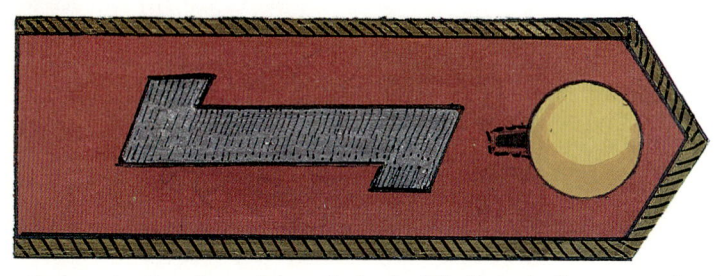

Prior to the introduction of a special arm badge for HJ adjutants, they wore a silver hooked bar on a carmine shoulder strap which was piped in gold and had a gold button.

## MEDICAL BRANCH

Special greyish-blue shoulder straps were introduced for the HJ medical branch in April 1935. At this time the ranks were:

1 — Oberfeldscher: Aesculapius staff and snake in silver,
2 — Hilfsarzt: As above, but with a silver bar,
3 — Truppenarzt: As above, plus two silver bars,
4 — Hauptarzt: As above, plus silver bar and star,
5 — Hauptstabsarzt: As above plus two silver bars and one silver star.

At this time pharmacists (Apotheker) had only two grades indicated on greyish-blue shoulder straps:

1 — Apotheker: Pessel and snake emblem in silver,
2 — Hauptapotheker: As above, plus silver bar.

In January 1936 these gradings were enlarged to become:

1 — Apotheker: As before,
2 — Hilfsapotheker: Pessel and snake emblem and silver bar,
3 — Truppenapotheker: Pessel and snake emblem and two silver bars,

4 — Hauptapotheker: Pessel and snake emblem and one silver bar,
5 — Hauptstabsapotheker: Pessel and snake emblem and one silver star and two silver stripes.

In September 1938 the use of the traditional symbol for medicine, the Aesculapius staff and snake, was replaced in all Nazi Party formation by the so-called "Life Rune." The arrangement of medical officer ranks was also slightly amended at this time:

1 — Oberfeldscher: Life Rune in silver,
2 — Hilfsartz: Life Rune in silver, plus one silver bar;
3 — Truppenarzt: Life Rune in silver, plus two silver bars;
4 — Hauptarzt: Life Rune in silver, plus one silver star;
5 — Hauptstabsarzt: Life Rune in silver, plus one silver star and one silver bar.

(a) Hauptarzt. 1st design. (b) Hilfsapotheker (assistant pharmacist) 2nd design (1936). Both are light blue-grey with silver piping and silver insignia.

*Truppenarzt*, shoulder strap (April 1935 to January 1936).

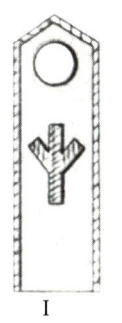

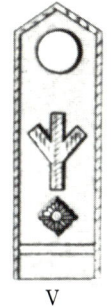

(i) Oberfeldscher
(ii) Hilfsarzt
(iii) Truppenarzt
(iv) Hauptarzt
(v) Hauptstabsarzt
Light blue-grey straps with silver piping and silver insignia.

I  II  III  IV  V

(1) RS (Rundfunk Spielscharen) Broadcasting groups. Red *RS* and red piping.
(2) B (Blinde) Special unit for blind boys. Red *B* and red piping.*
(3) G (Gehörgeschädigte) Unit for Deaf or hard-of-hearing. Red *G* and piping.*
(4) A (Akademie) Youth Leadership Academy. Silver *A* and silver piping.
(5) AHS (Adolf Hitler Schule) For pupils red *AHS* and red piping.
(6) AHS (Adolf Hitler Schule) For Staff silver *AHS* and silver piping.
(7) BS (Binnenschiffahrt) Inland Waterways, Marine HJ Yellow *S* and piping.
(8) S (Seeschiffahrt) Sea-going unit, Marine HJ Yellow *S* and piping.
(9) NPEA (Nat. Pol. Erziehungs-Anstalt) White *NPEA* and white piping.
(10) Hauptgefolgschaftsführer in Admin. Branch. Special three-pointed stars.
(11) Oberbannführer in Reserve. Silver bar behind end of shoulder strap.

* Created in April 1935. Shoulder straps were at this time *khaki* and the piping and letter was *black*.

50

A pre-1933 photo showing HJ boys in the soft peaked cap of the period and with the two colour piping to the shoulder strap then in use. The piping was in the *Landesfarben,* or colours of the German *Land* (State) concerned. For a full list of these colours, see section on lanyards.

## HJ BELT BUCKLES

It was not until 1933 that any degree of standardization was brought into force with regard to the type of belts and buckles worn in the HJ. Prior to this a wide variety of privately produced buckles had been worn. These usually featured a swastika (in one case, a swastika flag in full colour). During the time the Hitler Youth was a subformation of the SA, its members wore a "junior version" of the SA belt buckle.

In 1929 a first version of the leader's buckle was introduced. This is a pebbled swastika within a circular wreath of laurel leaves. It was made in a silver and a gilt version, the latter being (presumably) for the more senior leaders.

In 1933 what was to become the standard HJ buckle made its first appearance. This featured a closed-wing eagle within a circle, holding in its claws the diamond-shaped emblem of the HJ. Above the head of the eagle was the HJ motto: *Blut und Ehre* (Blood and Honour). It was intended that this would be worn by all ranks, officer and others alike.

From October 1934 all buckles had to carry the RZM mark on the reverse as well as the name, or logo, of the commercial company producing them. The following year the commercial marking was dropped and thereafter only the RZM mark plus a numbered code, prefixed by "4/...." was permitted.

Belts were brown until December 1935 when a change to black was ordered by the RJF. This orders caused some confusion and it was not

WIM SARIS

Officer's full dress belts and buckles. Gilt for highest ranking leaders, silver for others. This version of the leader's buckle was introduced in 1936.

Early semi-official NSDAP Youth belt buckle.

(a) and (b): Two versions of the standard belt buckle for non-commissioned ranks. (a) is rather poorly made in pot metal, (b) is a well finished nickle type. Both probably pre-1939. Most commonly found in greyish white metal.

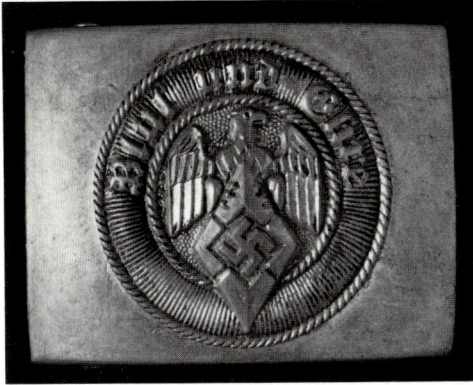

until November 1936 that black became standard. Aluminum began to be employed in January 1936 for HJ buckles as it was for those of the armed forces. This became the sole authorized material for HJ belt buckles, although, as with the black leather, it took almost a year before this became standard.

In November 1936 a special officers buckle was authorized. It is circular and of the same design as the centre piece of the boys buckle. This was worn with the black leather belt or with the ceremonial brocade belt which was introduced (officially) in September 1938, although, in fact, belts of this sort were worn by the HJ delegation to Rome in May of that year. The brocade belt is silver and black with a silver buckle, or, for highest ranks, gold and black with a gold buckle.

In practice officers wore, with working dress, either a plain twin-claw buckle or the boys rectangular type rather than the special officers version. No belt was worn with commissioned ranks "office dress" (*Gesellschaftsanzug*) or "walking out" dress (*Ausgehanzug*), i.e. that order of dress where black trousers and shoes were worn instead of breeches and top boots.

With the coming of war the order that only aluminum was to be used for the manufacture of HJ buckles was rescinded and a variety of materials found their way into use. Quality and "finish" declined as the war progressed. During the first eighteen months of the war the use of the leather cross strap was forbidden lest this result in a shortage of leather for the armed forces, but in February 1941 this restriction was lifted after the victories of the previous summer had resulted in an ample supply of leather being available.

The use of *white* leather belts and cross straps, etc. was extremely rare and may have been confined to delegations making official visits outside the Reich.

(c)

(c) Early semi-official NSDAP Youth belt buckles. (d) "Junior version" of SA buckle worn when the HJ was under SA command. (e) Officers buckle, 1929 type. Found in both silver and gilt.

(d)

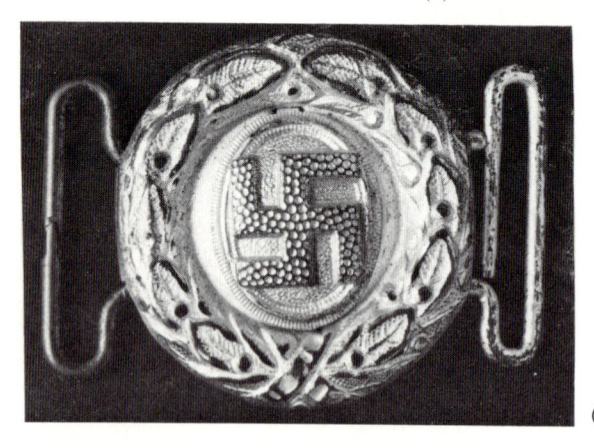

(e)

Two examples of early unofficial youth buckles. The flag (left) is in full colour. The background is red for buckle on right.

# HEADGEAR

The first *official* headgear worn by the HJ appeared around 1929; it was a soft-brimmed peaked cap in light khaki with a brown or black leather chin strap. On the peak was the first design of HJ badge. It was round with a rising sun and swastika, surrounded by the designation: *Deutsche Arbeiter-Jugend HJ.*

[Left] First design of HJ cap (c. 1929).
[Above] First design of HJ cap badge.

Pre-1933 cap with round "Deutsche Arbeiter-Jugend" badge. Note also the two-colour piping round the shoulder straps which was typical of this period.

In 1933 this type of headgear was replaced by a new pattern of peaked cap. It was, again, of light khaki, but of a slightly more formal shape and exhibited the second form of HJ emblem, the well-known diamond- (or rhombus-) shaped badge. Boys (*Hitlerjungen*) wore this badge on the cap top, or peak (*Mützendeckel*), but "leaders" wore it on the cap band, with, above, the then-current version of the Nazi national emblem (eagle and swastika).

The cap was piped in the *Oberbann* colour (red, yellow, green, etc.). The caps worn by all ranks had a black leather chin strap. For *Bannführer* and above, the soft brim was replaced by a black leather visor. Senior leaders had a coloured cap band which corresponded to the colour of their shoulder straps, thus a *Bannführer* had a white band, an *Oberbannführer* a yellow band, a *Gebietsführer* a bright red band and a staff officer a carmine band.

Cap of a *Kameradschaftsführer* to *Unterbannführer* (1933-1936). Yellow piping for *Oberbann* 2. The Eagle-and-swastika badge was worn on peak by "leaders." Boys wore on the peak the HJ diamond.

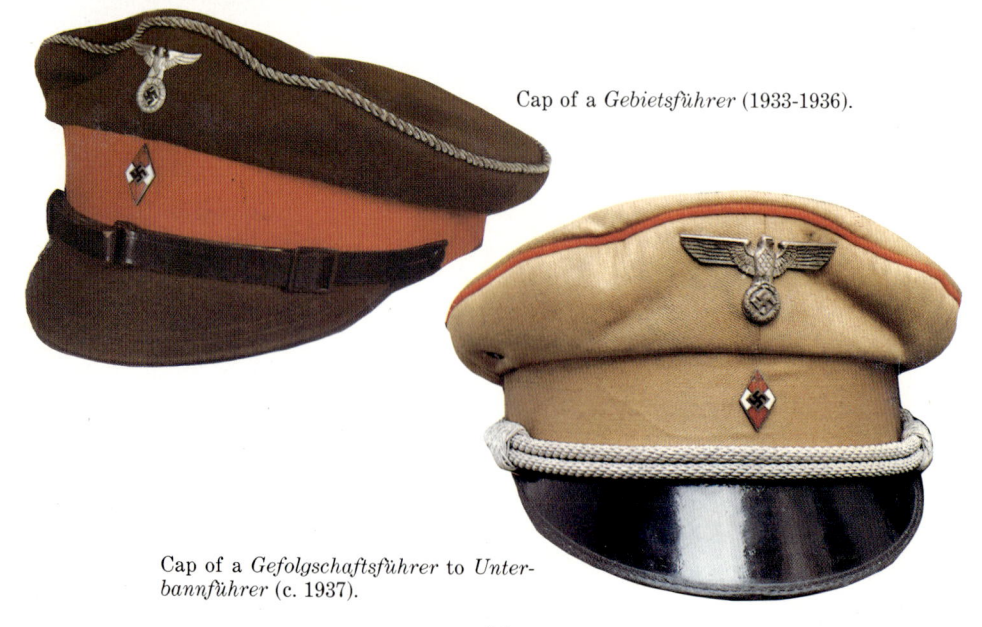

Cap of a *Gebietsführer* (1933-1936).

Cap of a *Gefolgschaftsführer* to *Unterbannführer* (c. 1937).

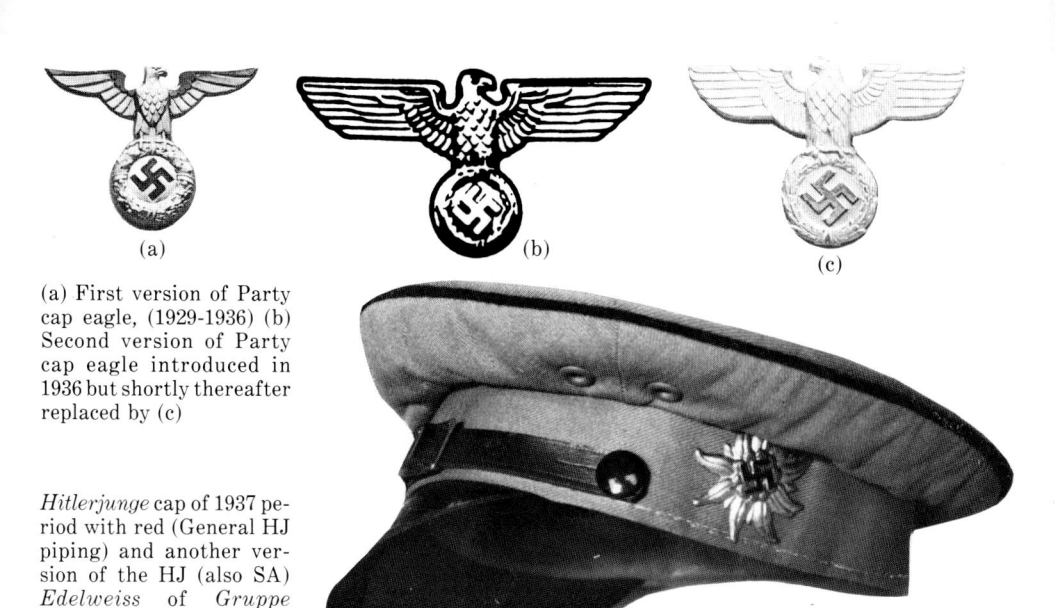

(a) First version of Party cap eagle, (1929-1936) (b) Second version of Party cap eagle introduced in 1936 but shortly thereafter replaced by (c)

*Hitlerjunge* cap of 1937 period with red (General HJ piping) and another version of the HJ (also SA) *Edelweiss* of *Gruppe Hochland*.

ULRIC OF ENGLAND

An *Oberstammführer* on the staff of the RJF with the 1936 type leader's cap and type (b) eagle and swastika.

Cap of a *Bannführer* to *Hauptbannführer* (1936 to 1939) or of a *Stammführer* to *Hauptbannführer* (1939-45). Silver piping, silver braid chin strap, black cap band. Silver eagle and swastika cap badge of type (c).

57

In 1936 a further modification took place. Peaked caps became yet more formal and militaristic. All ranks now had a black leather visor; the HJ diamond-shaped badge was now worn on the cap band with the second pattern eagle and swastika national emblem on the peak.

The ranks *Hitlerjunge* to *Oberscharführer* had a black leather chin strap. The cap piping was now red, and no longer in the *Oberbann* color. *Gefolgschaftsführer* to *Unterbannführer* (with the later expansion of HJ ranks, these became *Gefolgschaftsführer* to *Oberstammführer*) wore silver braid chin cords on their caps, instead of the aforementioned leather chinstrap, and their caps were piped in silver. *Bannführer* to *Hauptbannführer* (changed in 1939 to *Stammführer* through *Hauptbannführer*) wore a visored cap with a black band, silver chin cords and piping. The ranks of *Gebietsführer* and above wore caps with a black band, gold cap cords and piping, and a gold national emblem (all others had the national emblem cap badge in silver).

In January 1936 a "summer cap" was brought in for noncommissioned ranks. It was a light-weight khaki forage cap piped in red for the General HJ,* with the HJ diamond in either cloth or metal on the front, with an eagle and swastika above this, again either cloth or metal.

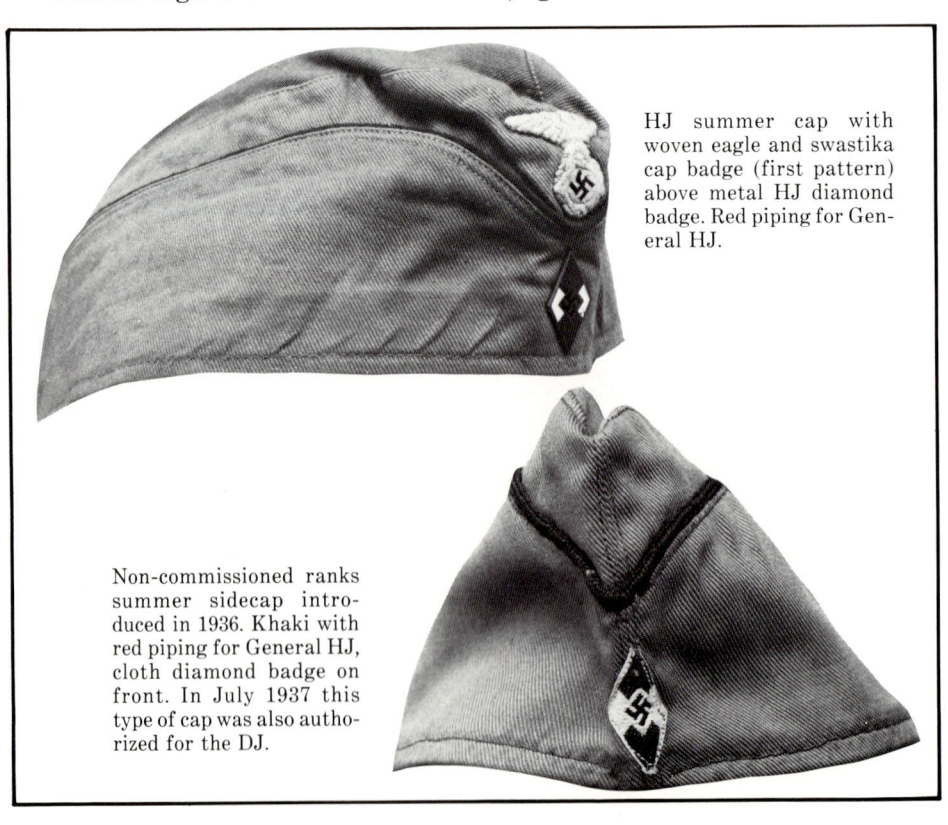

HJ summer cap with woven eagle and swastika cap badge (first pattern) above metal HJ diamond badge. Red piping for General HJ.

Non-commissioned ranks summer sidecap introduced in 1936. Khaki with red piping for General HJ, cloth diamond badge on front. In July 1937 this type of cap was also authorized for the DJ.

---

* Other branches of the HJ had the piping in their particular *Waffenfarbe*.

Non-commissioned ranks winter cap. Dark blue. Badge on front can be (as here) cloth or metal.

In 1933-1934 boys of the HJ who participated in ski competitions were allowed to wear a black ski cap with the HJ diamond on the front. Later this became standard wear for both the HJ and DJ winter uniform.

Members of the HJ and DJ in *Hochland* and *Deutsch-Oesterreich* Districts (southern Bavaria and Austria) were allowed to wear on the side of their caps (as well as the right collar of their uniform) a metal *Edelweiss*. This came in two versions — one with only the flower head, the other the flower with the stem and leaves.

In practice, especially in summer, headgear was more often than not dispensed with altogether.

Ski cap of an officer *Hochland* or German-Austria. Cap is piped in silver wire.

Metal *Edelweiss* worn on side of the cap, or in Austria on wearer's right collar.

BRASSARDS

Precisely how the swastika came to be adopted as the Nazi symbol is uncertain. It may have come from Finland, where it is the national emblem, and where German volunteers had fought for a brief period at the conclusion of the First World War. It may have originated with the *Freikorps*, some of whose units sported this ancient sun symbol. Whatever its origin, it rapidly became the outward and visible token of Hitler's followers.

The first brassard worn by a Nazi youth organization was that of the *Jungsturm Adolf Hitler*. It was black/white/red (the German national colours) with a black swastika on a white square.

At the Weimar Party Rally of 1926 the HJ wore what was to become the standard red/white/red brassard with a black swastika, although in this case it was on a *round* white background. Since the HJ was, at this time, a sub-section of the SA, it was necessary to provide some clear distinction between the two — hence the addition of the white band to the brassard.

Jungsturm Adolf Hitler brassard

Brassard worn at 1929 Rally

Standard HJ brassard (here in Bevo weave variety)

Regulations relating to the proper proportions of the white and red parts of the brassard were published but not always strictly observed. Officially the relationship is a 25mm wide white band between the two 40mm wide red ones, but white bands as narrow as 15mm are not uncommon, and the overall width of the brassard can vary from 100 to 120mm. Quality and "make" also vary, some are merely printed, others made up in separate pieces.

Boys in the special HJ unit for the blind wore the traditional armband of a German unsighted person — a yellow brassard on which there were three black circles.

Due to the historic link between the *Freikorps Rossbach* (see Chapter 1) and the Hitler Youth, the armband of this company of freebooters was, at one time, worn by veterans of the *Korps* on the lower left sleeve of their Hitler Youth (or other Nazi) uniform.

Brassard of *Freikorps Rossbach*

## DISTRICT TRIANGLES

On the left upper arm of their uniforms all members of the HJ wore a triangular cloth badge which indicated the unit to which they belonged. Normally this showed the name of the *Obergebiete* with the *Gebiet* place-name below. But those in special formations, such as the *Landjahr*, training schools, the RJF, etc., had arm triangles with the name or initials of their particular unit. For the sake of convenience these devices are referred to as "District Triangles."

Males had district triangles in black with yellow lettering; females wore black triangles with white lettering. District triangles were first introduced in 1933, although girls did not receive theirs until April of the following year. *Banne* which had been in existence prior to Hitler's accession to power in January 1933 were authorized to add a gold "bar" to the base of their triangles to indicate that they were what was known as "tradition units."

South East: Carinthia (Austria) with "traditions" gold bar.

Central: "Midlands" (Here for BDM. White on black)

The *Gebiete* place-name appears below the *Obergebiet* name, and they have to be read as though there is a full stop between the two. Thus, *Nord Berlin* does not mean "North Berlin" (as distinction from South, East or West Berlin), but *Obergebiete Nord, Gebiete Berlin*. Similarly *Südost Wien* is not Southeast Vienna but *Obergebiete Südost, Gebiet* (city of) Vienna. Some confusion might arise from the fact that there is a district triangle with the designation, "*Ost Berlin*." This is explained by the fact that there was a rearrangement of the HJ *Obergebiete*. Originally Berlin was part of *Obergebiet Ost*, but later this was made *Obergebiet Nord*. Among other changes were, for example, the disbandment of *Nord Ostsee* in 1938, the transformation of *Bayr. Ostmark* to *Tirol-Vorarlberg,* and *Mittelrhein* to *Hessen-Nassau*.

*HJ-Stabsführer* Helmut Möckel addresses an international sporting rally (note the Hungarian officer second to his left with an Italian officer directly behind). Möckel's "district triangle" has simply *RJF* and a "traditions" bar.

*RJF* Staff (with "traditions unit" bar at the base)

Academy at Brunswick

East: "General Government" (Poland)

*Landjahr* (Land Year)

*RJF* Staff Guard Berlin

South: Bayreuth

North: Hamburg

East: Sudetenland

West: Hesse-Nassau

For a complete list of the various *Gebiete* and *Obergebiete* as featured on district Triangles, see the section on the "Organizational Structure of the HJ."

The terms *Obergebiet* and *Gebiet* applied only to the HJ/DJ. In the BDM/JM these were known as *Gauverband* and *Obergau* respectively. The "traditions" bar for the BDM/JM was silver, not gold.

Other special district triangles included:

RJF;
RJF Stab;
RJF Stabswache Berlin;
RJF Stabswache München (Munich);
RJF Rundfunkspielschar (broadcasting unit);
Rundfunk HJ Potsddam (a second version of the above;
RJF Funktech. Bereitschaft (Radio Technicians Emergency Squad);
RJF Gefolgschaft;
Wachgefolgschaft;
RJF Reichsausbildungslager (National Training Camp).*

All the NPEAs had *NPEA* and a place-name (e.g. NPEA Potsdam) the Adolf Hitler Schulen normally had *AHS* and a place-name (e.g. AHS Weimar), but an example exists which has simply *Adolf Hitler Schule*.

The *Landjahr* triangle was unique in being green. It was worn, in this form, by both sexes.

Before the dissolution in November 1936 of the *Obergebiete* as an HJ organizational form, staff of an *Obergebiet* wore a "district triangle" which had simply the single word *Nord, Ost, Mitte, West,* or *Süd*. These were, of course, discontinued after that time.

Adolf Hitler School at Weimar

KLAUS BENSELER

---

* This was a precursor of the Military Toughening-Up Camps.

## LANYARDS

In the HJ/BDM etc., coloured lanyards were employed as an indication of both grade and function. A boy who held the rank of *Rottenführer* (and wore on his shoulder straps the single silver bar appropriate to this grade), but who acted as the leader of a *Kameradschaft* was entitled to wear the red and white lanyard of a *Kameradschaftsführer*. With the rapid expansion of the HJ in the mid 1930s, and again during the war, the function indicated by the lanyard was often much higher than that shown on the shoulder. This applied particularly to the leaders of the DJ.

Prior to the introduction (during the war) of special BMD/JM officer insignia, the lanyard was the sole indication of rank in both the girls' organizations.

The colour, or combination of colours, of the lanyard was the same for equivalent grades in both the male and female branches of the Hitler Youth.

An *HJ-Scharführer* with green rank lanyard. The use of the 1929-1936 pattern cap eagle is certainly unofficial with this type of uniform.

An HJ *Kameradschaftsführer* (and DJ *Jugenschaftsführer*) lanyard was worn from the button on the left breast pocket to the third button on the front of the shirt, i.e. the button on approximately the same level as the pocket. All other lanyards were worn from the left shoulder to the left breast pocket, with one exception. This was the lanyard of an *HJ-Hauptscharführer* ( or *DJ-Hauptjungzugführer*) and was worn in the manner of an adjutant, from the *right* shoulder to the right breast pocket. It indicated function rather than rank and was green/black.

Since the DJ uniforms had a shoulder strap on the right only, it was necessary to add a button to the left shoulder to accommodate the lanyard of boys above *Jugendschaftsführer* grade.

Originally the lanyard of a *Kameradschaftsführer* was in the *Landesfarben,* or colours of the various States (*Länder*) of Germany. Later this was changed to the colour of the *Oberbann* (as listed previously, e.g. red for *Oberbann 1*, yellow for *Oberbann 2*, etc.). Finally, in 1936, a red and white lanyard was adopted as standard for this grade or its equivalents in, the DJ, BDM and JM.

The *Landesfarben* were as follows:

Black/white
> Prussia, Ostland, Kurmark, Silesia, Ostsee (Baltic Coast) Nordmark, Nordsee (North Sea Coast), Lower Saxony, Westphalia, Lower and Middle Rhine, Westmark, Hesse-Nassau, Kurhessen, Mittelland.

Red/white
> Hamburg, Bremen, Oberhessen, Thuringia, Austria, Starkenburg

Blue/red
> Weser-Ems, Birkenfeld

Blue/white
> Franconia, Hochland

Blue/yellow
> Brunswick

Green/white
> Saxony

Red/yellow
> Baden

Blue/red/yellow
> Mecklenburg Lübeck

There were two strands of each colour interwoven. Medical officers wore a blue lanyard until September 1938 when its use was discontinued.

## LEADERS LANYARDS (*FÜHRERSCHNURE*)

(a) Kameradschaftsführer     Red/white (originally in
     Oberkameradschaftsführer     *Landesfarben*);

(b) Scharführer     Green (for Hauptscharführer,
     Oberscharführer     a green/black lanyard);

(c) Gefolgschaftsführer
    Obergefolgschaftsführer
    Hauptgefolgschaftsführer        Green/white;

(d) Stammführer
    Oberstammführer                 White;

(e) Bannführer                      Red;

(f) Oberbannführer
    Hauptbannführer                 Red/black;

(g) Gebietsführer                   Black;

(h) Obergebietsführer               Black/silver;

(i) RJF Staff                       Black/gold.

Exactly the same colour combinations were used by equivalent ranks of the DJ.

68

# HJ QUALIFICATION BADGES

Driver (*Fahrer*). Silver *F* on pink. Instituted in March 1937 and worn by headquarters drivers on HJ/BDM etc. staff (not connected with the *Motor-HJ*).

HJ boys under training with NSKK, 1st design. Silver on red/white diamond of the HJ.

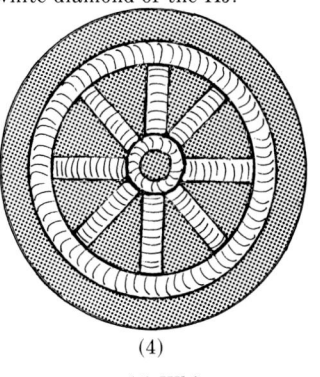

HJ boys under training with NSKK, 2nd design (colours as before).

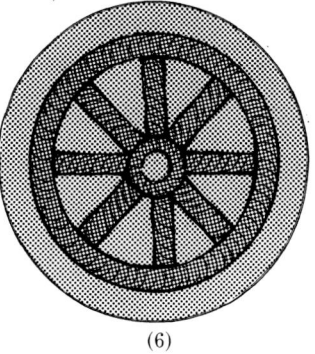

(4) White or grey cotton wheel on pink: members of the Motor-HJ. Regular personnel (e.g. staff of the Motor Sport School at Nürnberg) had silver wire wheel on pink.
(5) Yellow cotton wheel on pink: "Qualification Badge" (*Prüfungsabzeichem der Motor-HJ*).
(6) Matt gold wire wheel on pink: *Gebietsinspecteure* (Regional Inspectors of the *Motor-HJ*).

*Luftsportscharen* (Air Sport Squads) White wings and propellor on red circle. Background is khaki. Discontinued after January 1938.

A rare photo of the HJ adjutant's badge being worn.

HJ adjutant: silver "bar" on carmine, but if Adjutant to a Political Leader, the background is royal blue.

*Flieger Jugend.* Silver or white on sky blue. Worn between 1933 and 1938

Right: HJ Leaders who were members of the *Auslands Organisation* (Foreign Organization) were allowed to wear its badge — a silver wire *AO* on a black diamond — on the left cuff of their tunics (The style of the A and the O varies slightly with different "makes" of this badge).

Left: Administrative official's badge. This is found in five different types:
(i) A white cotton *V* on green for *Gefolgschaft* level;
(ii) Silver wire *V* on green for *Bann* level;
(iii) Silver wire *V* on green with silver wire surround for *Gebiet* level;
(iv) Gold wire *V* on green for Inspectors or Auditors (*Revisoren*) on the staff of the RJF;
(v) Gold wire *V* on green with a gold wire surround for Departmental Chiefs (*Amtsleiter*) on staff of RJF. Introduced in December 1935 but discontinued in December 1937. An administrator in the Marine HJ had a yellow V on a navy blue circle.

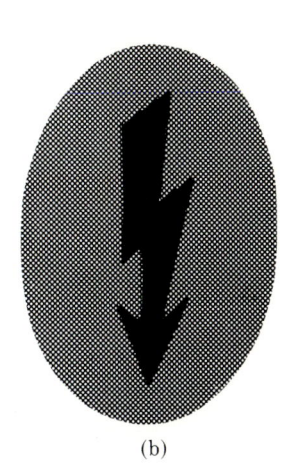

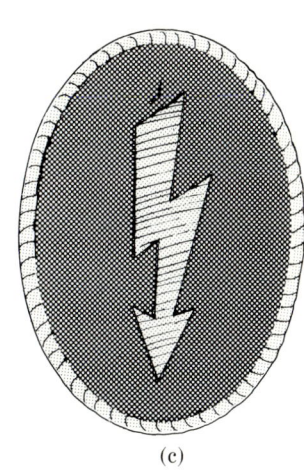

(a) (b) (c)

(a) Signaller's badge 1st design. Yellow cotton *Blitz* on green;
(b) Signaller's badge 2nd design "A" test: black cotton *Blitz* on green;
Signaller's badge 2nd design "B" test: Silver wire *Blitz* on green;
Signaller's badge 2nd design "C" test: Gold wire *Blitz* on green;
(c) Holder of an HJ Signals Instructor's Certificate (*HJ Nachrichten Lehrschein*). Gold wire *Blitz* on green with a gold wire surround.
The second design of *Blitz* is identical to that of an armed forces Signaller.

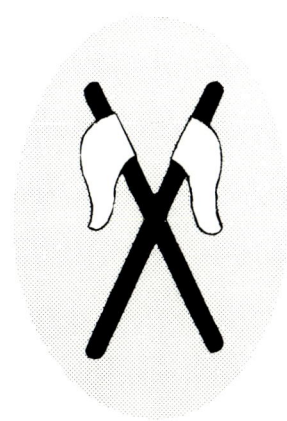

Holder of an HJ Riding Certificate (black lances, white pennants, on yellow background).

Holder of an HJ Pioneer Certificate (white on black).

Cloth version of the HJ diamond. This was worn o the following:
(a) Left upper arm of BDM/JM winter jacket (*Klette jacke*);
(b) Front of sports singlet at first by all youths, lat (with the introduction of a special singlet for HJ boy worn only by DJ boys and BDM/JM girls;
(c) Front of girls black bathing suit;
(d) Left arm of HJ, etc. ski jacket;
(e) Left upper arm of working overalls (as in t *Landdienst*, etc.);
(f) Left upper arm of BDM *Landdienst* short raincoa
(g) Front of white BDM nursing apron;
(h) Left breast of track suit (known in German *Sportschutzanzug* or *Traininganzug*);
(i) On left upper arm, in place of HJ brassard, b *Marine-HJ* when wearing working "whites" (aft January 1939).

An interesting and rare photograph of early HJ when this was a sub-section of the SA. The boys wear SA-type black collar patches. Note the absence of shoulder straps, neckerchiefs, headgear or swastika brassards. (Date: 1929).

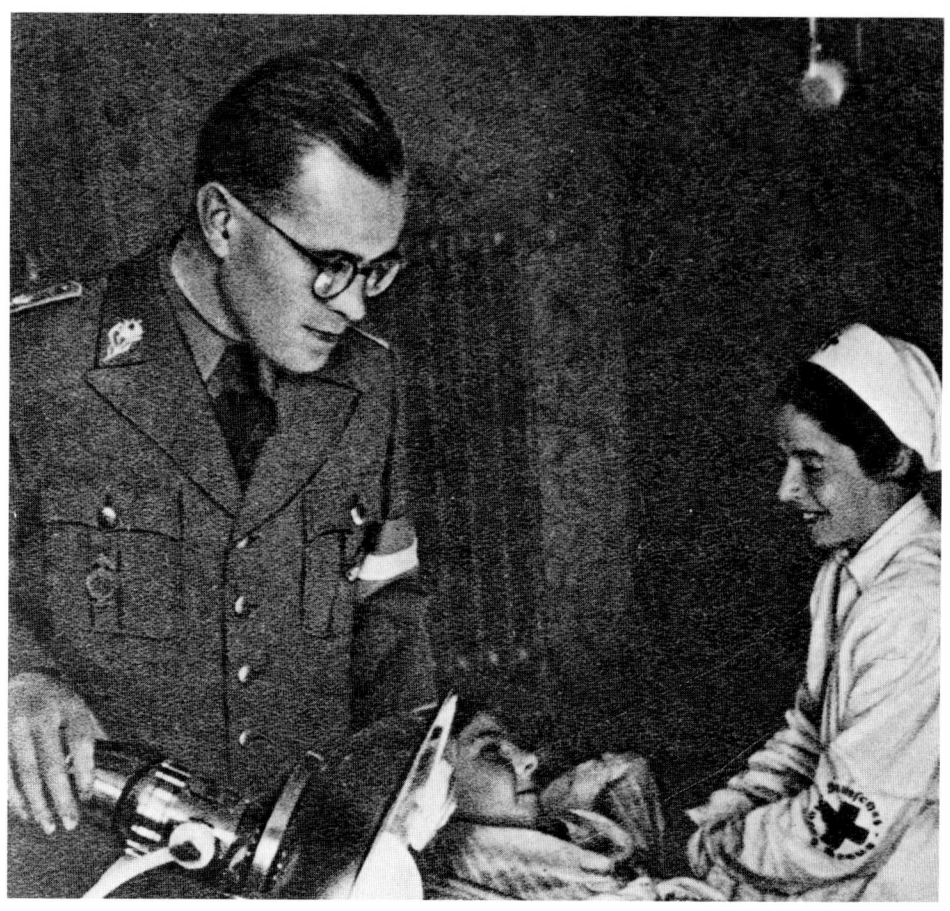

HJ doctor ("the rune" emblem just discernable on shoulder strap) gives sun-lamp treatment. Note the *Edelweiss* badge worn on his collar indicating that he belongs to an HJ unit in Austria or the Bavarian *Gruppe Hochland*.

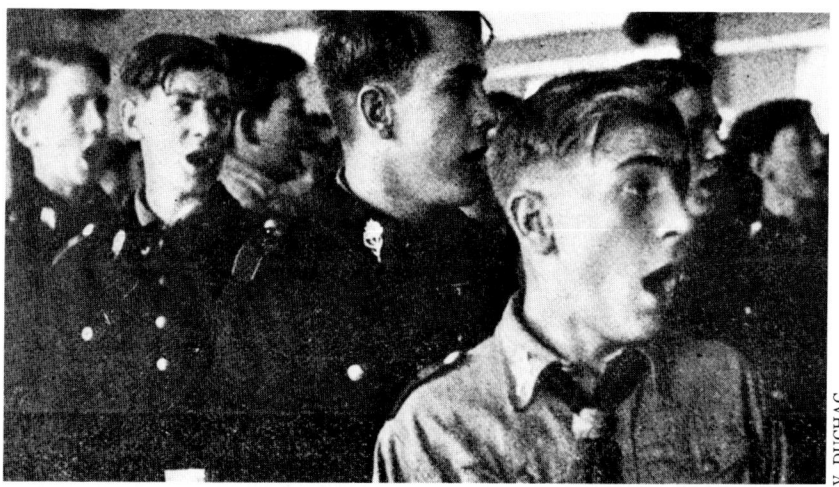

Boys of the Austrian branch of the HJ with Edelweiss badge on right collar.

# Flags and Pennants

What must certainly count as the first "Hitler Youth" flag was in fact devised before the Hitler Youth received its name. On January 23, 1923, at the time of the first Party Day of the NSDAP in Munich, the predecessor the HJ, the *Jungsturm Adolf Hitler*, was granted a flag, or more properly a pennant *(Wimpel)*, which showed a blue anchor and swastika on a white field. This device was supposed to symbolize the fact that the *Jungsturm* was achored in the NSDAP. To the casual onlooker it was more likely to have suggested naval connotations. Any possible confusion which may have existed could, however, been but short lived since, after a public fracas of the type common enough in the streets of Germany at this time, the pennant was seized by the Munich police. When Hitler came to power ten years thereafter, this "sacred" relic was retrieved and, on commemorative occasions, paraded in a place of honour.

At the national rally of the NSDAP at Nürnberg in August 1929, some 2,000 lads from all over Germany took part and were presented with the first proper HJ flags. These were referred to as *HJ Gaufeldzeichen*. They featured a black sword (representing nationalism) crossed with a black hammer (representing socialism) on a red field.

Prior to the seizure of power in 1933, and for some time afterwards, a wide variety of flags and pennants were used by the HJ and DJ with designs which could range from skull-and-crossbones to a Viking ship. The banners of the non-Nazi nationalist youth groups forcibly incorporated into the HJ survived only briefly until they, like their organizations, ceased to exist.

The sword and hammer *Gaufeldzeichen* was later combined with the eagle of Prussia to form the flag of an HJ *Bann*. The Prussian eagle held in its claws a sword (justice) and a sceptre (authority), but in the Hitler Youth version the sceptre is replaced by a hammer; a swastika is added to the eagle's chest, thus symbolically combining Prussian military tradition with National Socialism. Above the eagle's head is a scroll with the *Bann* number. The whole is set on a red/white/red field. This same type of field, but with simply a swastika in the centre, is the flag of both a *Gefolgschaft* and a *Schar*, the difference being one of size and the unit identification rectangle in the upper left quarter. Smaller formations had individually-marked pennants.

Flag poles were bamboo with a metal standard top, that for a *Gefolgschaft* being a bayonet, that of a *Bann* the more conventional ball-

and-spike. HJ standard bearers wore, as in the armed forces, a gorget and an arm badge. The eagle with sword and hammer, which features on the *Bann* flag, also appears on the gorget of a *Bann* standard bearer. On the gorget the *Bann* number is above the eagle; on the arm badge it is below. The standard bearer of a *Gefolgschaft* did not rate a gorget, only an arm badge. It shows a white eagle holding the HJ diamond on a black background. The standard bearer badge of both the *Bann* and *Gefolgschaft* was worn on the right upper arm. Both the gorget and the arm badge were introduced in July 1938.

Officials of the HJ from *Bannführer* (or its equivalent in the DJ, BDM, or JM) upwards were entitled to individual car pennants. In the case of the higher ranks these had an eagle holding the HJ diamond on a yellow field. The pennant for *Bannführer* was a red/white/red square with a black swastika with the *Bann* number and place-name in black Gothic lettering.

Locally-produced pennants in the early period were often crudely made, sometimes being nothing more than pieces of cloth or tape sewn onto coloured fabric.

The flag of the HJ as an organization was, like the brassard, a black swastika on white against red/white/red but, unlike the brassard, the white was the *same* width as the two red parts.

The flag for an HJ *Gefolgschaft* exhibits the same design of both sides, and measures 180cm by 120cm with red/white/red in equal proportions (40cm). The *Schar* flag is the same design, only smaller, 150cm by 100cm (red — 35cm, white — 30cm) and smaller swastika (both actually and relatively compared to that of *Gefolgschaft* flag). In the upper left quarter is an identification rectangle (there can be more than one rectangle, depending on the number of sub-units). The rectangle is black (later white) for *Gefolgschaft*, brown for *Schar*. Other rectangle colours are: *Motor-HJ:* Pink rectangle, black numbers, black surround; *Nachrichten-HJ* (signals): Yellow rectangle, black numbers, black surround; *Marine-HJ:* Navy blue rectangle, white numbers, white surround; *Flieger-HJ: sky-blue rectangle, white numbers, white surround; Landjahr:* green with *Landjahr* in white.

Tentative sketch of the *Jungsturm Adolf Hitler* pennant (January 1923). Based on two (rather unclear) photos.

76

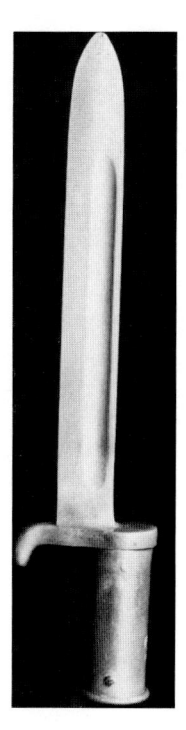

"Bayonet" flag top for HJ *Gefolgschaft* or DJ *Fahnlein* standard.

HJ *Gefolgschafts* flag. Same design both sides, measures 180cms by 120cms with red/white/red in equal proportions (40cms). *Schar* flag is same but smaller, 150cms by 100cms (red 35cms, white 30cms) and smaller swastika (both actually and relatively compared to that of *Gefolgschaft* flag). In upper left quarter is identification rectangle (can be more than one, depending on number of sub-units). This is black (later white) for *Gefolgschaft*, brown for *Schar*. *Motor-HJ:* pink rectangle, black numbers, black surround; *Signals HJ:* yellow rectangle, black numbers, black surround; *Marine-HJ*: navy blue rectangle, white numbers, white surround; *Flieger-HJ*: sky blue rectangle, white numbers, white surround; *Landjahr;* green with *Landjahr* in white.

Gorget for standard-bearer of a *Bann*. This was introduced in July 1938.

DJ model-makers. Boy on left wears arm badge of a standard-bearer of a DJ *Fahnlein*.

Arm badge for a standard-bearer of an HJ *Bann* or DJ *Jungbann* (silver wire on black)

Arm badge for a standard-bearer of an HJ *Gefolgschaft* or DJ *Fahnlein* (white/red/black cotton)

Car pennant which belonged to Gebietsführer Karbach of Obergebiet 12, Moselland. The pennant could also be flown on the cars of Karbach's immediate aides while on official business.

Pre-war parade of Hitler Youth led by standard-bearers. (note Bann standard-bearer's gorget and badge of right upper arm.)

Chief of Staff of the HJ: (Second design)

Departmental Leader of the RJF.

HJ Gebiet Leader (here for Württemberg)

79

HJ Bann Leader (here Neustettin)

Leader of a DJ Gebiet. Obverse and reverse

Leader of an BDM Unter- gau (here Pfalzsaar)

Leader of a JM Obergau. Obverse and reverse

Left: pennant for RJF and Gebiet staff, other than those entitled to the above individual pennants.

HJ *Bann* flag. Same design on both sides. It measures 200cms by 145cms. Red is 50cms white only 45cms *Bann* number on gold scroll.

80

# 6

# Specialist Sections of the Hitler Youth

MOTOR-HJ

The largest of the specialist sections of the Hitler Youth was the *Motor-HJ*. It was also the earliest, created in 1933 by an agreement between von Schirach and Konrad Hühnlein, the *Korpsführer* of the NSKK (Nat. Soz. Kraftfahrkorps — the Nazi motorized corps). Boys could transfer to this branch of the HJ at 16-years-old (the age at which a driving licence could be granted). Training was, in the early days, mainly on motorcycles, since the NSKK possessed far more of these than it did cars.

The new service proved to be enormously popular and expanded rapidly. In 1933 there were some 3,000 members, by the following year, 10,000, and by 1936 this had risen to 60,000; by 1938 the figure had almost doubled with 102,000 members. At the start of the Second World War, there were some 150,000 lads in 3,342 Motor HJ *Scharen*, making up 946 Motor HJ *Gefolgschaften* and 83 Motor HJ *Stämme*. The service had, by this time, 690 "homes" and 333 workshops or repair units.

An open motor sport competition was held annually in Germany for which the Motor HJ regularly carried off top awards, more than holding its own against the adult competitors!

Training was, as in other branches of the HJ, based on the *HJ Leistungsabzeichen*.\* The tests in the first two parts being the same as those for the general HJ, the specialist test formed the third section. For these, more than mere ability to drive was required. Against a minimum of 80 hours driving, an annual minimum of 105 hours practical mechanical work was required. Boys had to be conversant with not only the workings of the car and/or motorcycle, but also to have a thorough knowledge of traffic and road regulations.

The Motor HJ had pink piping like that of the army's motorized and armoured elements.

---

\* See section on *Honor Badges and Awards*.

Boys of the *Motor-HJ* receive instruction from an NSKK man in the repair of a puncture. The boys wear NSKK crash helmets and NSKK overalls.

# FLIEGER-HJ

The second most popular specialist section of the Hitler Youth was the *Flieger-* (flying) *HJ*. At the outbreak of war it had some 78,000 members. It began life in 1933 as the *Fliegerjugend*. In September 1935 the *Deutscher Luftfahrt Verband* (German Air Sport Association, or DLV) set up *Luftsportscharen* in which HJ boys could learn gliding. The younger lads in the DJ had their *Modellbaugemeinschaften* (model-making groups).

The Treaty of Versailles had forbidden Germany a military air army, but in 1935 Hitler felt strong enough to defy this and the Luftwaffe was born. In April 1937 the DLV was replaced by the NSFK *(Nat. Soz. Flieger Korps)*. The erstwhile *Luftsportscharen* were linked with the *Fliegerjugend* to become the *Flieger-HJ*.

The NSFK agreed to undertake the flying training of the Hitler Youth, but due to a shortage of powered aircraft this was done exclusively on gliders. Where real gliders were unavailable, the new "fliers" had to make do with building model ones. However this proved to be a very popular activity and an all-Germany model glider competition was held annually from 1936 onward. Prizes (badges and plaques) were awarded by the NSFK. Where real gliders were on hand, the *Flieger-HJ* lads could train for an award of the International Gliding Badge.

When the "Flak Helpers" came into being during the war, some *Flieger-HJ* units were simply incorporated into this organization wholesale.

The summer uniform was like that of the General HJ, but with light blue piping. The winter uniform was the ski-type in *Luftwaffe* blue-grey. Leaders had a winter tunic of the same style and colour of a *Luftwaffe* officer. Their winter greatcoat did not have black lapels, unlike that worn by regular HJ leaders.

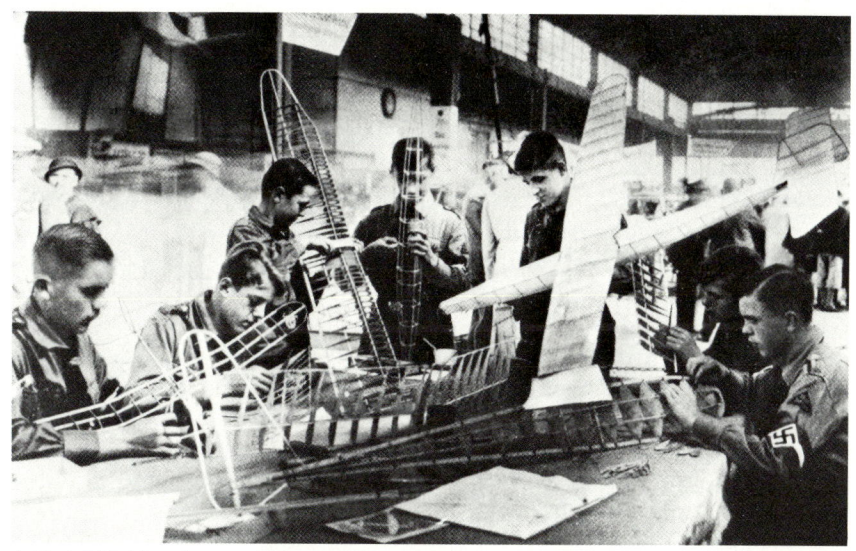

A Model Making Group of *Flieger HJ* at work on gliders.

NSFK officials conduct an HJ model glider meet.               TOM SHUTT

## MARINE-HJ

The third largest specialist section of the Hitler Youth was the *Marine-HJ*. This naval Hitler Youth had a membership of 62,000 boys by 1935. Actual seagoing could, given the geographical nature of Germany, be undertaken only by those units located along the North Sea or Baltic coasts, but sailing and rowing were possible on inland lakes or large rivers. Not far from Berlin was an important "Sea Sport School." Lake Constance (Bodensee) on the German/Swiss border was the locale of another noted *Marine-HJ* school.

During his first year of service, an MHJ boy was expected to gain the normal Achievement Badge *(Leistungsabzeichen)* of the HJ. The first two sections of which — athletics and shooting — contained the same tests as for the General HJ, but the third section — field exercises *(Geländesport)* was limited to map reading and distance judging. The other parts of this section, being more appropriate to infantry, were replaced by special "sea sport" exercises.

During his second year the boy could enter for the MHJ Sea Sport Badge *(Seesportabzeichen)*, indicated by a red fouled anchor. Subsequently, he might progress through the three higher grades, the A, B and C tests indicated by, respectively, one, two or three red chevrons added below the anchor. The A Test could be taken at *Gebiet* level, but for the B or C grades it was necessary to attend a National Sea Sport School, of which there were four.

On the inland lake and waterways, yachts and cutters were used for training purposes, but the MHJ did possess one seagoing vessel, the sailing ship "Horst Wessel" (which today is the training ship for the United States Coast Guard). The MHJ was also permitted the use of the Navy's three-master, "Gorch Foch," until, at the outbreak of war, the *Kriegsmarine* appropriated *both* for its own training requirements. There was a floating Sea Sport School, the three-masted schooner "Admiral von Trotha," anchored in the Stettin Lagoon, and a marine youth hostel, the sailing ship "Hein Godenwind," tied up in the harbour at Hamburg.

## UNIFORMS

The uniform of the *Marine-HJ* was closely patterned on that of the *Kriegsmarine*. Basically it was the virtually international sailor suit of navy blue woolen "vest" and "bellbottom" trousers, worn with a wide collar, knotted with white cord in front. On the left upper arm the HJ brassard was worn. The belt was, with this uniform, black with the normal HJ buckle. Headgear was the German Navy sailor's cap with a light blue band with the unit location in white. Two examples:

*M H J Kiel,*
*3/26 MAGDEBURG 3/26*

Originally the lettering was in white *Block* (Latin) script, but in 1938 that was altered to gold *Fraktur* (Gothic).

This MHJ lad wears the pre-1938 cap with HJ diamond *and* M29 national emblem.

*Marine-HJ Matrosenmütze* or, more commonly, "Donald Duck" cap. *Schiffsjungenschule HJ* cap tally.

JOHN COY

Winter uniform of *Marine HJ*. Light blue cap band has *1/162 LÜBECK 1/162*. Note lanyard indicating rank. The boy does not wear a district triangle arm badge.

In summer a white shirt could replace the navy blue "vest" and a white top could be added to the cap, but for both summer and winter *working* dress, a white moleskin uniform was worn. This comprised a loose fitting, shirt-like tunic worn over white trousers (not the bell-bottom type).

The 1934 dress regulations stated that, for winter, ratings had the addition of a navy reefer jacket worn with a black belt and cross strap. Petty Officers and officers had, at this stage, a double-breasted tunic with twin rows of five buttons, black shoulder straps, navy blue trousers, brown shirt and black tie. Their headgear was a peaked cap with, on the band, a gilt oak leaf wreath enclosing the HJ diamond badge.

Rather oddly, "full dress" *(Grosser Dienst)* consisted at this date (1934) of a brown shirt, brown shorts (or breeches for winter), brown shoulder straps piped in navy blue and a brown belt. A gold anchor on a navy blue circular backing was worn on the upper right sleeve. Headgear was the khaki HJ side cap piped in navy blue.

In 1934 there were only six ranks:

(i) *Oberjunggast:* A large chevron (yellow for the navy blue garb, cornflower blue for "whites") worn on the right upper arm, corresponding to the Navy's rank of *Matrosengefreiter;*

(ii) *Kameradschaftsführer:* A cloth star on the right upper arm on a navy blue circle. The star was yellow for the blue uniform and cornflower blue (on a white background) for working dress;

(iii) *Scharführer:* Two cloth stars on the upper right arm. The stars were placed one above the other and could be, as before, either yellow on navy blue, or cornflower blue on white, depending on the order of dress worn;

*Kameradschaftsführer*
(Gold star on navy blue).

*Scharfuhrer* (Two gold stars on navy blue).

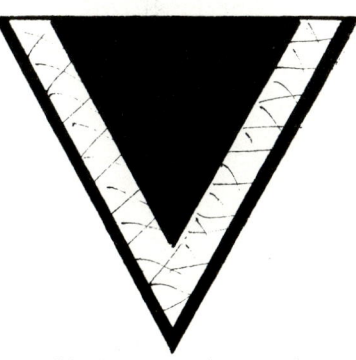

*Oberjunggast (renamed Rottenführer* in 1935). Gold chevron on navy blue.

Coxswain of a cutter (*Ruderbootsführer*). Red chevron on white oval.

Coxswain of a sailing craft (*Segelbootsführer*). Two red chevrons on white.

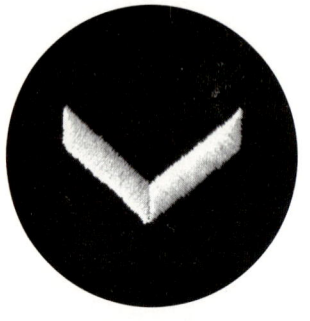

Rottenführer

Oberrottenführer

Kameradschaftsführer

Oberkameradschaftsführer

Scharführer

Oberscharführer

The above scheme of ranks was introduced in September 1938 and applied to Petty Officers below the age of 18 years. On navy blue uniform the stars and chevrons are grey on navy blue circle; with summer white, or white working dress they are cornflower blue on white.

When, in 1935, the General HJ introduced the new grade of Rottenführer, the *Marine-HJ* replaced the former Oberjunggast rank with this designation — the grade being (as in the DJ of the time) represented by a silver chevron on the lower right arm. Even after the introduction of the above scheme of ranks a *Marine-HJ Rottenführer* continued to wear his rank on the cuff (all the others were worn on the right upper arm). It was not until May 1939 that the type of Rottenführer rank pictured above was adopted and worn in the same manner as the rest.

(iv) *Gefolgschaftsführer:* This was officer grade and was therefore worn on the shoulder. It consisted of three matt gold stars on a black shoulder strap (both sides). A green-white lanyard was also worn:

(v) *Unterbannführer:* Four matt gold stars worn on both (black) shoulder straps. With this, a white lanyard;

(vi) *Bannführer:* A single gold oak leaf on the black shoulder straps. A red lanyard was also worn;

Functional, or trade, badges consisted of:

(a) *Signaller:* Crossed signal flags on a blue or white circle;

(b) *Technical Personnel:* A cog wheel, red on a blue or white circle;

(c) *Musicians (Spielleute):* Two inverted chevrons, in red on either a navy blue or white oval;

(d) *Sick Bay Attendant (Feldscher):* A white cross on red.

Somewhere between rank and functional badges were the devices worn by coxswains of cutters and sailing vessels. The former were denoted by a single red chevron, the latter by two red chevrons.

With the later expansion of the Marine-HJ, new rank insignia and new trade badges were introduced. The final rank scheme for ratings resembled that used by the DJ, although the nomenclature was different. The chevrons and stars were grey on navy blue, or cornflower blue on white, according to the order of dress. Petty officers under the age of eighteen wore their rank insignia in this manner on the right arm; those over that age wore theirs on the shoulder straps of their short jackets.

Signaller (*Signalgast*). Red and white signal flags on yellow sticks on navy blue circle

Technical personnel, Red cog wheel on white.

Sick Bay Attendant (*Feldscher*). White cross on red.

Boys of the *Marine-HJ* are instructed in the art of steering on board the training ship "Horst Wessel." On his left cuff the officer wears the white and blue band which the boys wear as their cap tally. They are in the white moleskin uniform which was worn as working dress. This photo must have been taken before the war since (a) the "Horst Wessel" was taken over by the *Kriegsmarine* at the start of hostilities and (b) the boys still wear the HJ brassard which in January 1939 was replaced on this form of dress by a cloth version of the HJ diamond.

Commissioned officers had a uniform which was in general appearance similar to that of a naval officer, except that rank was worn on the shoulder straps. Shirts were khaki; white was worn only with "office dress." This "office dress" was a single-breasted tunic of a kind unknown in the *Kriegsmarine*. Around the right cuff Petty Officers and officers wore what on ratings uniform was the cap tally — this is, a light blue band with the unit name and/or number in white.

For all ranks the piping, *Bann* number, rank stars and bars, etc. were yellow. All the standard accoutrements of the General HJ (belts, cross straps, *Fahrtenmesser* for ratings, *Führerdolch* for officers, marching and camping kit, etc.) were also issued to the Marine HJ. All ranks wore a "district triangle" above the normal HJ brassard. After January 1939 a cloth version of the HJ diamond emblem replaced the brassard (which tended to get crumpled) on "working whites."

A yellow fouled anchor on a navy blue circle was worn on the right upper arm at one stage, but was later discontinued. The first design of the Radio Telegraphist's badge was similar to that worn by the army — a lightning flash, or *Blitz* (red on dark blue). Later this became a lightning flash around an anchor. An advanced grade had one chevron below (on the working uniform the red *Blitz* was replaced by one of cornflower blue upon a white background).

*Marine-HJ* units which served on inland waterways had the letters *BS (Binnenschifffahrt* — inland shipping) in yellow on their shoulder straps and *Bann Binnenschifffahrt* on their cap tallies. Seagoing units had a yellow *S (Seefahrt)* on their shoulder straps and a district triangle with:

*Bann*
*Seefahrt*

The first type of headgear for boys was a soft peaked cap with a gold oak leaf wreath enclosing a fouled anchor on the band. Sometimes this was accompanied by the first model HJ badge, worn on the peak of the cap; but sometimes it was omitted. Later, when the traditional sailor's cap was adopted it had on the peak both the HJ enamel diamond *and* the Party national emblem, but in 1938 this was altered to the HJ emblem only. In 1944 a navy blue side cap, like that worn by the *Kriegsmarine*, piped in yellow, replaced the round sailor's cap as *Marine-HJ* headgear.

The four National Sea Sport Schools *(Reichsseesportschulen)* were:

1 — Prieros (South East of Berlin)
2 — Seemos (Bodensee)
3 — Ziegenort (Pomerania)
4 — Neusiedl am See (lower Austria)

*Marine-HJ* boys had the opportunity for active duty at sea during the war when lads in the upper age groups were allowed to serve as auxiliaries on board German merchant ships, mainly in the relatively peaceful Baltic.

Badge worn on left cuff of *Fahrtenanzug* (Walking-out dress) Gold anchor on dark blue.

Sea Sport Badge worn on right upper arm. Navy blue on white for summer dress.

Radio Telegraphist, 1st design. Red on navy blue

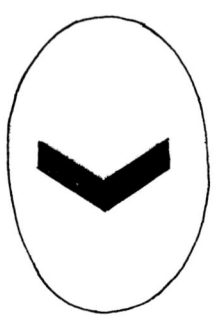

Three grades of preliminary tests leading to award of Sea Sport Badge.

Radio Telegraphist, 2nd design with advanced grade chevron. Red on navy blue (winter).

Winter uniform

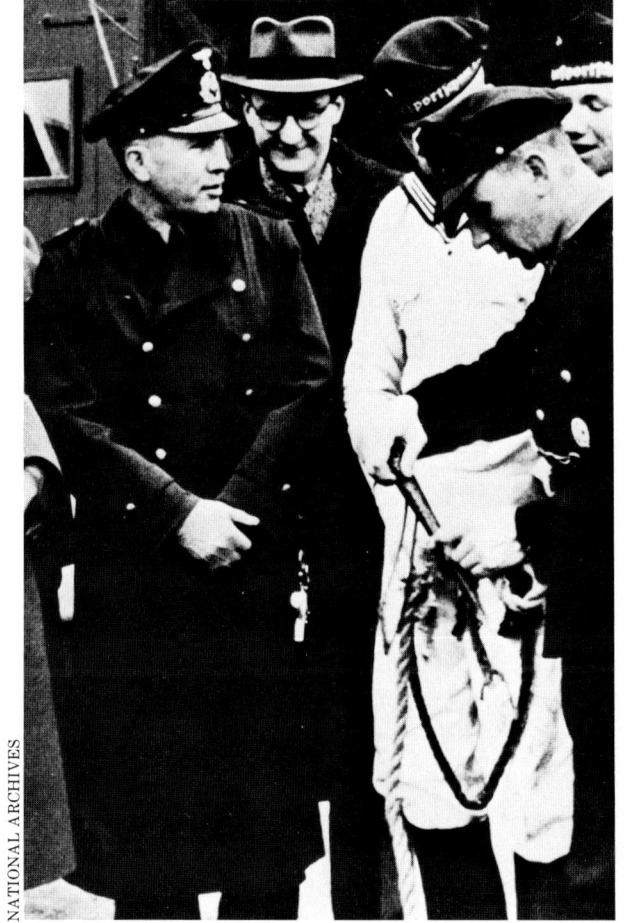

Peaked cap of a *Marine-HJ* leader. It is virtually the same as that of a German Naval officer except that the cap badge is silver not gilt and the *HJ* emblem replaces the national rosette in the centre of the wreath.

A *Marine-HJ* leader with cadets at the *HJ Seesportschule Berlin* during the war. The man on the right may be Marine SA since that organization often assisted in the training of the Marine HJ.

Boys of the Berlin *Marine-HJ* receive instruction in navigation from an adult Petty Officer. There are two points of interest about his uniform; (a) anchor on shoulder strap (b) the *MHJ Berlin* band worn (as is correct for officers) around the cuff.

3 Reichssee

Cap (or cuff) band of the no. 3 National Sea Sport School

M. H. J. KÖI

Cap (or cuff) band of the MHJ North Cologne

HISTORICAL RESEARCH UNIT

portschule 3

NORD I/53

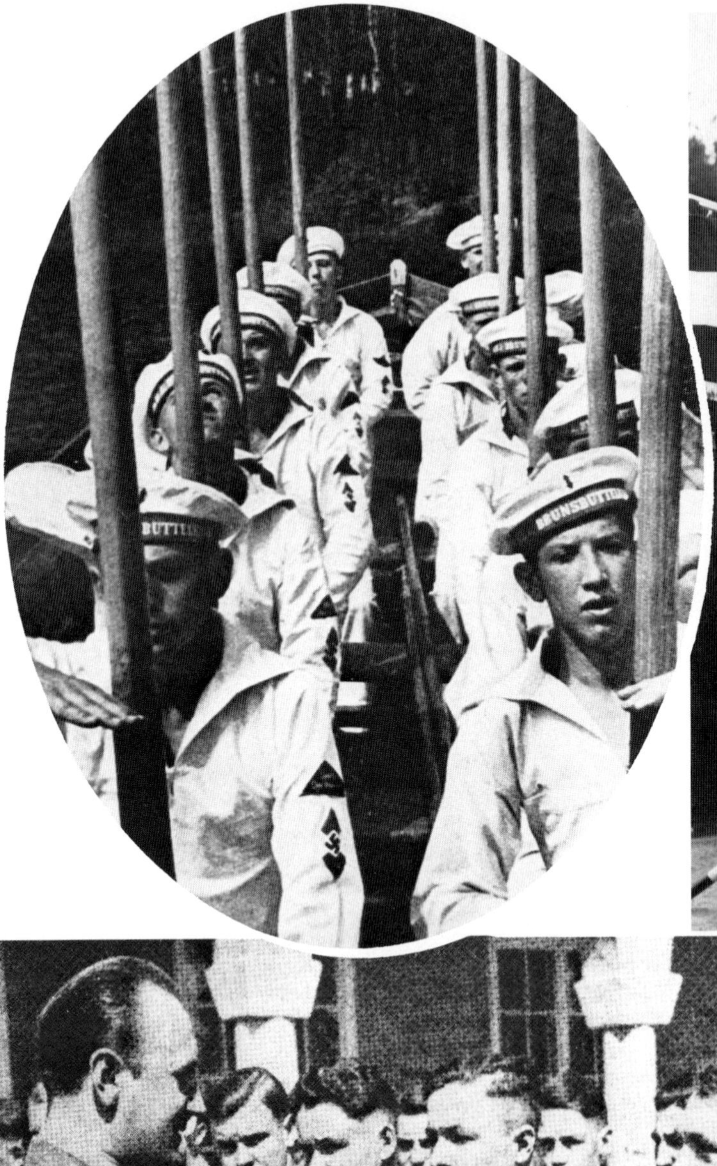

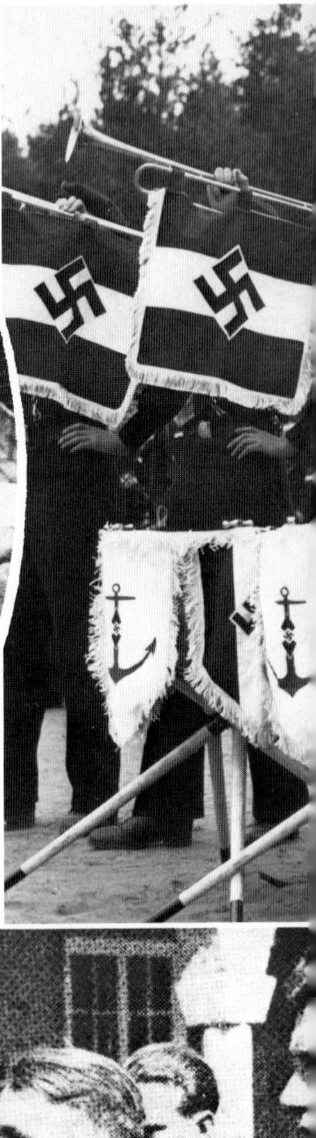

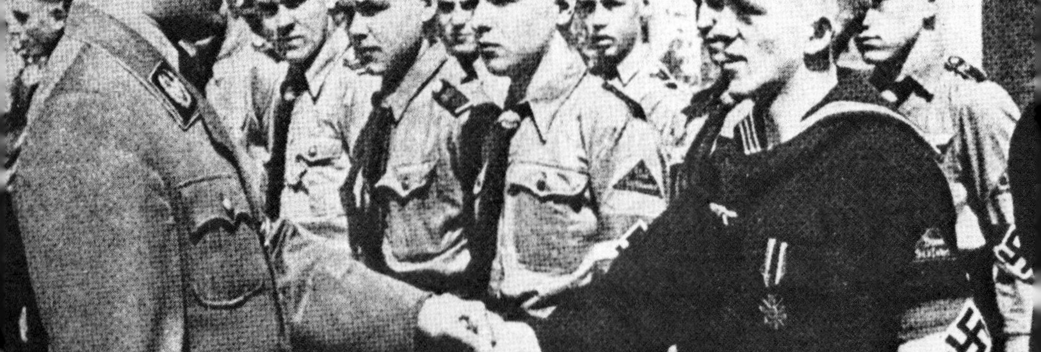

*Marine-HJ* trumpeters and kettle-drummer (note *Marine-HJ* drum skirt).

Above Left:
Boys of the *Marine-HJ* at Brunsbüttel (on the River Elbe) receive instruction in rowing a cutter.

May 1943: Artur Axmann awards the War Merit Cross 2nd Class with Swords to a *Marine-HJ* boy (Georg Ochs). Ochs was a member of the HJ *Bann Seefahrt* (this appears on the "District Triangle" on his left upper arm). Axmann shakes hands with his left as his right arm was lost during his time as a front line officer in Russia.

## NACHRICHTEN-HJ

The *Nachrichten-* (signals) *HJ* was the smallest of the four main specialist groupings in the Hitler Youth, with a membership, on the outbreak of war, of around 29,000 lads.

In addition to all the athletic and para-military training customary in the General HJ, the *Nachrichten-HJ* undertook a comprehensive course in signals work, which could last up to three years. The basic element normally took about six months to complete, at the end of which the boy could enter for an "A" certificate. This was indicated by a black *Blitz* on green (the signaller's emblem in the German army), worn on the left cuff. During the rest of the course, spread out over the following two to two-and-a-half years, he was expected to try for the more advanced "B" and "C" certificates (indicated respectively by a silver and a gold *Blitz*, upon a green oval backing).

Boys in the seventeen- and eighteen-year-old age group worked in close cooperation with the signals branches of the army or Luftwaffe. All boys received a grounding in theoretical physics, but most ot the work was practical and militarily oriented. In peacetime their duties might include such things as rigging up public address systems at rallies. They were also trained in the handling of messenger dogs.

Piping was lemon yellow like that of the army unit. Prior to the introduction of the three grades of certificates, there was only a single test, success in which was rewarded by a yellow cotton *Blitz* on a green backing.

In 1943 the *Strippenzieher* ("wire-stretchers"), as the *Nachrichten-HJ* boys were nicknamed, lost their identity and were absorbed into the Flak Helper *Flieger-HJ* set up.

Holders of the HJ Signals Instructor's Certificate (*HJ-Nachrichten Lehrschein*) were a gold wire *Blitz* upon a green oval with a gold wire surround.

## MEDICAL HJ

Until it was absorbed in the general HJ at the beginning of the war, the Hitler Youth ran a separate medical branch, which trained some 40,000 boys as *Feldschere* (literally "field surgeons" — an archaic word revived by the Nazis), and some 35,000 girls as auxiliary nurses. After the outbreak of war *all* HJ boys and BDM girls underwent first-aid instruction as part of their general training.

The first Medical Orderly Badge of the HJ (like that of the SA of this time) was a white Latin cross on a red circle. This was worn on the left cuff above any trade badge which might be worn there. Later this was replaced (again, as in the SA) by the Aesculapius snake-and-staff device. Orderlies wore this badge in yellow cotton on a dark blue oval, medical officers wore the same emblem, in gold wire on a purple backing with a gold wire surround. All HJ boys who passed the first aid test were entitled to wear this emblem in red on a white circle with "U D" (*Unfall Dienst* — accident service).

*Nachrichten* (Signals) HJ at Morse code practice.

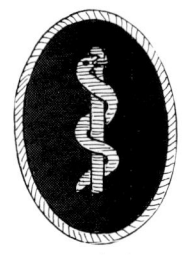

Doctor, 1st design. Gold wire on dark blue.

First Aid Badge (Unfall Dienst). Red on white.

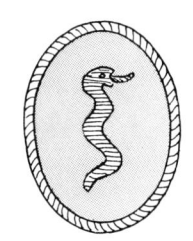

Veterinary Officer. Gold wire on light blue.

Doctor, 2nd design.

Pharmacist (*Apotheker*).

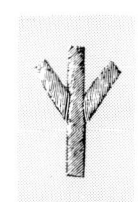

Dentist (*Zahnarzt*).

All the above are silver wire on light blue.

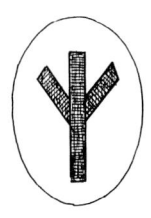

Left: Medical Orderly 3rd design. The first design was simply a white cross on a red circle. The second was as above Doctor 1st design except that it was yellow cotton and without piping round edge. Right: Medical Orderly of a *Gefolgschaft*. Red on white with green/white surround.

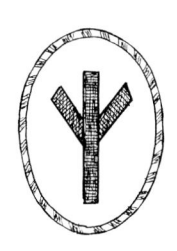

In September 1938 the internationally recognized medical emblem was replaced on all Party militias' medical services by the so-called "Life Rune." Medical orderlies now wore this in red on a white oval which, for those attached to higher formations, had a coloured surround, denoting the level of that formation. Medical doctors had a silver wire Life Rune on a grey-blue oval, pharmacists the same emblem, on an inverted triangle, dentists the same on a rectangular backing. The flag of a medical unit was a Life Rune in red on a white field.

Special shoulder straps for the medical branch were also introduced in September of 1938 (see section on shoulder straps), but the wearing of the former blue lanyard by medics was dropped. Piping on the khaki side cap was blue for medical personnel.

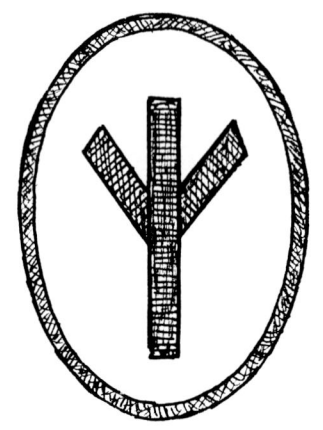

Medical Orderly of a *Bann* (red rune on white with red surround).

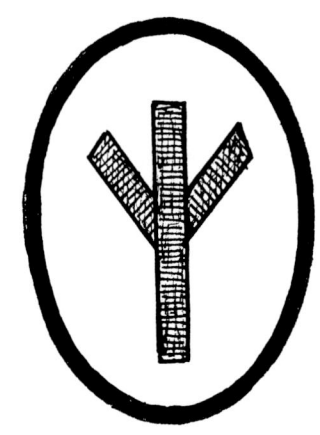

Medical Orderly of a *Gebiet* (red rune on white with black surround).

It may be noted that the colour of the surround corresponds to the colour of a Leader's lanyard — green/white for a *Gefolgschaft*, red for a *Bann* and black for a *Gebiet*.

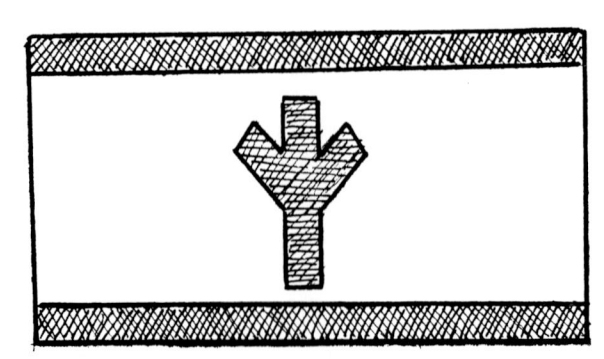

Special brassard for Medical Officers introduced in January 1939. It is a red "life rune" on white with red edges. The brassard for medical orderlies was the same but without the red edges.

Medical Officers on the RJF staff wore gold G (*Gesundheitsamt* = Health Office) on a brown circle with gold piping. The same in silver (with silver piping) was worn by doctors and pharmacists on the staff of a *Gebiet*. Whether this was a Gothic, or a Latin script "G" is not stated in the dress regulation order which specifies this.

REITER-HJ

In some country districts sections of the HJ trained on horses. These mounted, or riding HJ units had the same uniform as the others but, as horsemen, were allowed to wear black riding breeches and hightop boots. Those who earned the Riding Certificate wore a yellow oval with crossed cavalry lances (black with white pennants) on their left sleeve. Veterinary officers attached to the *Reiter-HJ* wore a yellow serpent (the army's veterinary symbol) on a light blue oval with a yellow outer edge. This badge appears in the 1933 dress regulations but disappears again shortly thereafter, possibly due to a lack of persons actually eligible to wear it (the *Reiter-HJ* was a fairly minor affair and its horses, usually farm animals, were doubtless cared for by the local civilian veterinarian). There was no special shoulder strap piping for the *Reiter-HJ*, although, logically, it should have been golden yellow, had army paradigms been followed in this case.

HJ-STREIFENDIENST

What amounted to a military police for the Hitler Youth was brought into being by a decree of December 1, 1936 under which a *Streifendienst* (literally "Patrol Service") was created. Its functions were policing HJ rallies and transport movements, supervising HJ hostels, assisting youth at railway stations and, according to its foundations order, "... defending youth against criminal elements and counteracting juvenile crime...." Each member was issued with a special *Ausweis* (authority card) and a black cuff-title with the designation *HJ-Streifendienst* in gold.

On August 26, 1938, under an agreement between Himmler and the RJF, the *HJ-Streifendienst* was recognized as a sort of preparatory school of the SS. Its training was now placed in the hands of the SS, and boys were expected to "graduate" into the SS after leaving the service.

Apart from the brassard, the uniform of the *Streifendienst* was that of the normal HJ. Shoulder straps were piped in white. There was a proposal to create a *BDM-Streifendienst*, but it never became a reality.

Two versions of the cuff-title.

A Streifendienst boy on traffic control duty. Note his cuff-title. This would normally be worn on the lower left arm, but as this is obviously a hot weather occasion and his sleeves are rolled up, he wears it mid-arm.

## LANDJAHR AND LANDDIENST

The *Landjahr* (Land Year) and *Landdienst* (Land Service) of the Hitler Youth were not original concepts. Both derived from an earlier nationalist organization — the *Bund der Artamenen.*

Founded in 1924 by Hans Holfeder as the *Bund Artam* (the latter word being a coinage from the old Persian by the Anglo-German astrologer, William Herschel). Its aim was to furnish voluntary agricultural assistance in Germany's eastern provinces. The motivation behind this was entirely chauvinistic. As elsewhere in western Europe there had been since the turn of the century, a steady drift of labour away from the land and into the cities. In Germany this had meant a movement of population from east to west. To fill the vacuum left by departing Germans, Slav workers had begun to move onto the farms and great estates of East Prussia, Silesia and Saxony. That these migrants could easily become permanent settlers, thus turning the German *Grenzland* into an extension of Poland, was something that disquieted German nationalists. The Artamenen Movement was created to counter this incursion.

The first Artamenen camp was opened at Limbach in Saxony in April 1924. By the end of that year there were fourteen camps; by 1927 sixty. In 1925 Friedrich Schmidt replaced Holfeder as Leader (*Bündesführer*), and at the same time he joined the Dresden section of the NSDAP. The nationalistic and racist notions of the *Bund* were very much in accord with the Nazi "Blood and Soil" (*Blut und Boden*) precepts and several prominent members of Hitler's party, among them Himmler, Walther Darré and Alfred Rosenberg, were simultaneously *Artamenen* adherents. Von Schirach, although not a *Bund* member, often spoke at their meetings. He shared their basic tenet that the drift from the land should not merely be halted, but reversed and that Germany should seek expansion in the east. He also agreed with their doctrine that urban life, permeated with deleterious Jewish influences, was harmful and that a robust peasantry was the surest foundation for a reborn Fatherland. The fact that the podgy patrician von Schirach had never soiled his hands with manual labour in no way inhibited him from extolling its virtues or commending it to others!

The *Bund* was not, thanks to its influential supporters, unlike so many other non-Nazi organizations, immediately suppressed after Hitler's accession to power. It was, however, not spared from assimilation. In 1934 at Gustrow in Mecklenburg it was transformed into the *Landdienst der Hitler Jugend*. This new branch of the Hitler Youth aimed at sending urban lads for one year (*Landjahr*) to a farm. This, it was hoped, would imbue them with a love of the land and, ideally, induce them to opt for this as a permanent way of life. At this time the *Landjahr* was not restricted to HJ members; other young men could, if they so wished, also participate. With the gradual absorption of almost the entire youth of Germany into the HJ, this provision later became meaningless. The service was voluntary except in the case of university students who were obliged to perform their "Land Year" (it was, in reality, only nine months) before being allowed to graduate. By the end of its first year of existence the *Landdienst* had forty-five groups with a

"Landdienst" cuff-title.

total of some 500 young men. The following year (1935) this had risen to 240 groups with over 3,500 members (BDM girls were now included in the service). Expansion of the groups was rapid:

    462 in 1936 (with 6,608 members)
    1,175 in 1937 (with 14,888 members)
    1,452 in 1938 (with over 18,000 members)

Fanfare trumpeters of the *Landjahr* of the HJ (a pre-war photo, possibly at a Nürnberg rally).

At the outbreak of war in September 1939 the *Landdienst* had 26,016 members with girls outnumbering boys. Male volunteers had to be between 14 and 18-years-old; females between 14 to 21-years-old and have the written permission of their parents. They had to submit to a medical examination to assess their fitness for work, which could amount to between fifty-four and sixty hours per week. They received no pay apart from a nominal 5 Marks per month. The cost of transportation to and from the place of work was borne by the state and living was free, providing the peasant families with whom they were billeted.

No unit was smaller than ten boys or girls. Around forty-five to fifty young persons comprised a *Landdienstschar* (of which there were 1,753 by the spring of 1940), each under a *Landdienstscharführer* responsible directly to the local *HJ-Bannführer* (or *BDM Untergauführerin*). Several *Scharen* made up a *Gruppe*. A *Landdienstscharführer* could attend a course at the National Land Service School, (*Reichslanddienstschule*), and pass out as a *Landdienstgefolgschaftsführer*. Later he might, if successful, be promoted to *Landdienstreferent*. The *Landdienst* of the HJ had to work in cooperation with the *Reichsnährstand* (The National Food Estate) which ran its own *Abteilung "Landjugend"* (Land Youth Department). Less than a third of those who aspired to be HJ *Landdienst* leaders were themselves sons of the soil.

With the advent of war the nature of the *Landdienst* changed. It became closely identified with the SS. In February 1940 a *Siedlernach-*

*wuchsstelle "Ost"* (Rising Generation Settlers Office "East") was created under a joint agreement between the leadership of the SS and the Hitler Youth. Its aim was to train so-called *Wehrbauern* (literally "armed peasants"), that is to say, future settlers in a conquered east who would not only till the land, but should it prove necessary, also defend it with their lives. To further this aim, the *Landdienst* concept was extended to include the youth of the Nordic countries — Holland, Denmark, Norway, and Flanders. The newly enlarged service was renamed the Germanic Land Service (*Germanischer Landdienst*).

Another development was that whereas the annual "harvest help" (*Ernteeinsatz*) furnished by the HJ had always remained separate from the *Landdienst*, after 1940 the two concepts became increasingly intermingled. To "lend a hand on the land" became part of every HJ boy's and BDM girl's moral obligation. Britain met the problem of the shortage of male agricultural workers by creating a Women's Land Army; Nazi Germany got out of this difficulty by exploiting child labour! In 1940 the BDM introduced a special *Osteinsatz* (East Action), whereby girls could volunteer to do a minimum of six weeks service in the newly created *Reichsgaue* of Wartheland and Danzig-West Prussia (both carved out of pre-war Polish territory). Increasingly "land service in the east" came to mean propaganda work among these "new Germans" as much as actual toil on the land. The Reichs's new citizens had to be instructed in what being a German meant — even to the extent, in some instances, of being taught the language!

Tunic of a *Landdienst Scharführer* (the rank indicated by the green lanyard). Cuff-title reads *Landdienst der HJ*. Green *L* on shoulder straps, green "district triangle" with the word *Landjahr* in white.

A fanfare trumpet banner of the Germanic Land Service. The motto "Schwert und Scholle" translates to "Sword and Sod."

A boy from Westphalia (according to the original German caption to the above photo) takes part in a *Landdienst* course in the Ostland. Note his cuff-title: *Landdienst der HJ*.

The *Landdienst* did not have a special uniform but was distinguished by a green Gothic *L* on the shoulder straps, which were also piped in green. The district triangle was unique in that it too was green with the word *Landjahr* in white. There was also a cuff-title with the inscription, *Landdienst der HJ;* later when this was enlarged to include non-Germans, it became *Germanischer Landdienst.* Fanfare trumpet banners consisted of a green field with the word *Landjahr* in black letters. The emblem of the later-formed Germanic Land Service was an *Oldalsrune* pierced by a sword, and was used on fanfare trumpet banners. Sometimes the banners had only the *Odalsrune* on a green field, others had white swastikas in the corners of the green field with the motto: "*Schwert und Scholle*" ("Sword and Soil" or, literally, "Sword and Sod"). Regulation uniform was worn only on formal occasions. A variety of dress was adopted while working.

## OTHER SPECIALIST SECTIONS

(i) *HJ Wachgefolgschaft* (HJ Guard Company). Originally known as the *Wachgefolgschaft Baldur von Schirach*, this was, unlike the foregoing, *not* a separate branch of the HJ, but only a special unit within it. It furnished a personal or ceremonial guard for the *Reichsjugendführer* of the HJ (first von Schirach, later Axmann). It was distinguished by its special shoulder straps (see section on Shoulder Straps), and by the fact that its members carried a bayonet-type sidearm (see Daggers and Knives section) and wore black breeches.

(ii) *Disabled Youths:* There were two[†] special units for the disabled: (a) for blind boys, and (b) for the hearing impaired. The former had a Gothic *B* (*Blinde*) in red on their shoulder straps, the latter a red Gothic *G* (*Gehörigschädigte*). The staff of an HJ *Gebiet* also wore a Gothic *G* in red on their shoulder straps, but as this would have a numeral below it, it was possible to differentiate between the two. The blind have, reputedly, much keener hearing than the sighted, therefore blind boys received training in sound location techniques. Youths who were hearing impaired were instructed in sign language. The object of these special units was to ensure that disadvantaged boys did not feel they were excluded from the national community because of their disabilities. Blind youths wore a yellow brassard with three black circles; the hearing impaired wore the same, but on a yellow circular background.

(iii) *Rundfunkspielscharen* (Broadcasting Groups). One thing never underestimated by the Nazis was the power of propaganda and publicity. The HJ ran its own broadcasting service under a *Jugendfunkleiter* (Director of Youth Radio) in Berlin, under the direct control of the RJF. The broadcasting groups were joint efforts on the part of all sections of the Hitler Youth. Staff of the Broadcasting Groups had on their shoulder straps a red Gothic *RS* (*Rundfunk-Spielscharen*).

---

[†] A suggestion was made that a third special unit for the physically disabled be created, but nothing came of this idea.

(iv) *HJ Film Production Units.* The RJF had tentatively started making films as early as 1932. Their first effort in this connection being a cinematic record of the *1st Reichs Youth* day at Potsdam. Cinema-going proved so popular that a regular Youth Film Hour (*Jugendfilmstunde*) was included as part of the standard HJ training schedule. This began in April 1934 as a monthly event, but by 1936 it had evolved into a permanent Sunday feature. The films shown were not, however, those made by the RJF unit (which never aspired to feature films, only documentaries) but those of the commercial cinema, or more precisely those commercially produced films which, in the opinion of Dr. Goebbels, were *Jugendwert* (valuable for young people). Although rarely overtly Nazi in content, they did stress themes such as community spirit, self-sacrifice and military valour, regarded by the Ministry of Propaganda as reflecting the National Socialist ethos. There were, of course, a few which were specifically propagandist in the full Nazi sense. Among these, later reference must surely be made, since this work deals with the Hitler Youth, to one whose hero was an HJ lad. This was "Hitlerjunge Quex," a film of sufficient distinction to have earned for itself a place in general histories of the cinema. Based on the life and early death of Herbert Norkus, called in the film Heini Völker (*Quex* was his nickname, derived from *Quecksilber* — Quicksilver), it was premiered in Berlin in September 1933 and was the first undisputed success of the Nazi cinema.

It is interesting to note that a feature about the work of the Hitler Youth was, at the Berlin Radio Exhibition of 1935, the first film to be shown on German *television* (Hitler's Reich was somewhat ahead of Britain at this time in the development of this new medium. Hitler himself never appeared on television, although he was not slow to exploit the advantages of cinematic propaganda).

(v) *Gebirgs-HJ* (Mountain Units). Formed during the war the Mountain HJ trained boys who aspired to become members of the Alpine or Mountain Sections of the army. Their instructors were Army or Waffen-SS *Gebirgstruppen,* or civilians from the strongly Nazi German Alpine League (*Deutsches Alpenverein*).

(vi) *Spielleute* (Musicians). Since ceremony played a major part in its activities, it was natural that the Hitler Youth should have its own corps of bandsmen — the *Spieleinheiten der HJ.* By 1943 there were some 36,000 boys and girls in 1,200 different musical formations, ranging from full orchestras to fife-and-drum corps.

Would-be music teachers had to undergo a two-year training course at either the Berlin, Weimar, or Graz State High School. On graduating they were classified as *Musikerzieher de HJ* (Music Instructor). Courses at the state high schools were not confined to music, but included, like all HJ training, sport, athletics and "political awareness." Prior to the HJ being able to furnish sufficient teachers of its own, instruction had been undertaken by military bands of the army or NSDAP.

The most common HJ instruments were the fanfare trumpet, bugle and drum. The latter came in two sorts: (a) the small side drum which, along with fifes, provided music for marches, and (b) the larger, less

Lapel badge of the HJ Mountain walking group (*Bergfahrtengruppe*) of the DAV (*Deutsches Alpenverein*).

Boys of the *Gebirgs HJ* parade before setting out on a climb. They wear the formal military-style uniform of the *Wehrertüchtigungslager*. The boy, second right, although an HJ member, wears a DJ belt buckle — typical of the interchange of HJ/DJ insignia that occurred after 1940 (note *Edelweiss* of "alpine" troops on side of cap).

easily portable, *Landknecht* drum (supposedly patterned on a sixteenth-century original) used mainly *en masse* at rallies to furnish an appropriately "heavy" background to the shrill fanfare trumpets. These large drums were, at first, ornamented in a variety of individual designs, but latterly a black and white "flame" pattern became standard. Similarly the banners of the fanfare trumpets were, in the beginning, the subject of a good deal of individual fancy, but were eventually standardized for the HJ with a black swastika upon red/white/red and a silver *Sigrune* on black for the DJ. Some HJ units carried on their fanfare trumpet banners their name in black — for example, *Hitler-Jugend Chemnitz*, but this practice was later discontinued.

Side drum with bugle (the bugle is pre-Nazi army type).

*Landnecht* drum as used by both HJ and DJ.

Fanfare trumpet and regulation HJ banner.

HJ bugle (slightly dented!)

Members of military bands were entitled to wear the traditional "swallows' nests" (*Schwallbennester*) of the armed forces bandsmen at the end of their shoulder straps. Members of the Fife and Drum Corps (*Spielmannszug*) had "swallows' nests" in "artillery" red and white cotton in the proportions of 11mm (red) and 16mm (white). The leader (*Spielmannszugführer*) had the addition of a 5mm white woolen fringe.

Members of a military band (*Muzikzug*) wore swallows nests in the same proportions as above, but with silver replacing white. The bandmaster (*Muzikzugführer*) had the addition of silver fringe, 6mm in length. Swallows nests were attached to the shirt or tunic by metal hooks on the underside of the nests that fitted into corresponding loops around shoulder seams.

Officially "swallows' nests" were only red and white, but other colours *were* used. Even as late as February 1942 the RJF was obliged to issue a reminder that blue and white, or black and white, swallows' nests were *unvorschriftsmassig* (contrary to regulations).

NATIONAL ARCHIVES

HJ bandsmen with "Swallows Nests." Their headgear indicates the period 1933-1936.

Member of a Military Band (red/silver) (One non-standard variant had a large black swastika in the centre)

Bandmaster (red/silver) with silver fringe

Drum-major's mace. (There was also a smaller version for DJ drum-majors)

Swallows nests were worn only where taking part in music making.

A few of the larger HJ bands possessed that characteristic and colourful adjunct of a German military band — a *Schellenbaum* — or "Jingling Johnny."

111

# League of National-Socialist School Students NSS and NSSi

In its origins the Hitler Youth was largely lower middle- and working-class; indeed it proudly proclaimed itself the "Union of German Worker Youth" (*Bund deutscher Arbeiterjugend*). However an important pro-Nazi organization existed among young persons, almost exclusively the children of middle- and upper-class parents, who continued their education after the age of fourteen (the, then, school-leaving age). This was the *National-Sozialistische Schülerbund* (*NSS*), created in April 1929 by the writer and economist, Dr. Adrian von Renteln, who later became its national leader. Membership was drawn in the main from boys at the prestigious (and fee-paying) *gymnasien* and *Realschulen*. Although an affiliate organization, the NSBO *was* established in the same year to accommodate trainees at trade schools (*Berufsschulen*), this never really took hold and was dissolved in 1932.

Members of the NSS, and its parallel girls' organization, the NSSi (*Nat.-Soz. Schülerinnenbund*), regarded themselves as very much a cut above their comrades in the Hitler Youth — a fact which inevitably resulted in friction between the two organizations. The more circumspect attitude of the NSS towards active participation in the Hitler movement was further cause of irritation to the Hitler Youth. This caution was unavoidable, dictated by the fact that many school authorities disapproved of political gestures on the part of their pupils, while in some of the German *Läner* such activities were forbidden by law. The NSS was, consequently, not uniformed and could display the swastika only outside school. Protests from the HJ leader, Gruber, that the NSS should align itself behind the Hitler Youth were unavailing. Indeed the SA leadership (under whose jurisdiction the HJ at this time functioned) ruled, in November 1929, that the NSS should be "... an independent organization directly subordinate to the Party...." (i.e., the NSDAP), but it was suggested that NSS leaders might like to join the HJ

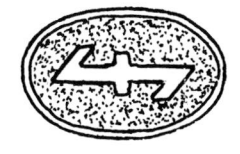

NSS lapel badge, 1st design.

NSS lapel badge, 2nd design. This is in two versions — one "solid," the other with cutaway background to the letters.

and attend its training sessions at least in the capacity of non-participating observers. Ironically it was the future HJ leader, von Schirach, at this stage head only of the NS University Students Union, who was behind this move. His covert motive was the hope that he himself might win control of school, as well as academic, students and keep them out of the hands of his rival, Gruber.

The economic blizzard of the early 1930s, with its threat to the future job prospects of the educated classes, resulted in a great growth of NSS membership; from 5,000 in December 1930 to 16,000 only one year later (HJ membership made an equally spectacular jump in the same period to around 29,000). The NSS now adopted a more overtly aggressive stance. Many secondary school teachers shared their pupils alarm at the crisis and the apparent failure of the Weimar Republic to deal with it, thus making them less willing to condemn participation by their charges in political manifestations of a type with which they themselves sympathized. The NSS began to speak about going into uniform and creating its own *Sturmtrupp* (apparently a junior version of the SS).

Belt buckle sometimes attributed to the pre-1933 HJ but much more likely to have been for the NSS. It is 35mm wide (i.e. "youth size") and has a white metal "wolf hook" on plain brass.

This intensification of NSS actively only served to increase disquiet among the HJ leadership. Gruber was bombarded with demands that the NSS should be disbanded or, at the very least, brought under the control of the Hitler Youth. But Gruber's position as *HJ-Reichsführer* was patently insecure. Criticism of his inefficient and ineffective leadership was commonplace not merely within the Party, but also in the HJ itself. He could not, therefore, risk crossing swords with an organization whose members were the sons and daughters of prominent persons on whose financial backing Hitler was increasingly dependent. Far from giving way to the demands of his critics, Gruber even granted the NSS the right to wear the brown shirt and swastika armband in July 1931, and form its own protection squads to police its meetings. This further incensed his detractors within the movement. His later manifest failure to make good a rather rash promise that he "... would double the size of the Hitler Youth...." resulted in his peremptory dismissal by Hitler in October 1931, who then installed Baldur von Schirach as "Reichs Youth Leader

(*Reichsjugendführer* — a new office, but still under the aegis of the SA. This subordination to the OSAF continued until May 1932). Renteln was nominated *Reichsführer* of both the HJ *and* the NSS (under Schirach's general control).

Gruber's legacy as HJ chief was a chaotic, inefficient and well-nigh bankrupt organization. Renteln's first task was to cut away the dead wood and rid himself of incompetent and, in some instances, corrupt subordinates. Twenty-eight of the forty-four *HJ-Gauführer* were relieved of their posts. Replacements came for the most part from the ranks of the NSS and NSDSt.B leadership corps. The dual HJ/NSS leadership proved more beneficial to the former than the latter. With many of its more able leaders transferred to the HJ, the NSS lost much of its dynamism. Membership actually declined during the course of 1932 — from 14,832 in January to 13,786 in December, while that of the Hj swelled to 55,356 in the same period. On June 16, 1932 von Renteln resigned his joint leadership and Baldur von Schirach assumed personal control over both organizations. A fortnight later (July 1) von Schirach terminated the independent status of the NSS and decreed that its members should transfer to the HJ. Since both organizations were, at this time, voluntary, the amalgamation decree stated that those not willing to adhere actively to the HJ could continue to do so as "passive members" (not entitled to wear its uniform). By December 1932 only 30% of the NSS had become active HJ, the rest opted for "passive" status. In April 1933, four months after Hitler's accession to power, the *NS Schülerbund* was officially dissolved and its members enrolled in the HJ. (NSSi girls were similarly absorbed into the BDM).

It could be said that the Hitler Youth "took over" the NSS, but it could as equally be said that the NSS took over the Hitler Youth, since it was largely erstwhile NSS members who formed the bulk of the new leadership. The social revolutionary radicalism of the earlier *Kampfzeit* gave way (much to the disgust of "old fighters") to a more staid and respectable image. What Hitler required now of his youthful votaries was no longer campaigning ardour but unquestioning submission to military-style discipline!

# 8

# NS Factory Cell Organization

The predecessor of the German Labour Front (DAF) was the National-Socialist Factory-Cell Organization (*National-Sozialistishe Betriebszellen-Organisation*, or NSBO). In September 1932 Artur Axmann and Heinz Otto created a youth section known as the NSJBO (*NS Jugendbetriebszellen-Organisation*) which aimed at winning converts among young factory workers and trade school apprentices. These latter had been, since 1929, theoretically, the concern of the *National-Sozialistische Berufsschul-Organisation* (NSBSO), but this National-Socialist Trade School Organization (an affiliate of the NSS) had remained largely an "on paper" setup and was now absorbed into the NSJBO.

Efforts to persuade young workers in industry to turn away from Marxism and adhere to Hitler were not notably successful, and the NSJBO was quietly wound up after being in existence for little over one year.

The DAF established its own *DAF Jugend* soon after, but this too ceased to exist when the "Law of the Hitler Youth" was promulgated in December 1936. This placed *all* youth groups under the authority of the Reich Youth Leader (Baldur von Schirach).

Lapel badge of DAF Jugend.

# 9

## *National-Socialist German Students Union (NSDSt.B)*

National-Socialist students groups had been formed at some German universities as early as 1922, but these were simply student companies of the SA. It was not until February 1926 that a separate student organization, the National-Socialist German Students Union (*Nat. Soz. deutsche Studentenbund*, or NSDSt.B), was established at Munich University by Wilhelm Tempel. It received Hitler's blessing in July and Tempel was confirmed as its *Bundesführer*. Before the end of the year there were some 20 groups in existence. In 1927 Tempel transferred to Leipzig University. It was not a move calculated to further his career as student leader since it removed him from Bavaria, the very heartland of the Nazi movement. His attempts to recruit "worker students" (he took the socialism of national-socialism very seriously) involved him in ideological conflicts with the Party and he resigned in July 1928.

His successor was a twenty-year old Munich student, Baldur van Schirach, who proved to be an energetic and competent leader. He organized the NSDSt.B into ten regions, each under a *Kreisführer* directly answerable to himself.

At first NSDSt.B members had to enroll in the NSDAP, but in 1929 this rule was waived. Membership of the NSDSt.B was now extended to include students at Technical High Schools, Trade Schools (*Fachschulen*) and business colleges (Many of whom would have been too young to be eligible for NSDAP membership which was limited to those over 18 years). The proportion of NSDSt.B members at established universities was actually lower than at these other centers of further education.

The removal of the necessity of belonging to the NSDAP meant that the NSDSt.B could no longer rely on financial support from the Party. It had to be largely self-financing, with the result that its leaders often had to pay for its propaganda material out of their own pockets.

Members were encouraged to join the SA and take part in the "War Sport" (*Wehrsport*) training which that organization provided. But less than half did so. For those who wished to avail themselves of this form of paramilitary exercise, an alternative was available in the Langemarck Student Companies (*Studentenring Langemarck*) established in 1929 by the Steel Helmet War Veterans Association. Many students found the atmosphere of Steel Helmet (under the patronage of no less a personage than the ex-Crown Prince) more congenial than that of the notoriously boorish and boozy SA.

At the time of Hitler's accession to power in January 1933 the NSDSt.B had only 6,300 male members and 750 female (These latter belonging to ANST — Working Community of Female National-Socialist Students).* In July 1933 the SA was granted a monopoly over all forms of *Wehrsport*. The Steel Helmet's *Studentenring Langemarck* voluntarily subordinated itself to the NSDSt.B, but in April 1934, like its Steel Helmet parent, it lost its identity altogether. The SA then tried to assert its authority over the entire student body. In September 1933 SA offices were opened at all German universities; students, whether NSDSt.B members or not, were exhorted to sign on in an SA unit. In February 1934 it became obligatory for them to do so. But the SA's dominance in this field was short-lived. In June 1934 Hitler "purged" the SA by having most of its leading members shot. The SA offices at universities throughout the country were quietly shut down. At the same time the NSDSt.B lost its former semi-independent status and became an integrated organ of the NSDAP. Enrollment in the NSDSt.B was not, however, made obligatory, indeed its membership was deliberately restricted to 5% of the student body.

Poster to commemorate 10th anniversary of NSDSt.B's foundation, 1926-1936.

Civil Lapel Badge

---

* *Arbeitgemeinschaft Nat.-Soc. Studentinnen.*

Each university, or institute of higher learning, had a *Stamm-Mannschaft* (regular company) limited to not more than sixty individuals, all of whom had already to be members of the NSDAP or one of its paramilitary affiliates (SS, SA, etc.). Since the student body was, by its very nature, a fluctuating society, it was decreed that membership of a *Stamm-Mannschaft* had to be for a duration of not less than three terms (Semesters). Every *Stamm-Mannschaft* had under it a number of *Stamm-Kameradschaften,* each of which was restricted to a total of not exceeding thirty members. The task of these units was to provide the "political leadership" of their fellow students.

When a new *Kameradschaft* was formed it was on probation for the first three months during which time it was known only by a designation number (K 6, K 7, K 8 etc.), but if accepted as fully "reliable" it was allowed to fly the NSDSt.B flag and apply for permission to adopt a name. This was usually that of some prominent person in German history (military leaders being much favored in this connection), but it could equally be that of a place or even a thing — for example, one of the *Kameradschaften* at the Technical High School at Karlsruhe adopted the name *Rote Erde* ("Red Earth" — an ingredient in the making of iron) while another at the same institution named is itself Carl Benz in honour of the celebrated automobile engineer (of Mercedes-Benz fame).

With its political enemies defeated, the NSDSt.B leadership now turned its attention to eliminating its rivals on the campus. Chief among these was the German Student Association (*Deutsche Studentenschaft,* or DSt.) to which all German students automatically belonged. The NSDSt.B sought to take this over by means of infiltrating its organization. The DSt. was, in no sense, an anti-Hitler body, indeed its leader, Gerhard Krüger, was an NSDAP member, but the DSt., encompassing as it did the entire student body, was much less politically reliable than the NSDSt.B. Antagonism between the NSDSt.B leader Oskar Stäbel (who succeeded to this post in 1933) and Krüger reached almost ludicrous proportions with each trying to get the other arrested for treason! Stäbel eventually won the day and was placed in control of both organizations, but had to be removed from this post after it was revealed that he had been embezzling DSt. funds! The two bodies reverted to their separate existences until the problem was finally resolved in November 1936 with the creation of a new office, that of *Reichsstudentrenführung* (Reich Student Leadership, or RSF) control of which was given to a high-ranking SS officer, Gustav Adolf Scheel.

Both Himmler and Deputy *Führer* Rudolf Hess (who, in his days at Munich University had been active in student politics) took a keen interest in NSDSt.B affairs. Hess even spoke of it as "... a sort of intellectual SS...." Himmler seems to have hoped it would furnish the future elite of the Party (which may have been the motive behind restricting membership to such a small percentage).

Another campus rival to the NSDSt.B was the fraternities (something more familiar in American than in British universities). The NSDSt.B sought to replace the Fraternity Houses with its own so-called

*Kameradschaftshäuser*, but this turned out to be impossible due to resistance, especially by the Catholic fraternities. Scheel had to be content with ordering NSDSt.B members not to join a fraternity. He then tried to subvert the fraternities by bringing pressure to bear on their alumni associations (*Altherrenbünde*) which were the source of much of their finance. In 1936 he set up his own *NS Altherrenbund der Deutschen Studenten*. A little later in the same year he revived the *NS Studentenkampfhilfe* (roughly: NS Student Fighting Fund) which had been set up first in 1931 as a means of raising money to support NSDSt.B propaganda. Through this latter agency he hoped to enlist the support of pre-Nazi era graduates, but by the end of 1937 it had a registered membership of only 15,000, which represented a very minor fraction of those eligible.

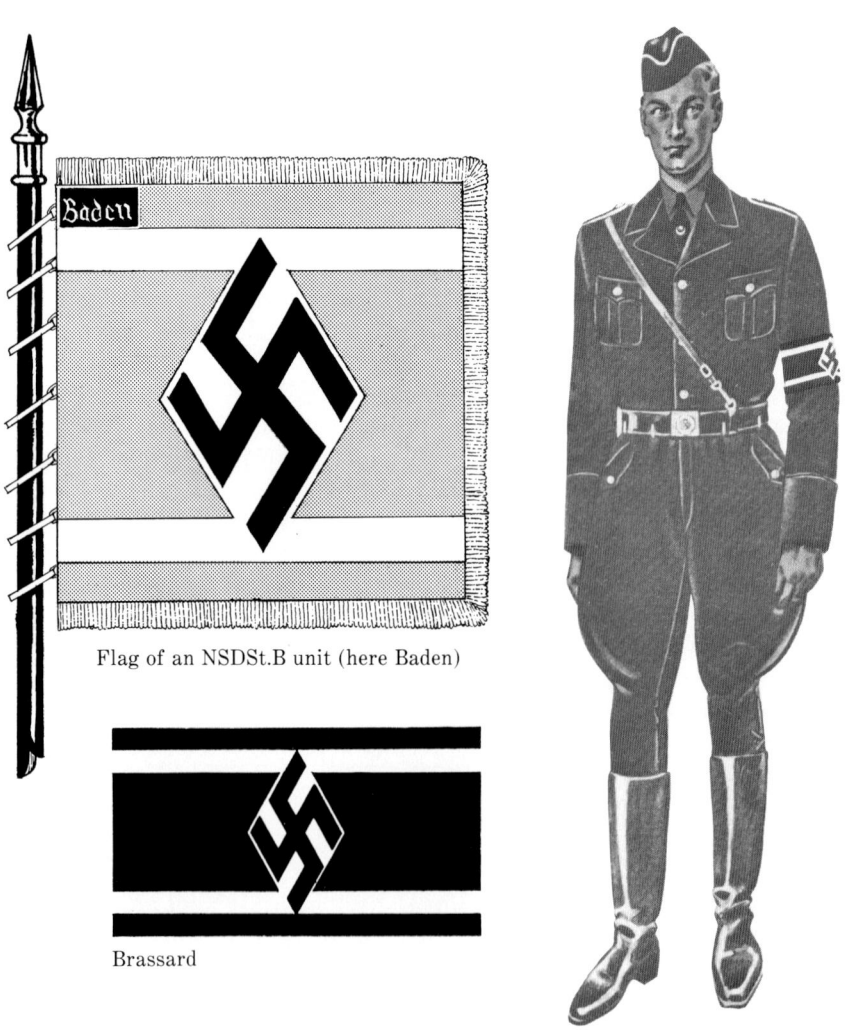

Flag of an NSDSt.B unit (here Baden)

Brassard

Member of a Stamm-Mannschaft (Regular Unit) or an Official (Amtstrager) of NSDSt.B.

The following year Scheel tried to blackmail the fraternity alumni associations into joining the National-Socialist *Altherrenbund* by threatening that if they failed to do so they would be barred from further participation in student life. This did succeed in bringing most to heel, although the Catholic alumni bodies refused to capitulate and were declared "politically intolerable" by Himmler and outlawed.

The coming of war in 1939 altered the composition of the student body radically. Whereas before the war only a small percentage of students had been women, by 1943 they comprised more than one-third of the total student population. Most of the NSDSt.B leaders left to join the armed forces thus leaving the political indoctrination of students in the hands of less committed individuals, many of whom had enrolled in the NSDSt.B merely as a way of advancing their careers. On the whole it can be said that the Nazis failed to make a significant impact among Germany university students, and in some cases universities became centers of resistance to them.

At first the NSDSt.B uniform consisted only of a brown shirt and special brassard, but later a full and distinctive garb was devised. This comprised a dark blue short jacket (without shoulder straps), dark blue breeches, top boots, khaki shirt, black tie and dark blue side cap. Later still the short jacket was replaced by a military style tunic. The NSDSt.B brassard is red with a white stripe inset from the upper and lower edge. In the center is a white diamond with a black elongated swastika. There were only five ranks:

Gruppenführer
Kameradschaftsführer
Arbeitsgemeinschaftsführer
Mitarbeiter in der Studentenführung
Mitarbeiter in der Gaustudentenführung

(a) Emblem for sports singlet. It measures 152mm across eagle's wings. There is a smaller version (104mm) in silver bullion which may have been intended for wear on the track suit.
(b) N.S. "old boys" (literally "old gentlemen") lapel badge. It measures 23mm in diameter but there is also a half size version.
(c) "N.S. Student Help in the Time of Struggle" lapel badge. It measures 23mm in diameter but there is also a half size version.

Brassard of a senior NSDStB leader. Red and white with *silver* edges. Made in high quality material like that of an NSDAP Political Leader.

It would appear that rank was indicated by the edging colour of the brassard, although this is not certain. Possibly lower grades were denoted by the use of a coloured lanyard.

Girls in the female section of the NSDSt.B wore a dark blue short jacket of the type used in the BDM with a white blouse and a dark blue skirt.

On the men's sports vest a large white cotton eagle (wing-span 152mm) was worn. In its claws it holds the NSDSt.B emblem. A smaller version (wing-span 120mm) in silver bullion exists and was probably worn on the track suit.

The civil lapel badge of the NSDSt.B is a black elongated swastika with red between its upper and lower segments and white between the lateral ones. The NSDSt.B Honour Badge (illustrated in the Awards Section) has a smaller version of this badge within a wreath of silver oak leaves. Like the Golden HJ Badge, it was awarded to those who had joined before January 1933.

At least three different versions of the NSDSt.B belt buckle are known to exist and are illustrated hereafter.

Two versions of NSDStB belt buckle. (i) was also worn by some NPEA students (e.g., at St. Wendel), while (ii) is found in two versions, one as above, the other with the rhombus placed horizontally not vertically.

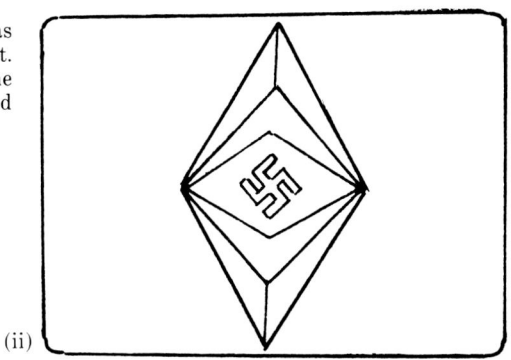

A trio of NSDStB "Langemarck" students in walking-out uniform.

JAN VINCX COLLECTION

Two non-German members of the *Langemarck Studium* (a Norwegian and a Fleming) work on a (slightly inaccurate!) model of an Me109. The cuff-title is clearly visible. Note the good quality gaberdine shirts.

# 10

# NSDSt.B Langemarck Scholarship

On November 11, 1914 a battle was fought at Langemarck (near Ypres) during which young German soldiers, many of them from volunteer companies of university students, advanced under murderous British artillery fire singing *Deutschland über Alles*. Their losses were heavy and the action, from the German point of view, a failure, but from it sprang a legend.

In October 1921 at the Garrison Church at Potsdam war veterans and students from Berlin University came together to form a Langemarck Committee. Until the coming of the Nazis in 1933 this body's principal concern was the preservation of the graves of the fallen of this battle and the erection of an appropriate monument. The Langemarck engagement passed into popular mythology as the symbol of heroic sacrifice on the part of German youth and as such was eagerly taken up by the Nazis. Baldur von Schirach instituted, in 1934, a *Langemarckspende* (Langemarck Fund) to which every member of the HJ had to contribute the sum of one Pfennig per month. By 1936 sufficient money had accrued to enable a Langemarck Scholarship *(Langemarck Studium)* to be set up. The object of which was to provide university training for a period of four semesters (two academic years) for young men (there was no provision for women) between the ages of 17 and 25 who were of academic standard but financially unable to afford any form of higher education. The training provided tended to be technically ordinate with courses in chemistry, physics and applied mathematics etc.

All participants were required to enroll in the NSDSt.B. During the Second World War the facility was extended to include students from the "nordic" lands. For example, at the Technical College (or, in German parlance, Technical High School) at Hanover, suitably qualified young Flemish, Dutch, Danish and Norwegian students were granted places, provided they too enlisted in the NSDSt.B. All students had a black cuff-title with *Langemarck Studium* in white.

# National Political Educational Institutes (NPEA)

If Germany were to become a "Leadership State" nothing could be more important than the training of future leaders. For this a new type of education — a National-Socialist education — would be required and, to provide this, a new type of school.

In 1933 an SA officer, Joachim Haupt, proposed the setting up of National Political Educational Institutes (*National Politische Erziehungsanstalten*, abbreviated to NPEA or *Napolas*, although this latter was unpopular on account of its italianate sound). These Institutes, at first staffed by SA or SS men, were something of a cross between an English public school and a Prussian cadet academy (Indeed many were located in former *Kadettenanstalten*). Three were opened during the course of 1933, the first at a seventeenth-century castle at Plön in Schleswig-Holstein, the other two at Potsdam (Berlin) and Köslin in Pomerania. Five more followed in 1934 with a further eight the next year. Favorite locations were army cadet schools, *Gymnasien*, requisitioned monasteries or refurbished castles.

A full academic education was provided for boys between the ages of 10 to 18 years but there was a strong emphasis on sport. Specialization, both academic and sporting, was encouraged. Some *Napolas* aimed at producing scientists, others linguistic experts, others still lent towards the arts and humanities. Similarly, since a high standard of proficiency in any given sport requires exclusive dedication to that discipline, boys were allowed to specialize in rowing, fencing, horse-riding, yachting etc., and, at those schools where facilities for it existed, gliding. Music also featured on the curriculum, each school having at least its own fife and drum corps if not full marching band or orchestra.

Religion remained on the syllabus until 1936 when it was replaced by "Germanic rites" (such as the pagan "summer solstice").

One of the more original features of the *Napolas* was the importance placed on *practical* training. The younger boys had to spend six to eight weeks of each year working on a farm; the older boys served down mines, or in factories; hopefully, they discovered the "nobility of manual labour" and avoided the temptations of class exclusivity. This was the socialist aspect of National-Socialism in practice. The nationalist half was manifest in the military orientation of much of the training — the end product of which was "a political soldier."

Pupils were known as *Jungmannen* and were divided into *Hundertschaften* (companies of one hundred). Each of these was sub-divided into three *Züge* (roughly platoons) with about thirty boys (i.e. a normal school class). In turn each *Zug* was split into three *Gruppen* of about ten boys apiece. The *Gruppenführer*, *Zugführer* and *Hundertschaftsführer* were pupils who fulfilled the combined function of a school prefect and a military academy cadet NCO.

All pupils, and most members of staff, wore uniform. At first the staff had been from the SA/SS (still under one command at the time of the creation of the *Napolas* in 1933) but latterly the SS came to dominate the work of the schools. Following the purge of the SA in 1934 Joachim Haupt, the *Napolas'* first mentor, was replaced by August Heissmeyer, an SS officer. Staff at the *Napolas* were granted honorary SS commissions. In theory control of the NPEA was vested in the civilian Minister of Education, Bernhard Rust, a veteran Party member. Heissmeyer was technically his subordinate, but as he was also a subordinate of Himmler; this resulted in something of a "split personality" for the unfortunate Heissmeyer, who was criticized by Himmler for not pressing the claims of the SS sufficiently strongly and suspected by Rust of sabotaging the work of his ministry in the interests of its rival!

Rust had to fight off incursions into his province by both Himmler and von Schirach. Although no boy could enroll at an NPEA without first being a member of the DJ or HJ, this did not imply that the Hitler Youth *controlled* the schools. Himmler increased SS influence by offering financial assistance and providing much needed equipment.

With the enormous expansion of the NPEA programme during the war (no less than 27 new schools were formed between 1941 and 1942) SS influence was ascendant and, in the case of schools outside the Reich, paramount. These extra-territorial establishments were known as *Reichsschulen* of which there were three. They took in young "nordic" boys as well as Germans.

Originally the Napolas had been conceived as male-only, but the first all-girls school was opened in 1941 at Achern in Baden, to be followed shortly thereafter by two more. Even some of the previously all-male schools subsequently admitted some female pupils and female staff.

UNIFORMS

At first pupils wore HJ uniforms with the letters *NPEA* in white on their (at this time) khaki shoulder straps. Their teachers wore either civilian clothes or SA or SS uniforms. Later a special NPEA uniform was devised for the upper age group boys. The younger lads continued to wear their normal DJ uniform with *NPEA* in white on their single black shoulder strap; on the left upper arm they had a black *Sigrune* on a white circle.

The uniforms for boys over 14 consisted of:

(a) For formal, parade or walking-out dress: an olive green single breasted tunic with dark brown collar, khaki shirt and black tie, black shoulder straps, piped in white with white *NPEA*, black belt with HJ buckle and black cross strap. A "Holbein dagger" (see Section on Daggers) was worn from a bayonet type frog. On the left upper arm was the normal HJ brassard. Long black trousers were worn with black shoes. Headgear was an olive green peaked cap with a dark brown band and white piping. On the band was an enamel HJ diamond badge and on the peak the national eagle-and-swastika emblem (slight variations of design here).

(b) Working dress: tunic as above but with the shirt worn open necked with its collar folded over the tunic collar. Shoulder straps were "school colour" (see below). Belt and buckle as above but without the cross strap. Olive green forage cap with HJ diamond on front surmounted by the national eagle-and-swastika, alternately a special version ski cap could be worn.

(c) Officers: tunic similar to that of students but with the brassard of the NSDAP (not HJ). Cap also similar to pupil's but with silver visor cord and, in place of the pupil's HJ diamond, the NSDAP rosette. On the peak of the cap an eagle-and-swastika of the SS type.[††] Officers also had a "Holbein dagger" but worn from a double chain in the correct dagger-carrying manner (as distinct from the bayonet type method for pupils). Both officer's and pupil's dagger bore the motto *Mehr sein als scheinen* (Be more than you seem). Officers wore black riding breeches and black top boots.

Studio portrait of a student at an NPEA. On black shoulder strap NPEA in white, piping is also white.

---

[††] The NSDAP/HJ eagle-and-swastika badge could be worn here instead.

Tunic of a *Gefolgschaftsführer*.

NPEA *Sommerbluse*.

132

An Instructor and pupils at the Reichsschule "Nederland" at Valkenburg with model gliders. All wear the olive green (or brownish) tunic of the NPEA. The officer has black breeches. Note the SS eagle worn on the left arm by the boys but not by the officer who wears to normal NSDAP brassard (as prescribed for NPEA leaders and teachers).

NPEA Pupils' tunic.

Cloth version of the SS eagle-and-swastika as worn by the boys in the photograph above.

133

[Right] Target practice (note here the narrow guage shoulder strap of an *Erzieher* or Instructor, and his SS-type eagle cap badge).

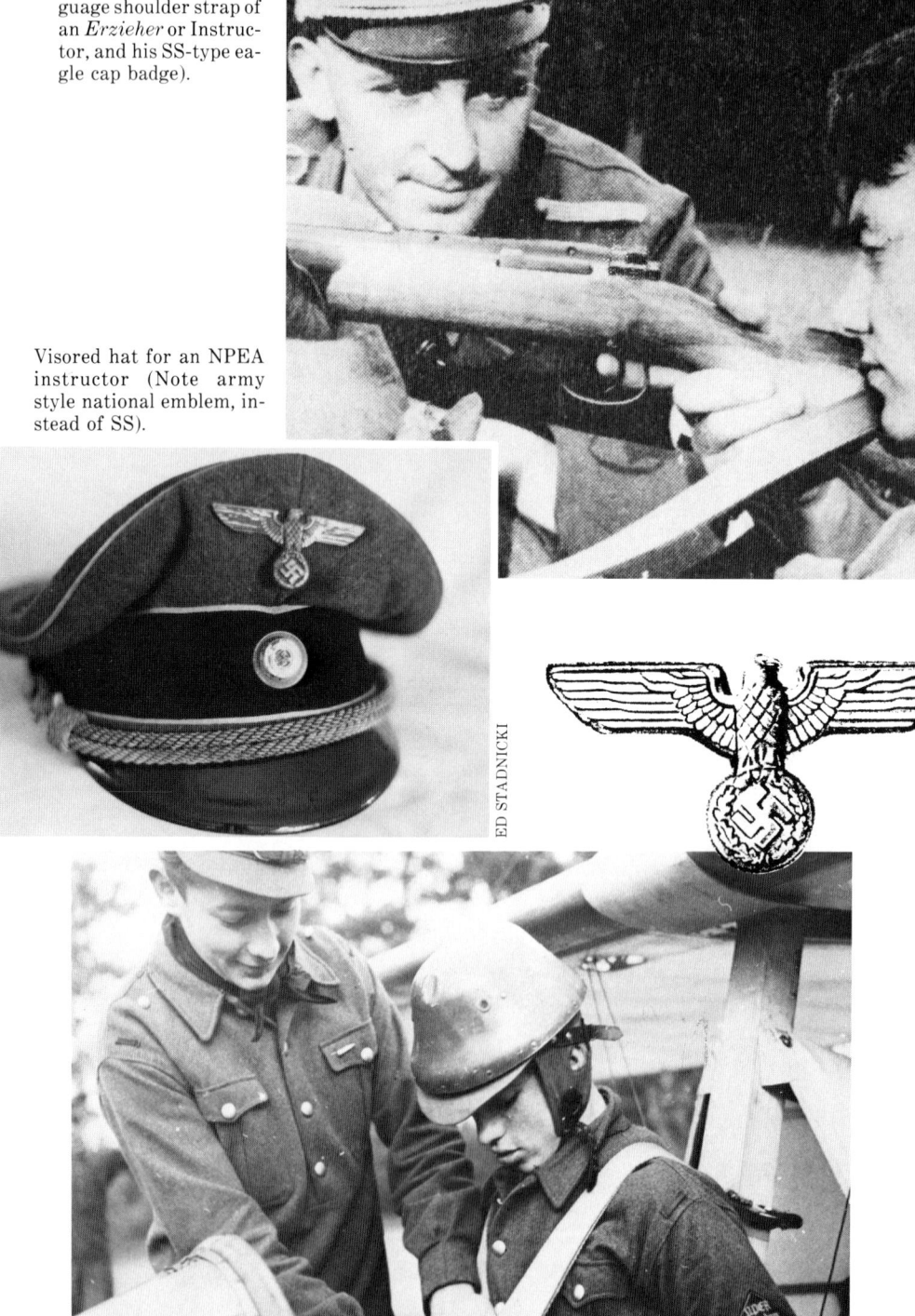

Visored hat for an NPEA instructor (Note army style national emblem, instead of SS).

ED STADNICKI

Gliding instruction at NPEA Potsdam (note this wording on the pupil's "district triangle").

134

(d) Rank insignia: a war-time German publication describes (but unfortunately does not *illustrate*) the special rank insignia devised for the NPEA. The accompanying drawings must therefore be regarded as only approximately accurate. The ranks are described as follows:

(i) *Jungmann-Gruppenführer*: a horizontal red/yellow twisted cord worn at the end of each shoulder strap.

(ii) *Jungmann-Zugführer*: an 18 mm wide yellow "bar" (or ribbon) with red central stripe worn on both shoulder straps.

(iii) *Jungmann-Hundertschaftsführer*: an 18 mm wide red "bar" with a yellow central stripe worn on both shoulder straps.

(iv) *Lehrer-Anwärter* (Probationary Teacher): 4 mm wide aluminum cord "which goes up and down once" (presumably like an inverted u) upon an underlay of the school colour.

(v) *Erzieher* (Teacher or Instructor): a 4 mm wide aluminum cord "which goes up and down twice." Underlay in school colour.

(vi) *Erzieher-Hundertschaftsführer* (Senior Teacher or Adult Leader of a "Company of one hundred"): a 4 mm wide aluminum cord "twisted twice" upon an underlay in the school colour.

(vii) *Anstaltsleiter* (Headmaster or Head of the Institute): a 4 mm wide aluminum cord "twisted thrice" upon an underlay of the school colour.

The document goes on to say that with their "service dress" (*Dienstanzug*) the underlay was in all cases white except for non-teaching staff such as Inspectors, Treasurers, etc., who had a grey underlay.

In March 1944 a new scheme of ranks was introduced for NPEA Staff. This was entirely SS in form. Other features of NPEA dress were a silver wire Aesculapius staff worn on the right cuff by medical doctors, a silver metal cog wheel worn by drivers, and a silver metal key for doorkeepers (both of these also being worn on the right cuff).

Normally pupils wore black shoulder straps but with their Field Service Dress (*Geländeanzug*) their shoulder straps were in the school colour. Members of the school military band or fife and drum corps wore "swallows nests" on both shoulders. These were white with "bars" in the school colour. The only exception to this was Spandau which, having white as the school colour, had black as the basic colour and white for the "bars" (making it in practice the mirror image of the Ilfeld "swallows nests").

[Above and right:] Shoulder strap and arm badge for 10-14 year-old NPEA pupils.

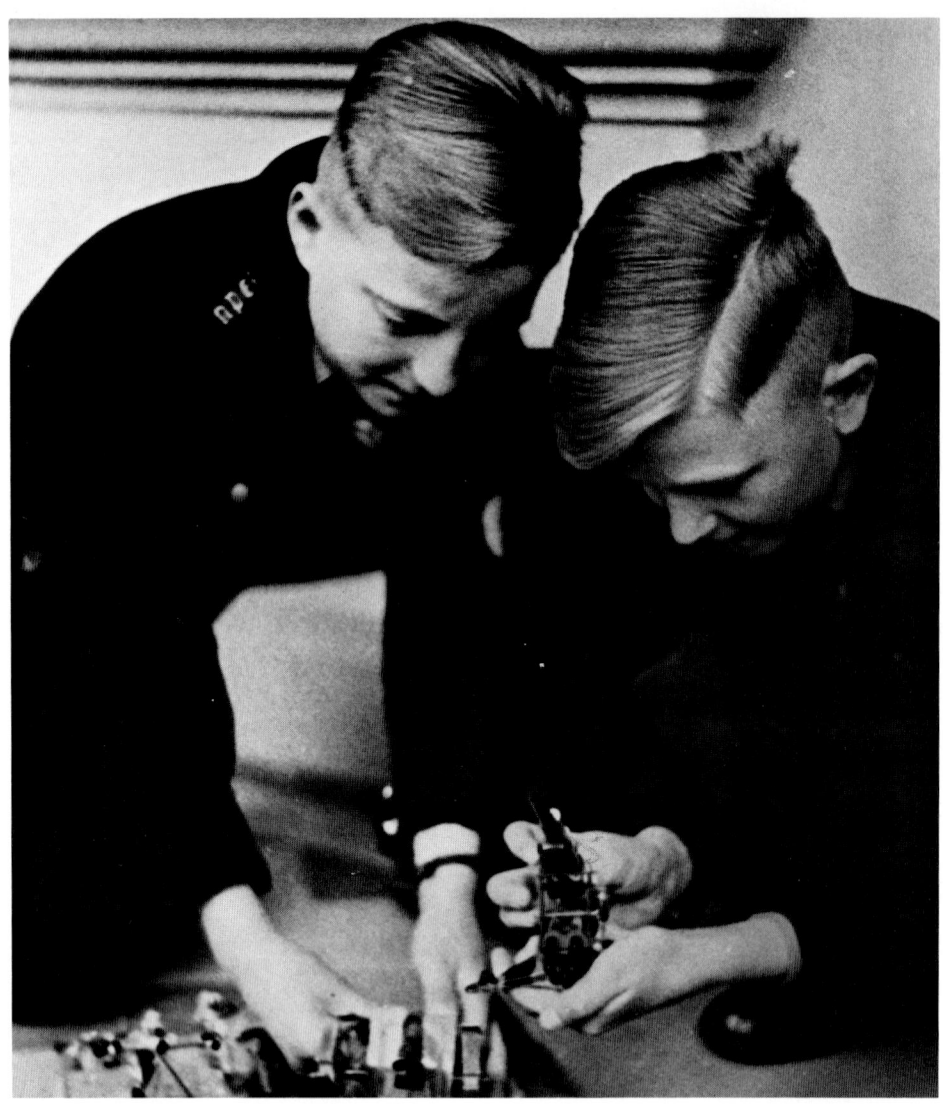

Young pupils at the NPEA at Naumburg.

Jungmann  | Gruppenführer (Red/yellow cord) | Zugführer (Yellow/red/yellow bar) | Hunderschaftsführer (Red/yellow/red bar)

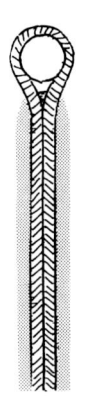

Lehrer Anwärter
(Probationary
Teacher)

Erzieher
(Instructor)

Erzieher-Hundert-
schaftsführer
(Senior Instructor)

Anstaltsleiter
(Establishment Chief).

NPEA Untersturmführer
(Referendar = Probationer)

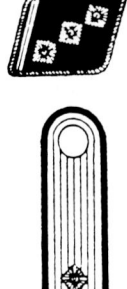

NPEA Obersturmführer
(Assessor)

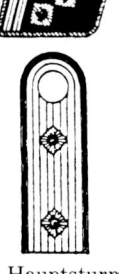

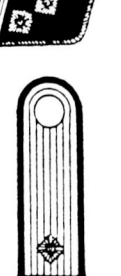

NPEA Hauptsturmführer
(Assessor with over
2 years service)

NPEA Sturmbannführer
(Studienrat = Student
Councellor)

NPEA Obersturmbannführer
(Oberstudienrat = Senior
Student Councellor)

NPEA Standartenführer
(Unterrichtsleiter = Deputy
Headmaster, also Min. Rat in
der Inspektion = School Inspector, ministerial councellor grade).

NPEA Oberführer (Anstaltsleiter =
Headmaster, of a small Institution also
Min. Dirig. in der Inspektion = School
Inspector, ministerial director grade)

NPEA Brigadeführer (Anstaltsleiter of
a large or combined Institution, also
School Inspector of Ministerial rank)

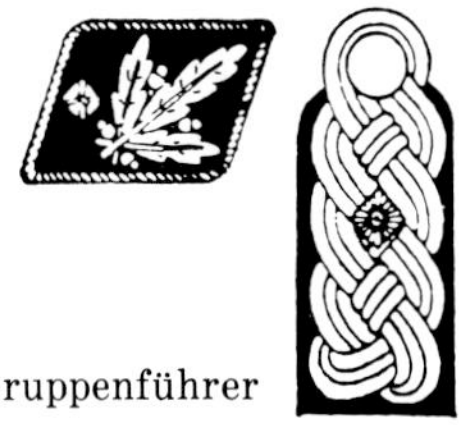

NPEA Gruppenführer

137

The following school colours are listed:

| | |
|---|---|
| Spandau | white |
| Ilfeld | black |
| Köslin | yellow |
| Wahlstatt | light green |
| Stuhm | light blue/grey |
| Potsdam | light red |
| Naumburg | dark red |
| Oranienstein | light blue |
| Plön | dark blue |
| Bensburg | brown |
| Schulpforta | light yellow |

The above are listed in the aforementioned document on NPEA uniform but it is by no means a complete list even at the time of its publication, and it is questionable if the concept of "school colour" could have been stretched to accommodate the final count of forty-three *Napolas* as listed below (the dates are the dates of foundation of each). The form of name and country of location are as existing at the time (several of these places are now in Poland or Czechoslovakia and have different names):

1933
Plön (Schleswig-Holstein)
Potsdam (Berlin)
Köslin (Pomerania)

1934
Spandau (Berlin)
Naumburg (Thuringia)
Ilfeld (Thuringia)
Stuhm (East Prussia)
Oranienstein (Hesse)

1935
Bensburg (near Cologne)
Ballenstedt u. Köthen (Anhalt, later renamed NPEA Anhalt)
Backnang (Württemberg)
Rottweil (Württemberg)
Klotzsche (Saxony)
Neuzelle (near Guben on the Oder)
Sculpforta (Thuringia, near Naumburg)
Wahlstatt (Lower Silesia — a former Cadet School attended by both
    Hindenburg and Ludendorff)

1936-1941
Putbus (on Rügen Island in the Baltic)
Loben (Upper Silesia)
Steckau (Styria, Austria)
Vorau (Styria, Austria)
Spanheim (Carinthia, Austria)
St. Wendel (Westmark)

*Gefolgschaftsführer* at NPEA Ilfeld.

Hegne (Bodensee)
Rufach (Alsace, in French, Rouffach)
Achern (Baden)

1942-1944
Marnheim (Kaiserlautern)
Haselünne (Emsland)
Reisen u. Wallenstein (Warthegau)
Annaberg (Upper Silesia)
Mokritz (South Styria)
St. Viet (South Carinthia)
Göttweig (Lower Austria)
Hubertendorf (Lower Austria): an NPEA for girls
Colmar (Alsace-Gau Luxemburg): an NPEA for girls
Raudnitz (on the Elbe in Bohemia)
Ploschkowitz (Sudetenland)
Kuttenberg (Protectorate of Bohemia-Moravia)
Breitsee (Vienna)

Theresianum (Vienna)
Traiskirchen (Lower Austria)
Burg-Strechau (Austria)
Lambach (Austria)
St. Paul (Austria)

*Reichsschulen*
1942-1944
Valkenberg (Holland)
Heijthuijsen (Holland)
Quatrecht (or Kwatrecht) Flanders.

NPEA Reichsschulen fanfare trumpet banner.

# 12

# NPEA Reichsschulen

(i) *Kwatrecht:* The *Reichsschule Flandern,* opened in September 1943 at Kwatrecht by Wettern in East Flanders, was intended to accommodate some 800 boys between the ages of ten and eighteen, but never, in fact, managed to enroll more then 120 lads — all of these under the age of fourteen. Of its three classes (of *Züge)* one consisted of Reich Germans, the other two were Flemish. As an adjunct to the Kwatrecht school there was also a so-called *Heimschule Flandern* (Home School Flanders) at Schoten about five miles from Antwerp. Both establishments were run by German SS officers — Kwatrecht by *SS-Obersturmführer* Paul Steck; Schoten by *SS-Obersturmführer* Heinrich Mangold.

By the following September Belgium was liberated. The schools were evacuated to various parts of Germany and kept constantly on the move by the rapidly deteriorating war situation. The Kwatrecht lads finished up at Ballenstedt, the Schoten pupils at Chiemsee. It is difficult to imagine that after September 1944 either group received much systematic education, especially since Flemish language textbooks were unobtainable in Germany.

The boys at the schools wore standard DJ uniforms of either the brown summer, or dark blue winter variety. Theoretically all pupils and staff at Kwatrecht wore a cuff-title with *Rijksschool Vlaanderen,* or its German equivalent, *Reichsschule Flandern,* but is doubtful if this was ever actually issued. Photographs of members of the school do not bear out its existence. However, they do prove that some, at least, of the pupils wore the correct black *Sigrune* on a white circle of an NPEA member of DJ age. Above this they wore a district triangle with *NPEA Kwatrecht.*

(ii) *Valkenburg:* The *Reichsschule Nederland* at Valkenburg in Limburg Province (southeast Netherlands, close to the German frontier) was opened in 1942 and took both Dutch and German pupils up to the age of eighteen. The younger lads, ages ten to fourteen wore standard DJ uniform, the older boys the olive-green NPEA uniform described above, but with one significant difference. In place of the HJ brassard they wore on the upper left arm an eagle-and-swastika of the SS type. An indication, perhaps, of how the SS had now established its supremacy over the *Napolas.* The *Reichsschule Nederland* was "twined" with its nearest counterpart, the NPEA at Bensburg (Cologne), and there were regular exchanges of pupils and staff between the two establishments.

There was, in addition to the above, a *Reichsschule Nederland* for girls, located at Heithuijsen (also in Limburg), which was run by a Dutch baroness.

Pupils at these schools were almost exclusively the offspring of collaborationist parents, usually SS men. Uniforms and education were both provided from German funds.

## Adolf Hitler Schools

Frustrated in his attempts to gain control of the *Napolas* von Schirach conspired with the leader of the DAF, Robert Ley, to create a new form of élitist education — national socialist grammar schools to be given the designation *Adolf Hitler Schulen* (AHS).

These were formally inaugurated, with Hitler's blessing, on January 15, 1937. The first opened at Krössinsee in April 1937. They remained outside the normal German state school system, thus beyond the control of Minister of Education Rust. The aim, never attained, was to have one in every *Gau* of the Reich.

Boys (there was no provision for girls) were selected at the age of twelve after attending a ten-day course at their nearest *Gebietsführerschule*. Each course consisted of between thirty and thirty-five boys from among whom the local HJ *Gebietsführer* and regional *Gauleiter* would, with advice from a doctor, select a possible nine or ten lads as suitable to go forward to an AHS.

By the start of the war there were ten such schools but many more were envisaged. War conditions greatly curtailed the building programme and only two more were added before all further construction was ordered to cease. School buildings were military in style, an impression reinforced by the presence of guards in sentry boxes at their gates. Some temporary war-time accommodation was found at the NSDAP's own *Ordensburgen* at Sonthofen and Krössinsee.

A school week consisted of twenty-nine hours of academic study and eight of sport or paramilitary exercises; a further eight hours were given over to "cultural activities" such as music or art. Schooling was, theoretically, free although parents who could contribute financially were invited to do so. The course was intended to last six years.

It was von Schirach's hope that the AHS would rival the NPEAs in producing potential leaders who would eventually fill the top posts in the Nazi hierarchy. Time was to run out before the scheme could be fully tested, but what results were available (the first graduates only "came off the production line" in 1942) were disappointing. Whereas the *Napolas* succeeded in producing, as all were agreed, "excellent officer material," the Adolf Hitler Schools never attained the same distinction. Significantly, few sons of prominent Nazis were to be found among the pupils at the AHS establishments!

## UNIFORMS

All boys were, of course, on admission already members of the DJ. As pupils they wore the standard DJ uniform with *AHS* in white on their single shoulder strap. At fourteen they became Hitler Youths and again wore the standard garb of that organization with, on their red piped shoulder straps, *AHS* in red. Staff, insofar as they were HJ officers, wore HJ leaders uniform with silver piped shoulder straps with silver *AHS*. All HJ members wore as their district triangle the name of the school with, above this, *AHS*. (For an example see "District Triangle" section.)*

The AHS motto was, like that of the NPEA *Mehr sein als scheinen* (Be more than you seem).

The 12 complete AHS establishments were:

    1 - Potsdam (Berlin)
    2 - Tilsit (East Prussia)
    3 - Waldbröl (near Aachen)
    4 - Koblenz (Rhine)
    5 - Plauen (Saxony)
    6 - Weimar (Thuringia)
    7 - Hesselberg (Franconia)
    8 - Chiemsee or Mittenwald (Bavaria)
    9 - Heiligendamm (Mecklenberg)
  10 - Landstuhl (Pfalz)
  11 - Wartha (Thuringia)
  12 - Iglau (Western Moravia in the "Protectorate" of Bohemia-Moravia).

An AHS pupil in summer khaki. Note his black shoulder strap with red *AHS* and red piping.

---

\* An example also exists which has no place name, but instead, *Adolf Hitler Schule* (in full).

Graduates of an Adolf Hitler School are congratulated by the School Leader.

Type of shoulder strap for AHS boys in the 10 to 14 age group (i.e. DJ lads).

145

Diploma awarded to an *Oberscharführer* for five years study at an Adolf Hitler School. It is dated Sonthofen, 10th November 1943 and is signed by Von Schirach and Dr. Robert Ley of the DAF (here in his capacity as National Organizational Leader of the NSDAF).

## NS Deutsche Oberschule Starnbergersee

Before concluding this summary of Nazi controlled education, reference must be made to the *NS Deutsche Oberschule* (National-Socialist German Secondary School) at Starnbergersee in Upper Bavaria. This high school, or junior college, located in a number of former holiday villas on the shores of the Starnbergersee (a lake some 15 miles south of Munich) was first opened in April 1934. It was, at this stage, conceived as an élite establishment for the training of future SA leaders. Its pupils, referred to as *SA-Jungmannen*, wore a junior version of SA uniform and carried a dress bayonet similar to that of the HJ *Wachgefolgschaft* (See Section on "Daggers and Knives") whose blade was inscribed *Ehre, Kraft, Freiheit* (Honour, Strength, Freedom).

In February 1936 the NSDAP took over control of the school, although most of the staff, including its head. Julius Goerlitz, continued to be SA leaders.

In 1941 all pupils were required to belong to the Hitler Youth and the school became an HJ *Stamm* in its own right. The boys, however, retained their former uniform, only their HJ identity cards indicating their new HJ status.

The staff wore, not HJ, but Political Leader uniform with a cuff-title *NSD Oberschule Starnbergersee* (silver letters on black with silver edges).

Parents had to pay for the privilege of sending their sons to this German equivalent of an exclusive English public school. Two of Martin Bormann's offspring were some-time pupils at the school.

# 15

# Leadership Courses

Perhaps the most pressing problem created by the rapid expansion of the HJ after the seizure of power in 1933 was the shortage of suitable leaders. The Hitler Youth could, of course, have simply taken over the leadership personnel of the various youth organizations which had been compulsorily integrated into it when it was declared the sole national youth organization, but this would have inevitably resulted in a dilution of the "purity" of the movement and introduced undesirable influences, from the Nazi point of view. The army expressed a willingness to second young officers as leaders but this, too, was rejected by von Schirach, who was anxious to preserve the independence of his organization.

There was, therefore, no alternative but to launch a crash programme of leadership training. Only a few centres of training (on a nationwide scale) existed prior to 1933, most of these the result of private initiative. For example, in Gau Munich, Emil Klein had founded a six-month leadership scheme, the first course of which commenced in November 1931, while in the same year Karl Hofmann of Gau Rhine-Pfalz started a "Horst Wessel School." The following year, at Flechtorf in Lower Saxony, von Schirach's deputy, Hartmann Lauterbacher, created a "Leo Schlageter School" (the name deriving from a Nazi proto-martyr, Albert Leo Schlageter, shot by the French in 1923 for resistance to their occupation of the Rhineland). In 1933 this school was removed to Potsdam (Berlin) and renamed the Reichs Leadership School (*Reichsführerschule*).

By the end of 1933, twenty-two *Gebietsführerschulen* (leadership schools at a *Gebiet* level, as distinct from the "national" school at Postdam) had either been opened or were already in an advanced state of preparation. Each of these schools ran a three-week "leaders course" (*Führer Lehrgang*), consisting of 149 hours, of which divided up as follows:

| | |
|---|---|
| Physical training | 30 hours |
| Field exercises (*Geländesport*) | 30 hours |
| "World Outlook" (Nazi dogma) | 29½ hours |
| Service training (*Dienstgestaltung*) | 20½ hours |
| Small arms shooting | 15 hours |
| Discussion periods | 6 hours |
| Cultural activities | 6 hours |
| "Home evenings" | 6 hours |

In August 1934 von Schirach claimed that these courses had produced 12,727 HJ leaders and 24,660 DJ leaders. Eventually there were some forty such *Gebiet* leadership schools.

The BDM had two *Reichsführerinnenschulen* (National Female Leadership Schools), one at Bad Godesberg (near Bonn) and the other at Boyden in East Prussia.

The HJ could not furnish from its own ranks sufficient professional men (doctors, dentists, lawyers, etc.) and had to seek these from outside, but here preference was given to "Old Fighters" (i.e. veteran Party members) to ensure their political reliability.

Graduates of the prestigious *Reichsführerschule* at Potsdam (where the course lasted eight, and not three, weeks), wore above their right breast pocket a badge with the letters *RFS* flanked on either side by oakleaves. This was on a brown background for HJ leaders, and on dark blue for DJ leaders.

To produce leaders of a higher calibre than those coming from either the *Gebietsführerschulen* or the *Reichsführerschule*, a special Academy for Youth Leadership (*Academie für Jugendführung*) was established at Brunswick in 1939. Entrance requirements for this were stiff, since it was hoped that its graduates would aspire to the top leadership posts of the HJ and or, at the very least, become full-time HJ leaders. The course was designed to last one year, but it could be embarked upon only after the candidate had completed his RAD (*Reichsarbeitsdienst*) and armed forces conscript service. In addition to the year at the Academy the student was required to have passed through the *Reichsführerschule* at Potsdam. He had also to have worked for not less than three weeks in a factory and spent up to six months with a German racial community outside the Reich. He had then to serve four months on the staff of an HJ *Gebiet*. Having done all this, he took a final written examination and, if successful, graduated as a full-time salaried *HJ-Stammführer*. He was required to sign an undertaking that he would serve for a minimum of twelve years with the Hitler Youth.

The BDM hoped to open its own *Akademie* at Wolfenbüttel (in Brunswick), but the coming of the war in September 1939 interrupted work on the building and it was never completed.

The war brought a second leadership crisis. Hundreds of young HJ leaders were called to the colours, or volunteered for service. The HJ slogan, "Youth must be led by youth" had to be translated into reality. Sixteen- and seventeen-year-olds were put through a new crash course of training, reduced from three to two weeks — the so-called *Führernachwuchsschulung* (leader trainee schooling) at a *Gebietsführerschule*. On completion of this they were given the designation of *K-Führer* (*Kriegsführer* — "war leader"). Boys of the HJ and DJ now were no longer lead by young adults, but by lads perhaps no more than two or three years senior to themselves.

# 16

# Shooting Courses

Systematic training in the use of small arms began in 1936 with the opening of the HJ's own Firearms School at Obermatzfeld in Thuringia. To encourage proficiency, an HJ Shooting (or Rifleman's) Badge was instituted the same year by von Schirach, higher grades being added in 1938 and 1942 (see "Awards" section). By 1939 the HJ had trained some 10,000 *Schiesswarten* (firearms instructors), who received the so-called "green licence" and a green cuff band. About 12,000 boys had by this date taken part in training courses using air rifles, and 51,500 had attained a sufficient skill to be awarded the Shooting Badge. The number of trainees increased significantly during the war when a further million and a half lads were put through shooting courses.

With a typically Nazi love of impressive statistics, the RJF announced in 1943 that seven million shots were fired *each month* by HJ trainees. What it failed to point out, however, was that twenty-seven people had been killed in shooting accidents, even before the outbreak of war and doubtless several more shared the same fate during the war years, although figures for this are not available.

The SA, which had lost its role in HJ training after 1932, came back into the picture in January 1939 with the creation of the *SA-Wehrmannschaften* (roughly: SA Militiamen). This new body was supposed to be responsible for the paramilitary education of German youth outside the armed forces. In practice the SA never made any great inroads into HJ training. The *Wehrmannschaften* had scarcely been properly formed before the advent of war in September 1939. The call-to-arms depleted its ranks to such an extent that it was incapable of fulfilling its allotted task. The army, and more importantly the Waffen-SS, took over the function of supervising HJ paramilitary training.

Pre-war shooting practice in the HJ on the range.

# Aeronautical Preparatory Technical Schools
# (Flieger Technische Vorschulen)

The first Aeronautical Preparatory Technical School (*Flieger Technische Vorschule*) was created by General Mooner of the Luftwaffe in 1937 with the object of providing a sound basic training for those wishing to make a career in the technical branch of the German Air Force. The idea proved so successful that before the end of the Second World War there were thirty-two such schools in various parts of Germany.

Strictly speaking these were not "schools" as such, but apprentice training schemes attached to some large commercial enterprise — usually an aircraft factory — but it could equally be an electrical or armaments business. The course was designed to last four years and was entirely free. It appealed mainly to sons of poor, or working-class families who saw it as an opportunity of obtaining a state-funded apprenticeship in a useful trade. The successful applicant began his training at the age of fourteen or fifteen years. Like so much else in Hitler's

Peaked cap of an officer at a *Flieger Tech. Vorschule*. It is Luftwaffe blue with black band. Embroidered Luftwaffe eagle above metal HJ diamond. Chin strap is silver speckled with blue.

Germany, these "schools" were conceived on paramilitary lines. The apprentices were known as *Militärschuler* (military pupils) and were enrolled as members of the *Flieger-HJ*. There was a *Hauptführer*, assisted by two *Zugführer* for every hundred boys.

In addition to the practical and technical training, the boys had to participate in all the normal activities of the Hitler Youth, particular emphasis being laid on sport and "political awareness." Although being trained primarily as ground technicians, the boys were expected to learn gliding and, hopefully, qualify for an A, B or C Certificate in this branch of sport. They also had to spend at least two hours per week in the construction of a glider.

On completing the four-year apprenticeship, the boy could, if he wished, go on to a further two-year course at a Luftwaffe Trade or Technical School (by that time as a member of the Luftwaffe).

UNIFORMS

The summer uniform worn by the boys was the same as that of the *Flieger-HJ*, that is to say, a brown shirt, black neckerchief, black shorts and a khaki side-cap, piped in light blue. The shoulder strap piping and *Bann* number was also in light blue. A black cuff-title with the name of the school in light blue lettering, e.g., *Fl. Tech. Vorschule Rudow* (Rudow is a suburb of Berlin), was worn on the left sleeve cuff.† The winter uniform was the same as the winter ski-type garb of the General HJ, but in Luftwaffe blue-grey material.

Badge worn on overalls by participant in course number *2* at the *Flieger Technische Vorschule* at Gotha. It is a blue badge with yellow lettering, borders and numeral.

---

† Other known examples of such cuff-titles are: Fl. Tech. Vorschule Magdeburg; Fl. Tech. Vorschule Berlin-Wedding; Fl. Tech. Vorschule Berlin-Reinickendorf; Fl. Tech. Vorschule Leipzig-Tauchau; Fl. Tech. Vorschule Brandenburg-Havel; Fl. Tech. Vorschule Braunschweig; Fl. Tech. Vorschule Stettin; Fl. Tech. Vorschule Oschersleben.

The above list may not be, by any means, a complete list. All were in the same style of Gothic lettering as the illustrated example of "Bremen-Oslebshausen."

# Deutsche Jungvolk

## HISTORY

The official birthday of the DJ was in December 1928 when, at a meeting of the entire HJ leadership at Plauen, it was decided to create a *Deutsch Knabenschaft* for boys between the ages of ten and fourteen. The following year the NSDAP in Vienna formed a similar young person's group giving it the name, *Deutsches Jungvolk* (a title which has been used in the *Wandervogel*, even before the First World War). On November 9, 1929 the *Gauleiter* of Vienna presented the DJ with its first flag — a silver embroidered *Sigrune* on a black field.

In August 1930 the Austrian DJ was formally linked with the *Deutsche Knabenschaft* under the appellation, *Deutsche Jungvolk: Bund der Tatjugend Grossdeutschlands* (German Young People: Union of Active Youth of Greater Germany) — a somewhat presumptuous title for a body whose total membership was little more than seven hundred! On March 27, 1931 the designation was altered to *Deutsche Jungvolk in der HJ*, and it was granted recognition as a subsection of the NSDAP. The silver *Sigrune* on black of the Austrian DJ was unanimously adopted as its official flag.

Membership of the DJ remained voluntary until December 1, 1936 when a law was enacted making membership of some branch of the HJ obligatory for all young persons from the age of ten upward (for both sexes). In practice compulsion was not applied until 1941.

Boys were "on probation" for the first six months of their service and were not accepted as full DJ members until they had passed a number of sporting and "ideological" tests (the latter comprised mainly a knowledge of DJ slogans, the words of DJ songs, and a general history of the Nazi movement). There was also a "test of courage," which could take the form of, for example, jumping from a certain height in full "marching order." If the boy passed these tests his initiation as a full member of the DJ was indicated by the presentation of a brown shirt,[††] black shoulder strap, and *Sigrune* arm badge, all of which he had to pay for!

---

[††] White shirts were worn by probationers.

Promotion from the DJ to the HJ took place annually on April 20th, Hitler's birthday. This continued even as late as April 1945, within days of the end of the war in Europe.

Originally a very formal division had existed between the HJ and the DJ, but during the late 1930's this was slowly broken down and formally abolished in 1940. Thereafter DJ leaders were only distinguished from those in the HJ by the colour of their uniform.

DJ training paralleled that of the HJ in that the main emphasis was on physical fitness and military preparedness, this latter included the use of a rifle (or air gun). Like their elders in the HJ, the youngsters of the DJ had to take part in gruelling route marches in full kit and participate in mock battles and other paramilitary exercises.

DJ UNIFORMS

Standardization of dress did not occur until well into the 1930's. Before this the only constants were the khaki shirt and the *Sigrune* emblem, even the latter varied in colour and style (the earlier versions being thinner than the later official type). The *Sigrune* was sometimes encircled in two coloured piping, this being the *Landesfarben*, or state colours, of the region of Germany in which the unit was raised (for listings of *Landesfarben*, see "Lanyards" section).

Early headgear was a beret (borrowed from the *Wandervogel)* or a khaki side cap, in a somewhat American style, piped in a single or double colour. More often than not the boys went bareheaded.

After 1933 tighter rules were formulated with regard to dress, but as every item had to be found at the boy's own expense, this did not result in immediate uniformity. According to the published regulations, the summer garb was to consist of a khaki shirt, black shorts (altered to dark blue in April 1935), black belt with cross-strap. A black neckerchief and leather toggle, similar to that of the HJ, was worn with the collar of the shirt open. A black side-cap, piped in the colour of the *Oberbann* was worn until April 1936, when the concept of the *Oberbann* was dropped. A plain black side-cap was then worn until being abolished in July 1937, when a khaki side-cap, piped in red, was authorized for both the HJ and DJ. (Members on the staff of a *Gebiet* or of the RJF had carmine piping on their side-capes.) Stockings were grey except in certain regions of southern Germany (and later Austria), where the "traditional" white socks were allowed. Shoes were brown, but black was optional.

The winter uniform was the same with the addition of a dark blue blouse until 1936, when a ski-type outfit in dark blue became standard winter dress for the HJ and DJ. With this form of dress the bottoms of the trousers were tucked into rolled-down blue socks. The blouse had three grey buttons down the front and a wide "floppy" collar. The black belt with cross-strap was worn with both the winter and summer dress.

In April 1935 shoulder straps were introduced for the first time. These were black and were worn on the right shoulder only. At first these showed the *Stamm* number followed by an oblique stroke and the

DJ boy wearing a brown beret with two colour *Landesfarben* piping. This form of headgear, deriving from the *Wandervogel* Movement, was unpopular and seems to have existed only for a short time.

DJ boys at Potsdam rally, 1932. Note their large "floppy" berets.

DJ boy of *Gruppe Hochland* (Highlands). On the side of his forage cap he wears the Edelweiss flower head of this Group. The badge he wears on his pocket is only a "day badge."

DJ forage cap with embroidered Edelweiss badge.

A more elaborate version of the Edelweiss emblem with stock and leaves.

(1) (2) (3)

(1) DJ *Jungzugführer* in winter uniform. His rank is indicated by his green lanyard.
(2) DJ drummer in summer uniform.
(3) DJ *Jungbannführer* (rank indicated by red lanyard) in the short "battle dress" type tunic introduced in February 1937.
(The above are from the 1937 edition of the *Organisationsbuch der NSDAP*).

Summer uniform (1933)

Winter uniform (1933)

Summer uniform: Khaki shirt, dark blue shorts; winter uniform: Same but dark blue blouse worn with it. Forage cap dark blue. Later ski type uniform worn in winter. "Die Uniformer der HJ" by Herbert Knötel (1933).

DJ boys (foreground) and HJ lads (behind) of the Hochland District.

(a)

(b)

Two examples of DJ shoulder strap (worn on right side only). (a) is the earlier type, in chain stitch with *Stamm* (1) and *Jungbann* number (133); (b) is the second type with woven *Jungbann* numeral only (539).

*Jungbann* numeral. Later only the *Jungbann* number (in white Arabic figures) was used. As in the Hitler Youth, units of the DJ in southern Germany (*Obergebiete:* Franken, Hochland, Bayr. Ostmark and Pfalz-Saar) and the unit number on the shoulder strap prefixed by a Latin *B*. Other letters which could feature on DJ shoulder straps were *G* (in Gothic) for *Gebiet* staff, *RJF* (in Gothic) for *RFJ* staff, *AHS* (in Gothic) for pupils of an Adolf Hitler School, and *J* for *Bann "Jungsturm"* in Nürnberg City.

Two standard features of all uniforms were the district triangle and the *Sigrune* arm badge. On the left breast pocket the enamel HJ diamond badge was worn. Prior to 1933 DJ boys wore on their left breast pocket a round enamel badge (as illustrated).

[Right] A slightly sea-sick DJ *Hordenführer*. Note the silver tress *"Winkel"* on his left lower arm which indicates his rank. The *Sigrune* on his belt buckle is obviously the gilt type (Picture taken during a DJ excursion which involved crossing the Baltic — which obviously not all the boys enjoyed!).

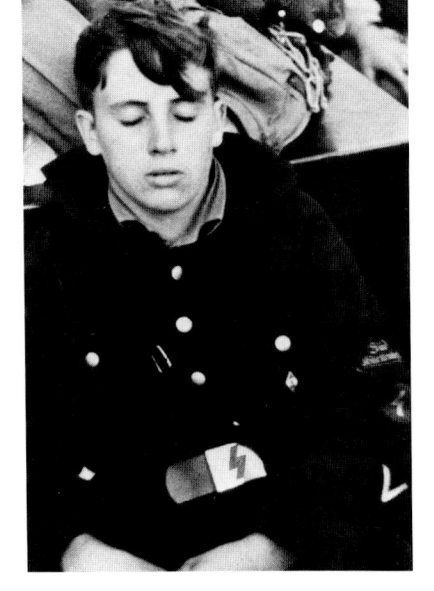

[Below] Two DJ boys in pre-1933 uniform with brown beret without piping. On the left breast pocket they wear the round DJ badge which in 1933 was replaced by the HJ diamond-shaped emblem. The beret was replaced by a black side-cap.

(a) First design and (b) second design of badge worn by DJ boys on left breast pocket prior to the introduction in 1933 of the diamond-shaped badge.

DJ leaders at first wore much the same uniform as the boys, but in September 1935 a special leader's képi was introduced — dark blue piped in silver with the eagle-and-swastika badge in white metal on the front. In February 1937 a short blouse (again in dark blue), somewhat similar to the British battle dress top, was authorized for leaders. A khaki shirt, black tie and black breeches was worn with it. The belt buckle was the same as for HJ leaders. Until May 1937 leaders wore only a right shoulder strap in plain black, their rank at this time being indicated by the colour of their lanyard and/or a special version of the *Sigrune* on the left upper arm. Thereafter DJ leaders wore on both shoulders HJ leaders insignia, although still retaining the former DJ nomenclature.

In June 1939 a further change was made to leaders' uniforms. Warrant Officers* were allowed to wear a dark blue version of the short tunic introduced the previous September for HJ Warrant Officers. A dark blue version of the full length tunic (for commissioned grade) was also brought in for DJ leaders of equivalent status. The use of the HJ brassard was also permitted.

In May 1937 the DJ was brought further into line with the HJ with the abandonment of the special DJ belt buckle (the *Sigrune*) and its replacement by the normal HJ type. The changeover had to be completed by January 1938. In some cases the former DJ buckle was simply "adapted" by having an HJ centrepiece soldered on top of the *Sigrune!*

During the Second World War the temporary *K-Führer* (usually boys from the upper age groups of the HJ) wore the same dark blue ski uniform as their charges. Only "regular" DJ leaders now wore the special leaders uniform described above.

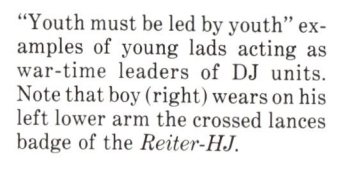

"Youth must be led by youth" examples of young lads acting as war-time leaders of DJ units. Note that boy (right) wears on his left lower arm the crossed lances badge of the *Reiter-HJ*.

---

* *Fahnleinführer* to *Hauptfahnleinführer*

## DJ RANK INSIGNIA

### 1st Pattern, 1933-1936

All noncommissioned ranks wore on the left upper arm a *Sigrune* in the colours of the *Oberbann* to which their unit belonged. These *Oberbanne* colours were the same as those of the HJ and were as follows:

Oberbann 1: red
Oberbann 2: yellow
Oberbann 3: green
Oberbann 4: blue
Oberbann 5: black
Oberbann 6: white.

Ranks within the DJ were indicated by coloured lanyards; senior officers had, in addition, a coloured background to their *Sigrune* arm emblem which corresponded to the colour of the cap bands worn by senior leaders in the HJ, namely (in rising order of seniority): white, yellow, bright red, carmine.

The scheme of ranks was as follows:

*Jungenschaftsführer:* red and white lanyard (orginally in *Landesfarben*)
*Jungzugführer:* green lanyard
*Fahnleinführer:* green/white lanyard
*Stammführer:* white lanyard
*Junnbannführer:* red lanyard. On left upper arm a silver *Sigrune* on a white circle outlined in the colour of the *Oberbann* (red, yellow, etc.).
*Oberjungbannführer:* red/black lanyard. Silver *Sigrune* on a yellow circle with a silver bullion outline.
*Gebietsjungvolkführer:* black lanyard. Silver *Sigrune* on bright red circle with silver bullion outline.
*Obergebietsjungvolkführer:* black/silver lanyard. Gold *Sigrune* on carmine circle with gold bullion outline.

Leaders on the staff of a *Gebiet* or on the RJF Staff had special arm emblems, introduced in November 1934.

DJ ARM BADGES (1933-36)
COMMISSIONED RANKS

*Jungbannführer.* Silver rune on white. Outer circle in colour of Oberbann. (Here green for Oberbann 3).

*Oberjungbannführer.* Silver rune and circle on yellow.

*Gebietsjungvolkführer.* Silver rune and circle on bright red.

*Obergebietsjungvolkführer.* Gold rune and gold bullion circle on dark red.

*Jungbannführer.* (Silver rune on white).

*Jungbannführer* on Gebiet staff. (Silver on red).

*Jungbannführer* on the Staff of the RJF. Silver rune on white. Inner circle pink, outer circle black. In November 1934 replaced by special Gebiet and RJF staff arm emblems.

*Oberjungbannführer* on Gebiet staff (Silver on red).

*Gebietsjungvolkführer.* (Silver on red).

(a)  (b)

Two examples of pre-1933 DJ arm badges. (a) red on white (b) white on blue with red/white piping which may be *Landesfarben* and indicate a unit from Hamburg/Bremen/Hesse (See Section on Lanyards). Note the different forms of the "Sigrune."

2nd Pattern, 1936-1937

In April 1936 the concept of an *Oberbann* was discontinued and with the use of *Oberbann* colours (red, yellow, green, etc.). All noncommissioned ranks now wore a white *Sigrune* on a red circle (on a "square" khaki background). The lanyard colours denoting rank remained unaltered. A new grade, that of *Hordenführer*, was introduced in January 1936 as the first step in the promotion ladder. It was the counterpart of the HJ *Rottenführer* grade and was indicated by a silver tress chevron on a khaki (or in winter, dark blue) inverted triangle worn on the left cuff.

DJ ARM BADGES
(1936-37)

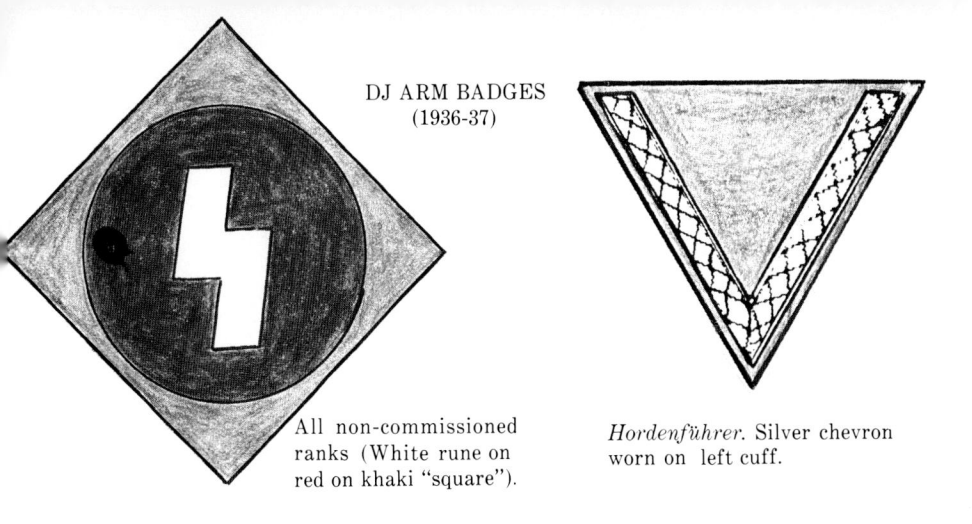

All non-commissioned ranks (White rune on red on khaki "square").

*Hordenführer.* Silver chevron worn on left cuff.

DJ ARM BADGES (1933-36)
(WORN ON LEFT UPPER ARM BY NON-COMMISSIONED RANKS)

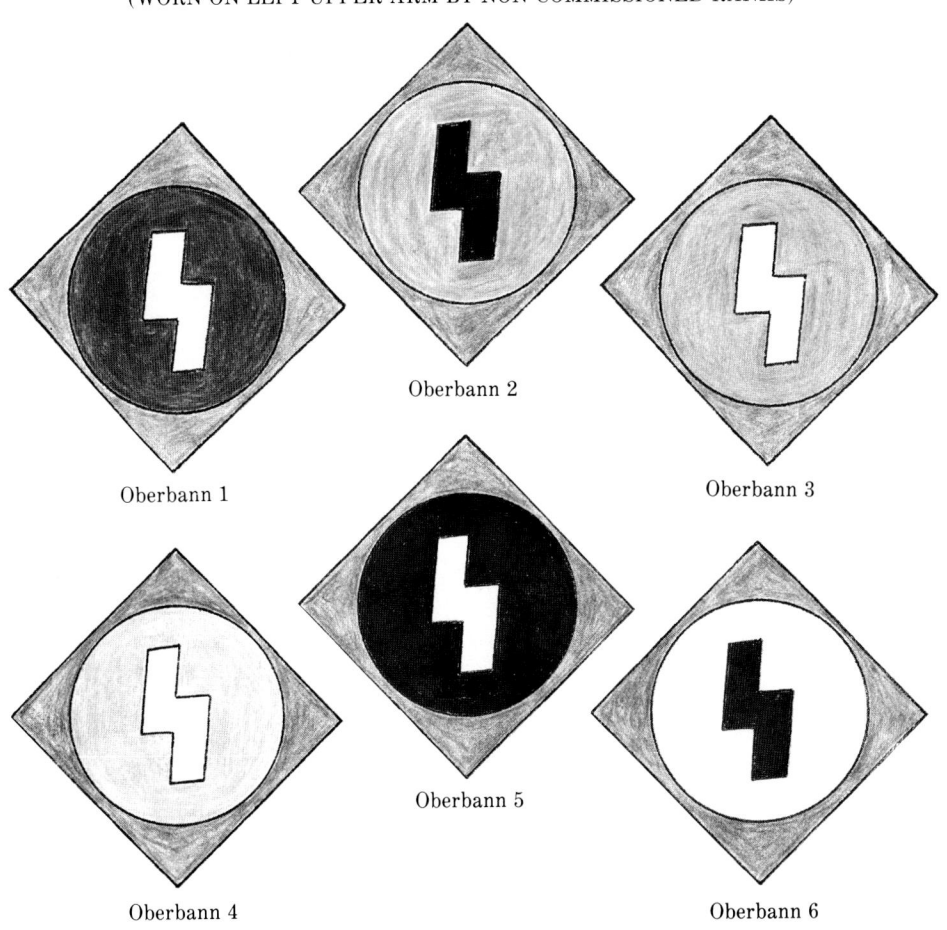

Oberbann 1

Oberbann 2

Oberbann 3

Oberbann 4

Oberbann 5

Oberbann 6

The colours of the DJ Oberbanne correspond exactly to those of the HJ Oberbanne, that is to say: red for Oberbann 1, yellow for Oberbann 2, green for Oberbann 3, blue for Oberbann 4, black for Oberbann 5 and white for Oberbann 6.

Hordenführer  Oberhordenführer  Jungschaftsführer

Oberjungschaftsführer  Jungzugführer  Oberjungzugführer

Arm badge for boys  Arm badge (officers)

Fahnleinführer  Oberfanhleinführer  Hauptfahnleinführer  Jungstammführer  Oberjungstammfü

A *Jungbannführer* (or indeed *any* person in charge of a *Jungbann* irrespective of his actual rank) now wore a silver *Sigrune* on a white circle on the left upper arm. On the staff of a *Gebiet*, however, a *Jungbannführer* wore the silver *Sigrune* on a red circle, an *Oberjungvolkführer*, the same with a silver bullion surround, a *Gebiets-Jungvolkführer* the same with a double silver bullion surround. Corresponding grades on all staffs (other than the RJF) had the same but on a carmine circle. Members of the RJF in these grades had gold in place of silver (the circle was carmine).

3rd Pattern, 1937-1945

A final revision of DJ rank insignia took place in the two years preceding the Second World War as the DJ was brought more and more into line with the HJ commissioned grades (*Jungstammführer* and above) were permitted to wear the HJ brassard. A silver *Sigrune* on a black circle with a silver surround was worn only by subalterns (*Jungstannführer* to *Jungbannführer*) and now on the left cuff, not the upper arm.

In September 1938 the RJF devised new DJ arm rank badges — their introduction to take effect from January 1939. These took the forms of chevrons and/or stars in silver-grey cotton on dark blue (for both summer and winter dress) worn on the right upper arm. The *Hordenführer* chevron, however, continued to be worn on the left cuff until May 1939 when (more logically) it was brought into line with the others. Noncommissioned ranks continued to wear the white *Sigrune* on a red circle but without the "square" khaki background. Noncommissioned grades serving on *Gebiete* or other staffs wore a white *Sigrune* on a carmine circle, later the colour of the circle was altered to pink.

The photo on right was taken in June 1941 and is interesting in that the ski cap has the national eagle-and-swastika emblem as the cap badge. His HJ rank is *Scharführer* (two stars on shoulder strap) but he wears the white lanyard of a DJ *Stammführer*.

167

The use of various coloured lanyards was continued, but especially under the circumstances of war these tended to indicate acting, rather than substantive rank (e.g., when HJ boys, often only the equivalent of lower or middle ranking NCOs, acted as "officers" for DJ units, they wore a lanyard appropriate to such a rank).

Jungbannführer   Oberjungbannführer   Hauptjungbannführer   Gebietsjungvolkführer   Obergebietsjungvolkführer

The above shoulder strap ranks were introduced in May 1937. It is possible that the two highest grades were only theoretical since at that level the two organizations tended to merge.

A war-time photograph of HJ and DJ leaders attending a training course at the Reich Leadership School in Potsdam (taken outside the Sans Souci Palace). It is interesting to note that the DJ leaders now wear the HJ brassard (not the pre-war Sigrune) and that their tunic is simply a dark blue version of that of an HJ leader.

## MARINE-DJ

The DJ had only one specialist section — *Marine-DJ;* even this would appear to have been short-lived. Details of its uniform feature in the 1934 dress regulations, but thereafter references to such an organization disappear. It may have been felt that this type of training was too rough for very young lads, or, conceivably, an insufficient number of volunteers may have presented themselves. Whatever the reason, the Marine DJ seems to have quietly faded away by the mid 1930's.

Its uniform was very similar to that of the *Marine-HJ*. Boys wore short navy blue trousers (in both summer and winter) with black stockings — these being rolled down to the ankles in summer. With this they wore a navy blue cotton sailor's vest with a broad collar with white stripes (exactly like that of the Marine HJ). In warm weather the wearing of a white shirt could be authorized at the unit commander's discretion. Headgear, both summer and winter, was a navy blue sailor's cap with a light blue cap tally on which was *Marine-DJ* and possibly (this is uncertain) the unit numeral or other designation.

In winter a short navy blue reefer jacket could be added. On the left upper arm a *Sigrune* badge was worn. The regulations do not state the colour, but since this was 1934 it was most likely in the normal DJ *Oberbann* colour combination. As working dress, summer or winter, the same white moleskin garb as worn in the Marine HJ was employed. Belts were black with the usual *Sigrune* emblem on the buckle. Leaders' uniforms are not described but it is stated that *Marine-DJ* leaders will wear, "... a *Sigrune* and piping corresponding to their DJ rank...." Again this would appear to relate to the type of DJ rank insignia current at that period, e.g., a silver *Sigrune* on a white circle to indicate the rank of *Jungbannführer*, etc., etc.

Standard DJ buckle for non-commissioned ranks. After 1934 DJ officers wore the same buckle as HJ Officers. Early in 1938 all members of the DJ were authorized to wear same belt buckle as HJ.

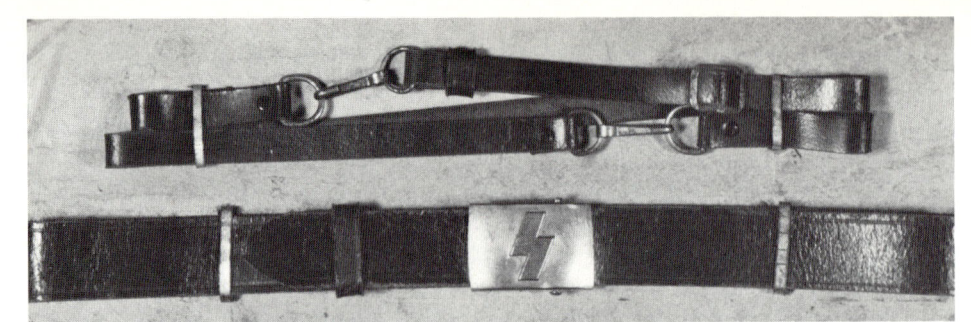

Complete belt, buckle and cross strap set. In some versions of the buckle, the *Sigrune* is (as here) gilt coloured.

Early version of DJ buckle with "lightning flash" type of *Sigrune*.

Variant based on pre-1933 badge design.

DJ boy with early version of *Sigrune* buckle.

170

DJ Jungbann flag (both sides the same).

DJ Fahnlein flag (both sides the same).

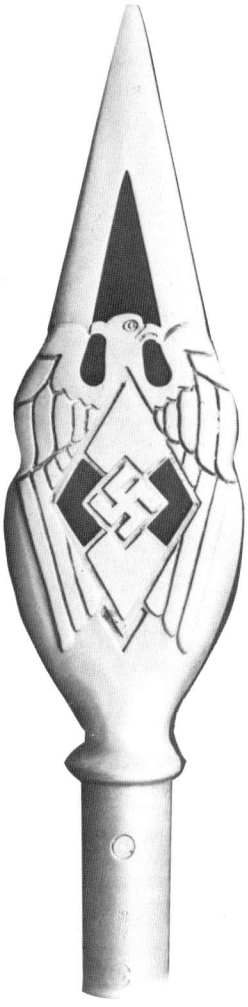

Standard top for a DJ Jungbann flag.

Jungzug pennant. Reverse can have individual design and colour.

DJ boys at summer camp with early design of flags.

Stamm flag. Reverse is of individual unit design and colour. Georg Preifer was the "honour name" of Bann 280 (Berlin-Weissensee).

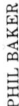

Variation DJ trumpet banner (reverse). White reversed *Sigrunen* on a black field. White horse, designation "Fä21/252," and border on red shield. The obverse exhibits a large white *Sigrune* on black.

Fahnlein pennant. Reverse can have individual unit design and colour.

172

Jungbann flag (both sides the same).

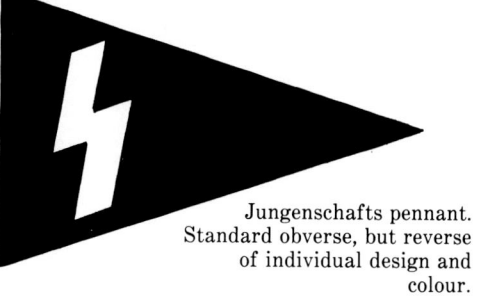

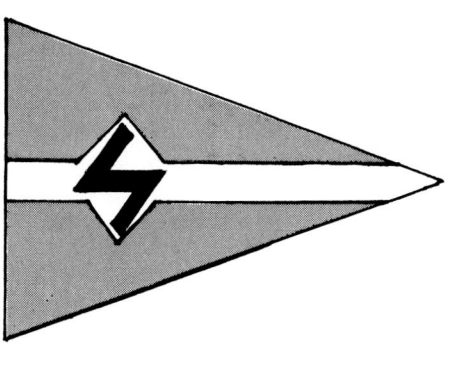

Jungenschafts pennant.
Standard obverse, but reverse
of individual design and
colour.

173

[Above (left)]: Flag party and fanfare trumpeters, probably c. 1939.

[Above (right):] Two types of *Sigrune* as featured on DJ fanfare trumpet banner — the upper one is the standard type, the lower an early semi-official variant. Other variants were a white skull and cross-bones or a mobile swastika, etc. After 1934 all such variants were forbidden and only the standard white *Sigrune* on black permitted.

DJ fanfare trumpeters with a rather unusual type of fanfare trumpet banner.

Flag party with second design DJ Jungbann flag, possibly c. 1935. Note diversity of "uniforms"!

DJ "swallows nests" in wear.

DJ fife and fanfare trumpet player. He wears a very unusual type of "swallows nest" with a black *Sigrune*. The banner of his fanfare trumpet (just visible) is also unusual. In January 1936 the wearing of "swallows nests" by DJ fanfare trumpeters and DJ *Spielmannzüge* (fife-and-drum corps) was forbidden. They were retained only by DJ bandsmen.

# 19

## *Bund Deutscher Mädel and Jungmädel (BDM and JM)*

The Hitler Youth had been in existence for two years before the creation of an official female section was even muted. At a meeting in Plauen in December 1928 Kurt Gruber and the regional leaders of the HJ agreed to the setting up of a *Schwesternschaft der HJ* (Sisterhood of the HJ). Its public launching did not take place until July 1929 at which time it registered a grand total of sixty-seven members. Exactly one year later (July 1930) the name was changed to *Bund deutscher Mädel* (League of German Girls, or BDM). It was open to girls over the age of fourteen. In April of the following year a junior branch, the *Jungmädelgruppe* (Young Girls Group, or JM), was established to take in girls below this age. Neither made much immediate impact. In March 1932 the BDM had only 5,184 members and the JM an insignificant 750. However, by the autumn of that year there had been a dramatic increase. At the celebrated muster of the HJ at Potsdam in October 1932 some 15,000 of the young participants were girls.

But the BDM had competitors in the market for the Nazi-minded female youth. The Women's Group of the NSDAP, originally called the *Deutscher Frauenorden* (German Women's Order), but, after 1931 known as the *Nat.Soz Frauenschaft* (NSF), took under its wing young girls in its *NS-Mädchenschaft*. The ladies of the NSF did not subscribe to the view that care of impressionable teenagers should be entrusted to the brash "Youth-must-be-led-by youth" enthusiasts of the BDM. The welfare of girls, especially those of the well brought up variety, was, in their submission, more wisely placed in the hands of mature women. Really well-bred young ladies eschewed both the largely working-class BDM and the maternalistic NSF's *Mädchenschaft* and inclined towards the *Bund Königin Luise* (Queen Louise League — a conservative, nationalist, although *not* national-socialist, ladies association, formed in 1923).

The BDM complained to Hitler that the NSF was "poaching" its girls. Rivalry between the two became so bitter than in July 1932 Hitler was obliged to decree that the BDM would, in future, be the sole authorized Party organization for girls and the NSF for adult women. This,

Membership badge of the
NS-Mädchenschaft
(GHF-*Glaube, Hoffnung,
Liebe,* or "Faith, Hope and
Charity/Love," the motto
of the NSF).

Badge of the
Bund Königin
Luise

however, left open the question of at what age does a girl become an adult woman — 18 or 21 years? This problem remained unresolved until it was finally settled with the creation, in January 1938, of the BDM *Werk "Glaube und Schönheit"* for young females between the ages of seventeen and twenty-one, which acted as a bridge between the BDM and NSF (both organizations having a hand in its running).

Another rival to the BDM's monopoly was the *NS-Schülerinnenbund* (National-Socialist School Girls League, or NSSi, this being the female counterpart of the boys NSS-*Nat. Soz. Schülerbund)*, which aimed at winning for the Hitler cause young people at secondary schools. Secondary education being class-biased, was incompatible with the classless "national community" of Nazi ideology. In July 1932 the NSSi was disbanded and its members ordered to transfer to the BDM. The NSF's *Mädchenschaft* soldiered on, despite the Hitler injunction, until well into 1933; while the *Bund Königin Luise,* rather surprisingly, survived until April 1934 when it too was dissolved.

The BDM placed as much emphasis on physical fitness as did the HJ, but, although disciplined and uniformed, it was less militaristic in tone. Women's role in life, it opined, was secondary to men's; women's place being in the home or hospital (there was a good deal of practical training in nursing). The BDM ran forty-seven *Haushaltungsschulen* (Home Economics Schools) with an average turnout of 1,300 graduates per year. Armed with their diploma, they lectured to schools or BDM units on child welfare and eugenics.

The girls, like the boys, had annual tented camps, nationwide sports competitions and, although on a rather smaller scale, organized trips abroad. Another feature that they had in common with the males was "back to the land." This policy actively encouraged girls to join farming communities in the summer and autumn, principally to assist with the harvest, although a girl might as easily find herself acting as an unpaid servant or "nanny" in a farmer's household. Theoretically allotted less strenuous tasks than the boys, the girls, especially after the outbreak of war, were not infrequently given work once performed by grown men. This provided a (voluntary) foretaste of what they might expect (compulsorily) when drafted, at age eighteen or nineteen into the Women's Section of the National Labour Service (RAD). Regular BDM officers, during the war, could (and did) transfer into, and out of, the RAD as leaders of girls' camps.

Like the rest of the Hitler Youth, much of the BDM's leadership corps was part-time and unpaid. Only a minority of officers were salaried "regulars." Potential BDM or JM leaders were personally selected by the *Mädelführerin* of each *Bann* formed into *Führerin-Anwäterinnen-Schaften* (Female Leader-Candidate Squads, usually abbreviated to *FA Schaften)*. It was necessary to have belonged to an *FA Schaft* for at least a year before an individual could be accredited as a "leader."

There were also full-time BDM training schools *(Reichsführerinnenschulen)* at Bad Godesberg (near Bonn) and Boyden in East Prussia. The projected BDM *Akademie* at Wolfenbüttel in Brunswick was never completed due to the outbreak of war.

Entry into the JM and promotion from it to the BDM took place annually on April 20th (Hitler's birthday). BDM/JM membership remained voluntary until December 1, 1936 when youth service was made obligatory under law for both males and females, but in practice compulsion was not fully applied until after the outbreak of war.

In March 1932 Elisabeth Greiff-Walden was appointed national leader of the BDM/JM with the title *Referentin für Mädelfragen in der Reichsleitung der HJ* (Referent for Girls Matters in the National Leadership of the HJ). This rather ponderous appellation was, in June 1932, changed to *Bundesführer des BDM*. In June 1934 Trude Bürkner-Mohr took over as BDM chief with the new designation of *BDM Hauptreferentin*. In November 1937 she resigned in order to have her first child and was succeeded by Dr. Jutta Rüdiger who was not designated *Reichsreferentin für den BDM beim RJF* (National Referent for the BDM within the Reich Youth Leadership). Dr. Rüdiger held this post until the collapse of the Third Reich in May 1945.

The gargantuan growth of the BDM/JM from a mere 4,036 in February 1932 to almost six million by the close of 1933 resulted in the same leadership crisis as the HJ. The solution was similarly a crash training programme of officers and lower ranking leaders.

The wartime tasks of the BDM/JM are dealt with elsewhere.

All members of the BDM/JM were expected to observe certain personal proprieties. Hair had to be worn short, or, if naturally long, pleated "Gretchen fashion." Makeup had to be kept to a minimum, preferably not worn at all — the German maiden was supposed to glow with natural good health. Smoking was forbidden on duty and generally strongly discouraged as being inimical to sporting fitness and liable to cause infertility, both cardinal sins in the Nazi calendar. The use of alcohol or any other artificial stimulant was, of course, taboo. Unseemly conduct in uniform, whether on duty or not, was treated with severity.

## UNIFORMS

The first girls uniform was a rather unsightly white collared brown "gym slip" worn with white stockings and black shoes. Sometimes a black beret was added.

It was Hitler who objected to this unalluring garb. "... We don't want our girls to be dressed in such a fashion that no man would give them a second look ...," he complained and commissioned a well known Berlin dress designer to devise a more becoming ensemble. The result was a summer uniform consisting of a dark blue skirt (the length of which varied considerably over the years with changes in female fashion), white blouse with two patch pockets, dark blue neckerchief and toggle, black leather belt with a plain claw buckle for leaders (girls had a slightly narrower belt with white ornamental studs). On the left breast pocket of this, and *all* BDM/JM uniforms, the small enamel diamond-shaped emblem of the HJ was worn.

Early BDM uniform. The girls belong to a group formed in Gau South Hanover-Brunswick in September 1929.

BDM girl wearing the *Kletterjacke;* ca. 1936-1937

BDM girl, ca. 1933. She wears the early type uniform with white collar.

(a) BDM girl in winter jacket and beret
(b) BDM girl in winter great-coat
(c) JM girl in summer uniform
(d) BDM *Untergauführerin* (a rank indicated by red lanyard) in summer uniform. (The above from the 1937 *Organisationsbuch der* N.S.D.A.P.). At first girls did not wear a badge on their berets, but during the war this badge was sometimes worn.

BDM girls. This photo must have been taken before April 1934 when "district triangles" were introduced for girls. Note the large "floppy" berets.

NATIONAL ARCHIVES

181

For autumn and winter wear a four-pocket short suedette tunic, known as a *Kletterjacke* (climbing jacket) could be added. This was originally fawn-coloured but, in September 1940, it was altered to dark blue to match the skirt or slacks (this latter innovation would have been frowned upon as too masculine prior to the war). The *Kletterjacke* had six buttons down the front and one on each cuff. On the left arm a cloth version of the HJ diamond was sewn with, above it, the district triangle (white on black). The district triangle was also worn on the left upper arm of the blouse.

An uncomely black beret topped with a large button was employed as winter headgear. At first this embodied no insignia of any sort, but later an eagle-and-swastika badge was added. This, however, was short-lived since the beret was jettisoned in favor of a dark blue hat with a turned up back-and-sides brim. In very cold weather a brown greatcoat could be worn. The HJ enamel badge was worn on the right lapel of this coat.

The JM uniform was simply a junior version of the above except that, the winter head covering, was a dark blue pixie cap (known in German as a *Teufelsmütze* — Devil's cap) with two vertical white bands down the centre. In rainy weather a brown rain-cape could be worn.

JM *Teufelmütze* ("devil's cap").

P. COLEMAN

An interesting feature of the BDM/JM greatcoat is that instead of the district triangle, a cuff-title was worn on the left lower arm (the positioning being described as "three fingers width above the end of the sleeve") on which was the name of the *Obergau* in white lettering on blue (for BDM) or white lettering on brown (for JM). Sometimes these cuff-titles are to be found with silver bullion on white — presumably for high officials when worn with the white summer tunic.

In winter, the white socks were replaced by brown stockings. The wearing of dark blue or black gloves was also permitted. This applied to both BDM and JM.

Even the young lasses of the JM were not exempt from having to don "full marching order" of rucksack, bedroll, water bottle, side-pack etc. on summer route marches or in transit to camp.

Before the war rank was indicated by means of various coloured lanyards, but around 1939/40 an entirely new scheme of insignia, along with much more elaborate officer uniforms, was introduced. Only the two lowest ranks (*Mädelschar* — and *Mäelschaftsführerinnen*) continued to use a lanyard as an indication of rank. Above these grades the new insignia (described below) were worn. There was also, at this time, a slight simplification of the former somewhat cumbersome (even for German) nomenclature, e.g., *Mädelgruppenführerin* and *Jungmädelgruppenführerin* were changed to *BDM Gruppenführerin* and *JM Gruppenführerin* respectively. Similarly the prefixes *Mädel* and *Jungmädel* were dropped from all other ranks and BDM or JM substituted.

A trio of BDM girls in marching order await the arrival of a train to take them to camp. Their pennant looks distinctly "home made."

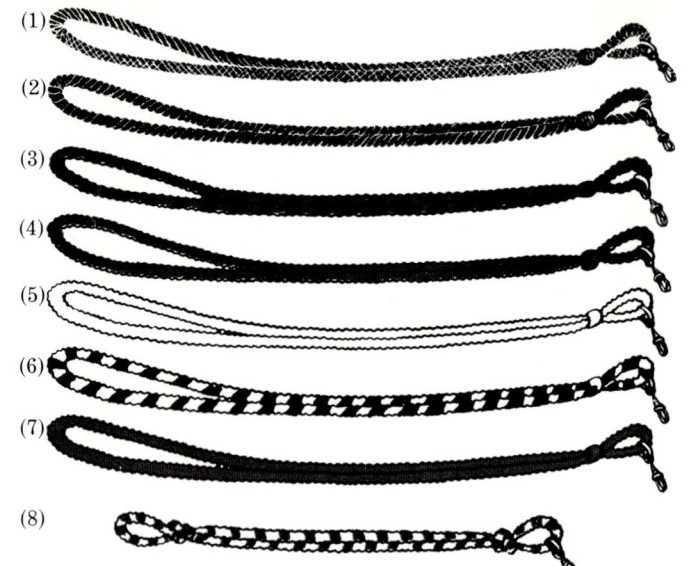

(1) Gauverbandsführerin: black and silver (This rank was later discontinued); (2) Obergauführerin): black; (3) Gauführerin: red/black; (4) Untergauführerin/J.M. Ringführerin: red; (5) Mädelring-/Jungmädelringführerin: white; (6) Mädelgruppen/Jungmädelgruppenführerin: green/white; (7) Mädelschar-/Jungmädelscharführerin: green; (8) Mädelschafts-/Jungmädelschaftsführerin: red/white (but originally in *Landesfarben*, then colour of the Oberbann)

Method of wearing lanyards 1 to 7, around the neck, under the neckerchief and through the toggle. The shorter Mädelschaftsführerin lanyard was worn from the left breast pocket button to the second button (i.e. the button level to it) on the blouse or Kletterjacke.

The new rank insignia took the form of a silver, or for higher ranks, gold bullion open-winged eagle on a black (or on summer dress, white) shield with various types of border to indicate grade. The unit number (where this was applicable) appeared above the eagle's head. These new devices were worn on the left upper side of the tunic above the enamel HJ badge.

The newly introduced officer uniforms were dark blue. Working dress (*Dienstkleidung*) comprised a single-breasted tunic with six black or blue plastic buttons down the front and three on each cuff, worn open-necked with a white blouse (no tie or neckerchief), dark blue skirt, brown stockings and blue leather high-heeled shoes.

Formal Dress (*Festkleidung*) took the form of a closed neck tunic with concealed buttons and two side pockets — the rest of the ensemble being as above. A new, and smarter, dark blue winter coat replaced the former mannish brown greatcoat, its broad collar could be worn as a hood. A sleeved rain-cape secured at the neck by an ornamental chain could be worn as an alternative to the winter coat. On all these uniforms, including the cape, the new rank insignia was worn on the upper left side.

ihrerinnendienftkleidung
(Sommer)

Jungmädel-Bundestracht
(Sommer)

Führerinnendienftkleidung
(Winter)

# R.J.F. Stab

RJF Staff cuff-title. Silver or gold (according to grade) lettering on black.

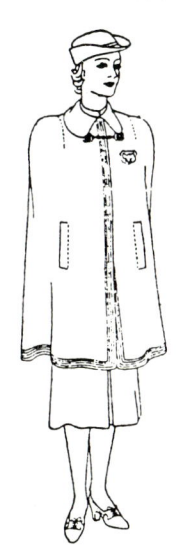

[Left:] Rain cape which can be worn with working, or formal, dress.

[Right:] Formal dress (*Festkleidung*) with RJF Staff cuff-title. Below rank badge is HJ/BDM badge and NSDAP membership badge. These forms of officer dress and those above were introduced at the start of the war but only the more senior ranks possessed the full range of authorized attire.

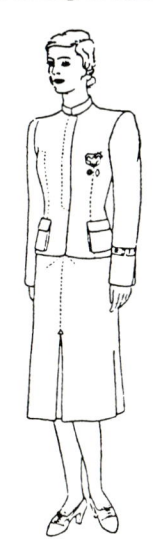

Members of the Reichs Leadership Staff wore a black cuff-title with, in silver, or for higher ranks, gold letters *RJF Stab*. This has a narrow inset stripe on the lower edge.

| | | |
|---|---|---|
| i<br>Gruppenführerin | ii<br>Ringführerin (single narrow silver border) | iii<br>Untergauführerin (double narrow silver border) |
| iv<br>Gauführerin (one broad, one narrow silver border) | v<br>Untergauführerin* | vi<br>Reserve Untergauführerin* (black edged silver "bar" behind badge) |
| vii<br>Gauführerin* | viii<br>Obergauführerin | ix<br>Reichsreferentin |

*On the Staff of an Obergau or of the RJF.
(i) to (iv) are silver (on black for winter uniform, on white for summer uniform).
(vii) to (ix) are gold (on black for winter uniform, on white for summer uniform).

| | | |
|---|---|---|
| Gruppenführerin | Hauptgruppenführerin (JM. u. M.) | Ringführerin (JM. u. M.) |
| Bannmädelführerin | Hauptmädelführerin | Gebietsmädelführerin |

BDM Reichsreferentin

With the dropping in 1943 of the terms Untergau, Gau and Obergau, it was necessary to change the nomenclature of BDM/JM officer grades. The German text states that "the eagles" are silver up to, and including, Hauptmädelführerin; gold for ranks above this (also gold for any grade of leader on staff of a *Gebiete* or RJF). Figure left is in Working Dress (*Dienstkleidung*). Figure right: Winter coat.

186

A lightweight white cotton tunic could be worn in high summer. This was first introduced in June 1939.

Leader of the BDM, Dr. Jutta Rüdiger (centre) with Penelope Testa, head of the *Giovane fascista* (Fascist Girls) of Italy (left in white summer uniform) and Pilar Primo de Rivera (right) of the Spanish Falangist Women's Organization. Dr. Rüdiger wears the white summer tunic of a BDM officer.

The BDM/JM, unlike their male counterparts, had few "trade" badges. Significantly those that they did have were exclusively medical.

Like the HJ, the BDM at first employed the internationally-recognized Aesculapius snake-and-staff emblem as its medical symbol. This was worn on the left cuff of the tunic or the left side of the blouse when the tunic was not worn. In September 1938 all branches of the Hitler Youth were ordered to replace this device with the so-called "life rune" BDM/JM doctors, dentists and pharmacists now wore exactly the same badges as their male counterparts, i.e.:

Doctors: Silver life rune on greyish-blue oval
Dentists: Silver life rune on greyish-blue rectangle
Pharmacists: Silver life rune on greyish-blue inverted triangle.

Medical Orderlies (known as *GD Mädel* — Health service girls) wore:

GD Mädel: Red life rune on white oval
GD Mädel (Gruppe): Red life rune on white oval with green/white surround
GD Mädel (Untergau): Red life rune on white oval with red surround
GD Mädel (Obergau): Red life rune on white oval with black surround.

# BDM-OSTEINSATZ

BDM "East Action" cuff-title. Dark brown with light brown lettering. (Forman Collection)

## Südost-Salzburg

BDM Staff Südost-Salzburg. It is silver bullion on white, but an example also exists which is silver on dark blue (presumably one is for summer, the other for winter, uniform). The dark blue example has a silver stripe at the bottom only.

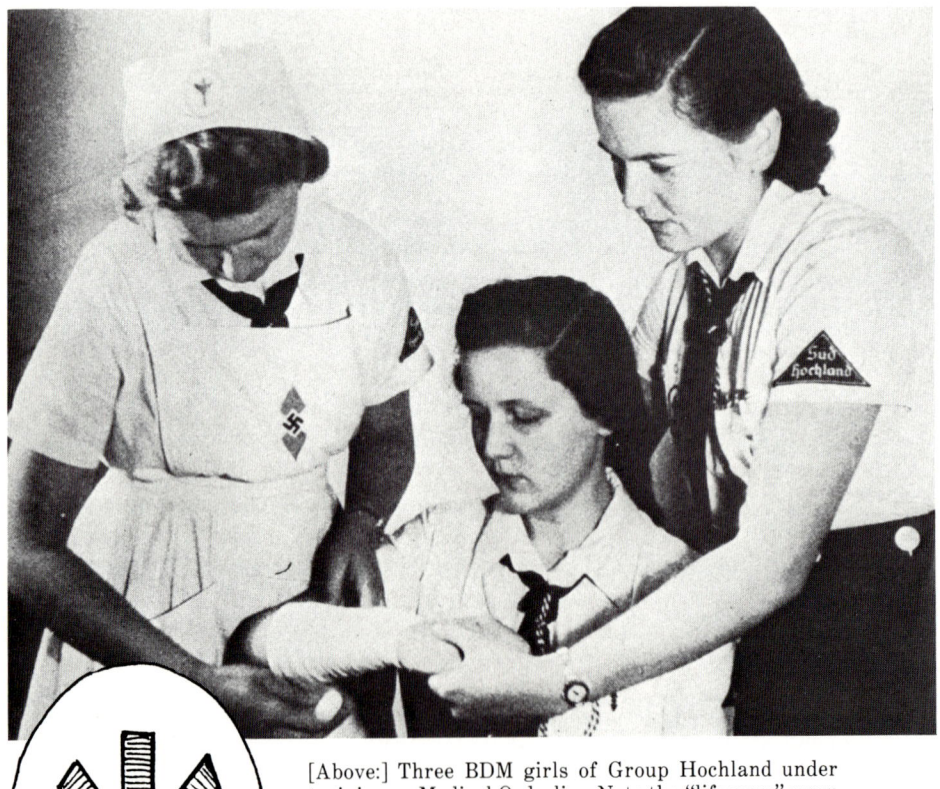

[Above:] Three BDM girls of Group Hochland under training as Medical Orderlies. Note the "life rune" worn on nurse's cap by girl on left. The other girls wear the "life rune" on left side of blouse.

[Left:] Like their male counterparts, BDM medical orderlies wore a red "life rune" on white (with the appropriate colour of piping surrounding it).

[Above:] BDM First Aid (*Unfall Dienst*) qualification badge. It is red on white with red surround.
[Right:] BDM girls of Berlin Group practice first aid. Note the *UD* arm badge.

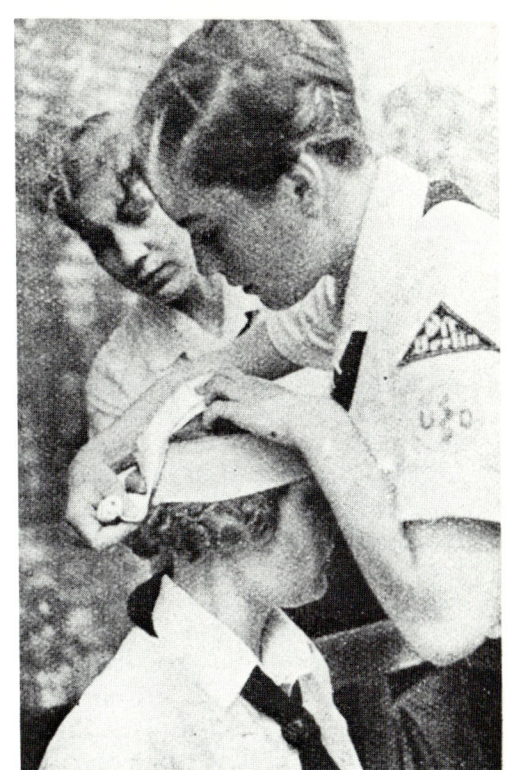

Pharmacist, 1st design. Silver bullion on black.

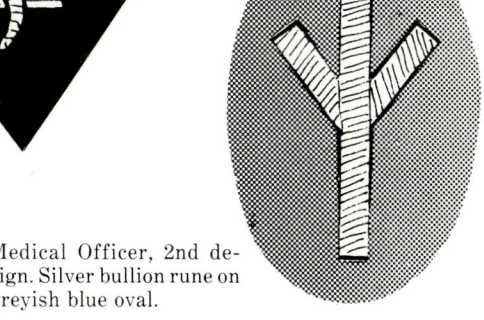

Medical Officer. 1st design. *Hilfärztin* (Assistant M.O.) had red on black. *Hauptärztin* (Senior M.O.) had (as here) silver on black. *Oberärztin* (Chief M.O.) gold bullion on black.

Medical Officer, 2nd design. Silver bullion rune on greyish blue oval.

189

The former First Aid Badge was discontinued after the introduction of these devices in September 1938.

## "FAITH AND BEAUTY" ORGANIZATION
(*BDM-Werk "Glaube und Schönheit"*)

Created in January 1938 as a "sporting, cultural, political, and practical working community," the BDM "Faith and Beauty" Organization was open to young women in the 17 to 21 age group who could serve for a minimum of twelve months and leave, hopefully, "... enriched in personal talents and interests...."

In its physical education aspects it was the counterpart of the British Women's League of Health and Beauty, its most popular activities being gymnastics and "eurhythmic dancing" (something of an international craze at that time). There were also riding, fencing, tennis, water and winter sports sections. The New German Woman was expected to be beautiful in a healthy, out-of-doors fashion, useful about the house and imbued with a "correct" political outlook. She should also be competent at first aid and willing to "lend a hand on the land." The *NS Frauenschaft* was adjured to adopt a "comradely attitude" and assist in training the girls in domestic science and child care. Despite the admonitions from on high there was, in reality, a good deal of jealousy and bad feeling between the two organizations.

Uniforms were that of the BDM with a special badge: a blue shield upon which a gold and a silver star, supposedly emblematic of faith and beauty, was placed.

War circumscribed the work of the *"Glaube und Schönheit"* girls to some extent, but as they were regarded as valuable propaganda for the Reich, some groups were allowed to travel outside Germany to give displays in the occupied lands. There was, for example, a successful and well publicized good-will visit to Holland in July 1942.

Emblem of "Glaube und Schönheit"

War-time BDM receive instruction in telegraphy from (perhaps significantly) an SS instructress.

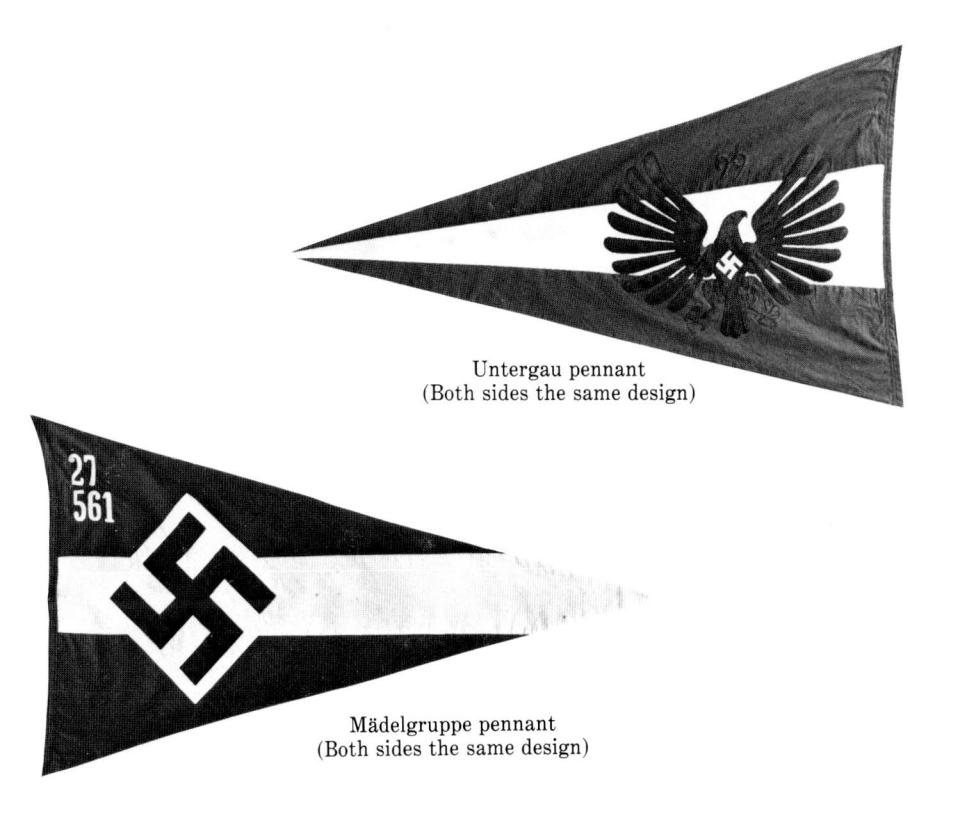

Untergau pennant
(Both sides the same design)

Mädelgruppe pennant
(Both sides the same design)

Mädelschar pennant.
Standard obverse (can be with, or without "BDM" — some examples also have place name). The colour and design of the reverse was optional and left to the choice of the unit in question.

First design of *Mädelschar* pennant with original type HJ emblem.

Parade of BDM girls through Grunewald Stadium in Berlin carrying pennants of this sort (undated but probably 1932). Note how long the skirt was at this time!

Untergau pennant, first design with name of Untergau (here Havel).

Untergau pennant, second type. Black and white.

Gruppen pennant.

J.M. Mädelschaft pennant (reverse). The obverse was the same as for the Gruppen pennant, but the choice of the design and colour of the reverse was left to the unit in question.

# Sport

The cultivation of physical, or more correctly, *fighting* fitness was a preoccupation of the Hitler Youth, taking precedence even over political education. As much as two-thirds of HJ training time might be devoted to *Körperertüchtigung* (bodily toughening-up). This applied to girls as much as boys. Sport played a prominent part in this process, but only those disciplines which had a bearing on military preparedness were practiced. The Hitler Youth did not teach ice dancing or golf! To shooting and marching, on the other hand, a great deal of time and effort was dedicated.

Von Schirach was quick to establish the HJ's hold over youth sport. The German National Physical Training Union (*Deutscher Reichsbund für Leibesübungen* or DRL) catered mainly for adult physical and sports training, but it also ran a youth section for the under-18s. The National Sports Leader (*Reichssportführer*), Hans von Tschammer und Osten (appointed to this post by Hitler in July 1933) came to an agreement with von Schirach in November 1934 that all youthful members of German sports and athletic clubs should enroll in the Hitler Youth. Despite this requirement the DRL's under-18s Section continued to carry on its own independent (or parallel) training until July 1942, even awarding a sports badge based on its own five-part test exercises; thereafter the HJ's monopoly on youth sport was total and further awards of this badge ceased.

The first so-called "sports mobilization" of German youth (military terminology was frequently applied by the Nazis however inappositely) took place on Saturday and Sunday June 22nd/23rd, 1935 when three and a half million young people took part in sports competitions in various parts of the Reich. By 1937 this figure had risen to nearly seven million.

Paramilitary training or field exercises, known in German as *Wehrsport* and *Geländesport*, were by no means a Nazi invention. The Treaty of Versailles had forbidden Germany military conscription and had limited her army to 100,000 men. Hitler did not feel strong enough to defy these restrictions until March 1935 when he re-introduced universal military conscription and expanded the armed forces. Prior to this, Germans of many differing political persuasions had formed clubs devoted to this aspect of "sport." In Hitler's party, the SA was the custodian of paramilitary training. Freed from SA dominion after 1933, the Hitler Youth set up its own *Geländesport* units.

Youth Sports Badge of the DRL

## SPORTS KIT

The basic sports kit, the same for both sexes and with no distinction between officers and others, was a white singlet, black silk shorts and black sports shoes (often worn without socks). On the front of the singlet was a cotton version of the HJ diamond. Later the HJ singlet was distinguished from that of the others by having a red/white/red band around the middle with, in the centre, a black swastika in the same proportions as the brassard.

For gymnastic displays the girls had short sleeveless white cotton frocks, again with the HJ diamond on the front.

Special ski outfits for HJ boys, BDM girls and DJ youngsters were devised. The HJ had a light brown blouse, laced at the neck and sides, with two breast pockets. A cotton HJ diamond was worn on the left arm with, above it, the district triangle. Dark blue "plus-four" type trousers were worn with brown side-buttoned gaiters over black boots. Headgear was a dark blue ski cap (later to become standard as winter head cover for both HJ and DJ). Girls had a dark blue blouse with side pockets. The HJ diamond and district triangle were worn on the left arm. Their dark blue ski trousers terminated in white rolled-down socks and black boots. In place of a hat, a dark blue headband was worn to keep the hair in place.

DJ boys wore what was later to be adopted as the universal HJ/DJ winter garb, the only difference being that the headgear was a dark blue woolen cap. For a brief period (possibly around 1933/34) HJ and DJ boys wore an indication of their rank on the left cuff of the ski blouse. This took the form of chevrons and/or bars. Later this practice was discontinued. With the introduction of the dark blue ski outfit as standard winter dress, this was often worn instead of the special ski blouse (although this latter *did* continue to be employed by those who possessed it — the evidence being wartime photographs).

Although swimming did not form part of the regular training schedule of the Hitler Youth, there was a proscribed costume. For boys this was dark blue trunks, for girls a black one-piece cotton costume with the HJ cotton emblem on the front. Use of a bathing cap (for girls) was optional. The girls of the *Glaube und Schöheit* group were permitted to

HJ boy and BDM girl in sports vest.

Ski uniforms for (a) HJ boys, (b) BDM girls (dark blue).

HJ boy in second design sports vest.

HJ boy in ski blouse (a war-time photo).

197

wear a form-flattering *white* bathing costume, although this was mainly for dry-land gymnastics and eurhythmic dancing (intended to display the healthy natural beauty and good development of the new German maiden).

Cycling was an approved HJ sport and there were even special bicycle units — the poor relations, perhaps, of their power-bike mounted comrades of the *Motor-HJ*.

On route marches or on one's way to, or from, summer camp, full marching order was worn. This consisted of the following items: large pack or ruck-sack (*Tornkister*) around which, attached by straps at sides and top, was (a) a blanket and (b) a *Zeltbahn*. This latter served the double purpose of either a waterproof ground sheet or an individual small tent — it was also possible to combine several to make a larger tent. Mess-tin, water bottle and "bread sack" (*Brotbeutel*) completed the equipment. With full marching order the *Brotbeutel* was attached to the belt, but otherwise was normally worn from a shoulder strap. Leaders were furnished with a leather map, or dispatch, case. "Pioneer" units carried an entrenching tool (short-handled spade). All the aforementioned were more or less standard military accoutrements. There was, however, an unusual additional item. Those at the front, or the rear of a night marching column, wore around their waists a special reflector belt so as to avoid being run down by road traffic — a device somewhat ahead of its time and slightly at variance with the more usual "live dangerously" philosophy of the Nazis!

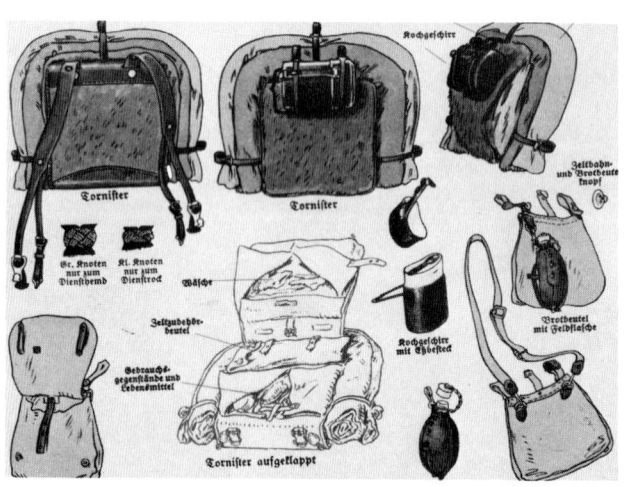

HJ marching items. Top row: front, reverse and side view of rucksack. Below left: (a) large (b) small toggle for neckerchief, "bread sack" open. Lower centre: rucksack opened out. Lower right: mess tin, water bottle and "bread sack" as worn from belt (in full marching order), below is the "bread sack" worn with a shoulder strap.

Full pack as worn by DJ boys.

Map, or dispatch case.

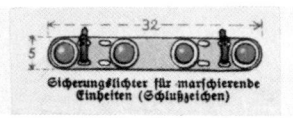

Reflector belt for night marching.

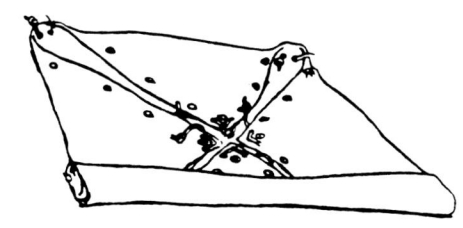

*Zeltbahn* opened out. A multi-purpose item; ground-sheet, small tent, part of large tent, or even, in an emergency, capable of being turned into a stretcher to move wounded!

Left: BDM ski blouse (closed at neck)
Above: HJ sports singlet second design.

"High School Sport, Berlin, Achievement Badge." Although bearing a swastika, this is an unofficial sports award of a private school in Berlin. Tolerated for a short time, all such fanciful pieces were eventually banned by the Nazis and only the official HJ sports awards allowed.

Left: Sports *Ausweis* (Record Card in which a boy's achievements were recorded).

200

Badge of the HJ Ski School at Hirschegg (in Austria). A very well made item with enamel badge and gilt wreath. Actual size is 62 mm (from an example in Forman Collection).

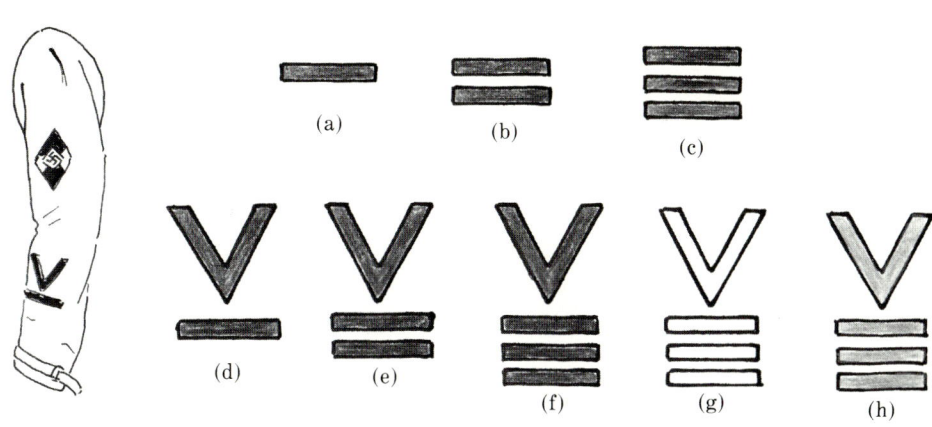

Above: Rank insignia of the HJ and DJ as worn on left cuff of ski outfit.

(a) Kameradschaftsführer
 Jungenschaftsführer
(b) Scharführer
 Jungzugführer
(c) Gefolgschaftsführer
 Fahnleinführer
(d) Unterbannführer
 Stammführer
(e) Bannführer
 Jungbannführer
(f) Oberbannführer
 Oberjungbannführer
(g) Gebietsführer
 Gebietsjungvolkführer
(h) Obergebietsführer
 Obergebietsjungvolkführer

BDM girl in track suit (right) talks to a Flemish contestant at an international youth sports meeting held in Germany during the war.

201

Cuff-title *HJ-Geländesportwart* (HJ Field Exercises Course), yellow on black.

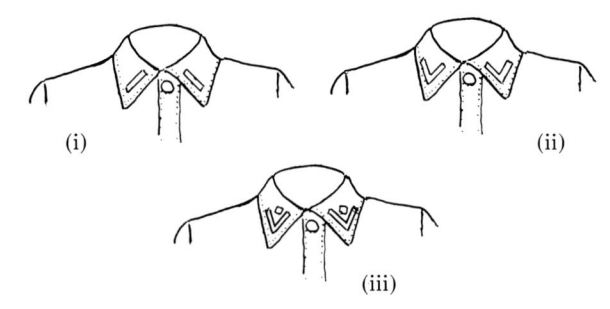

Staff at *Geländesport* courses or training schools wore on their track suits an indication of their status as follows:
(i) *Hilfsport-und Hilfsgeländesportlehrer* (Assistant Sport and Military Sport Teacher): a silver "bar" on both collars.
(ii) *Sport-und Geländesport-lehrer:* a silver chevron on both collars.
(iii) *Leiter der Führerschule* (Head of a Training School): a silver chevron and a silver star on both collars.
This form of identification was dropped in October 1938; thereafter staff wore HJ rank on black, carmine piped, shoulder straps with RJF.

Cuff-title *HJ-Sportwart* (approximately HJ Sports Course), red on black.

Cuff-title *HJ-Schiesswart* (HJ Shooting, or Marksmanship course), green on black.

There is also a fourth similar cuff-title, *HJ-Schiwart* (HJ Skiing Course). This is white on black. All the above were worn on the left cuff by supervisors. More than one could be worn at a time.

From 1934 until almost the end of the Second World War an annual all-Germany Hitler Youth Sports Festival (*Sportfest*, or *Jugendfest*), renamed in 1937 the National Sports Contest (*Reichssportwettkampf*) was held each summer. To encourage a good all-round standard of performance a little badge was awarded (on a points basis which varied from year to year) to any boy or girl who achieved an "above average" score in the three branches of youth sport — running, jumping and throwing (javelin or hammer). Each badge was accompanied by a *Führer-Urkunde* (Hitler Certificate). These little badges, unimpressive, sometimes even tawdry in appearance, were awards and as such must

National Team Ski Jump Competition, 1935/36

Victor in the Bann and Untergau Sports Festival, Gebiet Baden, 1939

Berlin v. Vienna District Challenge Competition, 1941. Light Athletics.

203

certainly be regarded as ranking above donation or "day" badges. They could be worn for one year.

The design of both badge and *Führer-Urkunde* varied, although sometimes the same design would be used for a number of consecutive years, only the date being altered.

Apart from the aforementioned National Sports Contest, victory in other important sporting events was rewarded by a variety of plaques or non-portable medallions. It would not be feasible to list all the many and different kinds and patterns, but a selection is shown below.

1934
(ceramic)
Dated: 22 Juni 1934

1935
(aluminium)

1936
1937
1938
(aluminium)

1938
(bronzed tin)

1938
Alternative design. It can be bronzed tin or plastic.

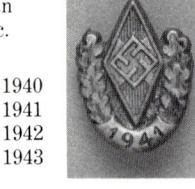

1940
1941
1942
1943

1943
Alternative design
(1940-43 are all in poor quality aluminium or alloy)

Obergau Challenge Competition in Swimming.
Vienna-Tyrol-Württemberg
15. 6. 1941

Example of an early *Führer-Urkunde*. It reads: "German Youth Festival 1934. In the sports competition of 23rd June 1934 Werner Fortmann achieved a victory with 58 points. In recognition we award him this certificate. Signed Baldur von Schirach and National Sports Leader, von Tschammer und Osten."

# Camps and Foreign Visits

Perhaps the most popular of all HJ activities was the annual summer camp. Usually of ten to fourteen days duration, some were extended to three weeks. All involved either travel within the Greater German Reich (after March 1938 this included Austria) or, for a fortunate minority, a trip abroad.

In 1936 there were tented camps in 1,977 different localities in Germany with a total participation of over half a million young persons. The RJF aimed at sending not less than 6,000 lads abroad each year while at the same time bringing ten or twelve times that number of foreign youngsters to Germany to witness the triumphs of the new Reich.

The year 1938, dubbed by the RJF "The Year of Getting Acquainted" (*Jahr der Verständigung*), was the high point of this international commuting. During it there were visits to and/or mutual exchanges between, Rumania, Hungary, Yugoslavia, Greece, Poland, Bulgaria, Spain, Portugal, the Baltic states and even places as remote as Turkey, Iraq and Bolivia, as well as a highly publicized visit to Japan by some thirty HJ leaders which so impressed the hosts that they struck a special "medal" to commemorate the event.

In 1939, even under the shadow of impending war, *Gebiet Nordsee*, for example, sent *Bann* 382 to Holland, *Bann* 59 to Finland, *Bann* 77 to Hungary and *Bann* 285 to Yugoslavia. The same year witnessed a rally of "young Nordics" at Straslund (on the Baltic Coast) with male and female guests from Denmark and Scandinavia.

The British were not excluded from these manifestations of Nazi beneficence. In 1937 a joint English-German *Jugendlager* was held at Rossfeldhütte with two weeks of "comradeship and sport" (the latter being mainly skiing).

If the scale of the camping activity was vast, so were some of the individual camps — at one in 1939 no less than 25,000 boys and their leaders took part.

A badge presented by the Japanese authorities to all the members of the above delegation (they can be seen wearing it above the left breast pocket). It shows the flags of Germany and Japan and has, in Japanese, "From the German and Japanese Youth Leagues." Each badge was presented in a small blue case.

(A)

(B)

Obverse (a) and reverse (b) of a medallion of the Congress of European Youth. The obverse shows flags of participating movements with, at the bottom, the name of the recipient: *Lien Van Eck*. The reverse shows Europa and the bull with, "European Youth Congress, 13-19 Sept. 1942 Vienna" (the dates *should* be 14-18 Sept.).

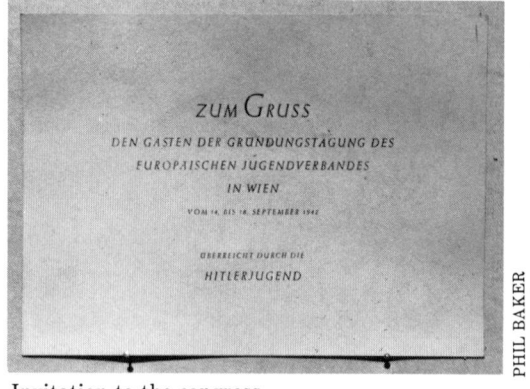

Invitation to the congress.

HJ visit to Japan.

The BDM indulged in camping on almost as extensive a scale as the boys (from whom, of course, they were carefully segregated).

War circumscribed, but did not terminate, trips outside the Reich. HJ delegations continued to visit allied or occupied lands — France being, as before the war, a notable exception. Indeed apart from one Franco-German Youth Meeting at Bad Reichenhall (in upper Bavaria) in August 1937, the HJ appears to have deliberately cold-shouldered the French. They were pointedly *not* invited to the "Rally of European Youth" held in Vienna in September 1942 which brought together youth leaders from Bulgaria, Finland, Croatia, Rumania, Slovakia, Hungary, Belgium, Denmark, Norway, Holland and Spain as well as Italy. At this rally a "European Youth Union" was proclaimed and September 14 pronounced "The Culture Day of European Youth" by von Schirach who proposed that this date should henceforth be commemorated annually by a great concourse of youth at Weimar, that shrine of German culture and learning. Doubtless von Schirach hoped that this display of European cultural concord would be hailed as an event of major political significance. Sadly, for him, the German press, on the orders of Dr. Goebbels, ignored it. Disaster at Stalingrad was still some months distant and Germany remained confident of final victory. She did not, at this stage of the conflict, wish to represent herself as some sort of equal partner in a European alliance — even it only a cultural one. Apart from the institution, by von Schirach, of a miscellany of literary and musical awards, the "Rally of European Youth" achieved precisely nothing.

Visit in 1938 by a group of specially selected HJ to Japan. A unique uniform was worn on this occasion with white leather belts and cross straps.

A visit by HJ and DJ to Bulgaria during the war. The official in the dark uniform (left) is German Ambassador Beckerle. The parade is taking place in the garden of the Embassy at Sofia.

Two young participants in the "Rally of European Youth" held in Vienna in September 1942. On the left a German DJ boy who chats to a very young member of the *Ustase* Youth from Croatia.

Meeting of "French-German Youth" at Reichenhall in August 1937. The brassards appear to be white and have the French and German national flags. It is not possible to read the writing on these but it may be: Jeunesse Franco-Allemand; Deutsch-Französische Jugend. Cooperation between German and French youth was extremely rare!

# National Vocational Contest

In February 1934 Baldur von Schirach came to an agreement with Dr. Robert Ley, leader of the German Labour Front (DAF), that their respective organizations would jointly sponsor an annual national vocational contest (*Reichsberufswettkampf*) to assess the levels of skill achieved by the rising generation of German workers in all fields — manual, intellectual and artistic.

In the first contest, held in May 1934, some 500,000 young people participated and there were 20 "national victors" (14 boys and 6 girls). In 1935 the number of top winners had increased to 38 (26 boys and 12 girls). The finals were at first held in Berlin but the contest proved so popular and the number of entrants increased so dramatically (over three and a half million by 1939) it became necessary to hold simultaneous finals in five other cities — Saarbrücken, Königsberg, Munich, Hamburg and Cologne.

Those eligible to enter were:

(a) Male manual workers between 15 and 18 years;

(b) Male commercial and technical apprentices between 15 and 21;

(c) Females between 15 and 21 years;

(d) Students, male or female, at universities, technical high schools, trade or commercial colleges;

(e) All entrants had to be members of the HJ or the DAF or some other Nazi organization.

The contest included, as well as practical test in the trade or skill, a written test of arithmetic and composition. Some familiarity with "political theory" (this of course meant Nazi dogma) was also called for, although latterly the Contest tended to lay its principal emphasis on the trade skill.

The contest was subdivided into twenty *Wettkampfgruppen* (Competitive Sections) each with its own standards. In some Sections (mining, heavy industry, etc.) only males could compete, in others (office practice, hotel management, handicrafts, etc.) the sexes competed on equal terms. There were three stages on the road to national victory. First was the Regional (*Kreis*) contest. The victors at this level could then proceed to the *Gau* contest. If again successful, they could enter for the National (*Reich*) final.

Until 1937 only certificates were awarded. *All* participants got a *Beteiligungs Urkunde* (Certificate of Participation), winners received a more elaborate one. The design of these certificates varied from year to year. The reason for this was practical — the design for the next year's certificates and all publicity material relating to the ensuing contest formed part of the tests in the current year's handicrafts and arts section.

Commemorative badges were issued in connection with each contest. These cannot, however, be equated with mere "day" badges, since they were restricted to contestants and organizers and furthermore, at the *Gau* and *Reich* levels, they presupposed success at the lower grades. In 1937 a national Victor's Badge was instituted. This is simply the HJ diamond emblem in coloured enamel upon a silver DAF cog-wheel. It was presented in a small square case not unlike that of the Iron Cross 1st Class along with an "award document" — a large folder which, when opened out, showed a portrait of Hitler on the left and a hand-drawn certificate of achievement on the right. The badge was worn on the left lapel of civilian clothes and (possibly) on the left or right breast pocket of uniform. All the *Reich* victors were presented personally to Hitler by Ley and von Schirach.

[Above:] National Victor's Badge, 1st type (1937) from an illustration (not to scale) which appeared in the German press at the time. Left: A German girl wears the National Victor's Badge, 1st type below what is possibly a Contest Participant's Badge.

210

There may have been some adverse comment that this rather insignificant-looking little badge failed to do justice to the high degree of proficiency required to become a *Reichssieger*, since, only a year later, it was cancelled and replaced by a much more impressive award. This new decoration was in the three grades: Regional Victor (*Kreissieger*), *Gau* Victor (*Gausieger*) and National Victor (*Reichssieger*). The HJ diamond and DAF cog wheel was retained but now placed in the talons of the national eagle which was upon a wreath of oakleaves, enclosing a white enamel circle upon which was *Kreissieger, Gausieger* or *Reichssieger* and the date of the contest. The eagle, cog-wheel and wreath were bronze, silver or gilt, according to the grade of the badge. The first awards of this new badge were made in 1938 and continued until 1944, by which time the quality of metals used had sadly deteriorated (the bronze now being grey metal) and the former enamel replaced by paint!

War-time Contest were known as *Kriegsberufswettkämpfe* (War Vocational Contests) and there was no longer any age limitation.

The largest Contest was that of 1939 when the following awards were made:

    Kreissieger .............................................. 40,000
    Gausieger ............................................. 6,600
    Reichssieger ......................................... 508

The 1935 Contest was honored by a postage stamp (in two values of the same design) and the 1939 Contest by a stamp showing the Victor's badge.

The badge was worn on the right (later left) breast pocket. There does not appear to have been a miniature.

*Reichssieger* (gold) badge of 1938 in case of issue.

*Kreissieger* (bronze) badge of 1939.

(i)

Participant's Badges of (i) the 1934 Contest and (ii) the 1935 Contest. Both are inscribed National Vocational Contest of the German Youth. Both have HJ (Hitler Youth) and DAF (German Labour Front).

(ii)

PETER GROCH

[Left:] Victor's Badge given to 3,224 boys and girls who passed the Gau (and, presumably, also the Kreis) levels of the 1937 contest and who sat the "finals" in Munich. This information comes from the *Leifsiger Tageszeitung* of 27th April 1937. The badge is gilt with the HJ emblem in coloured enamel. Wording is: *1937 Reichskampf München, Haupstadt der Bewegung* (National Contest, Munich, Capital of the Movement). It shows the Feldherrnhalle at Munich.

[Right:] Participant's badge of the 1938 "finals" held in Hamburg on 22nd to 29th April. The *Illustriete Kronen-Zeitung* of 23rd April 1938 illustrates this badge and describes it as being for participants and *Mitarbeitern* (in this sense, probably, "organizers") of the Contest. It is silver coloured with burnished highlights and HJ emblem in coloured enamel. It incorporates the civic arms of the city of Hamburg.

212

[Left:] Participant's badge of the 1939 "finals" at Cologne. It is a dull brownish colour with the HJ emblem in coloured enamel. It incorporates the arms of Cologne and a panorama of that city.

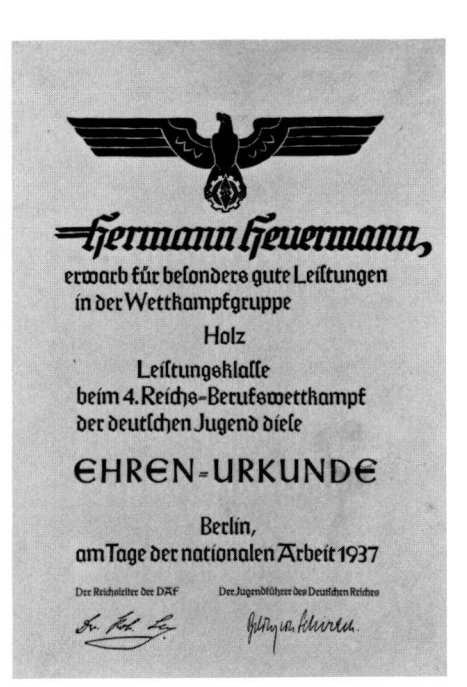

"Certificate of Honour" (Ehren-Urkunde) awarded to Hermann Heuermann "for especially good results in the Wood (work) Section of the 4th National Vocational Contest of German Youth... Berlin. On National Labour Day, 1937." Signed by Labour Front Leader, Robert Ley and Youth Leader Baldur von Schirach.

A further certificate to the same individual, Hermann Heuermann, "for outstanding achievement in the Regional (*Orts*) Competition of 1938... *Kreissieger* in the Wood (work) Section. Possession of this Certificate entitles him to wear the Kreissieger Badge. Berlin, National Labour Day, 1938." Signed by Robert Ley and Baldur von Schirach.

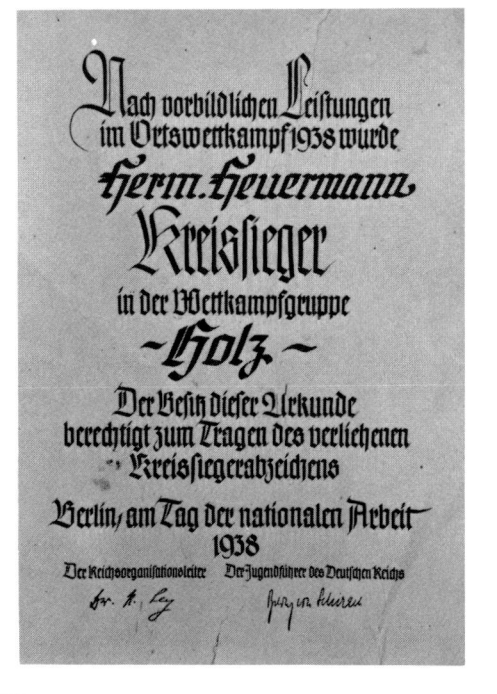

A poster advertising an exhibition relating to the Contest in Berlin "8th to 15th April 1934" (overprinted "extended to Wednesday 18th April.") "Open daily, admission free."

"Participant's Certificate" (Beteiligungs Urkunde) "Josef Grabinger is awarded this certificate for his participation in the Vocational Contest of all German Workers. Berlin, March 1939." Signed by an Obergebietsführer. These certificates were given merely for taking part in the Contest.

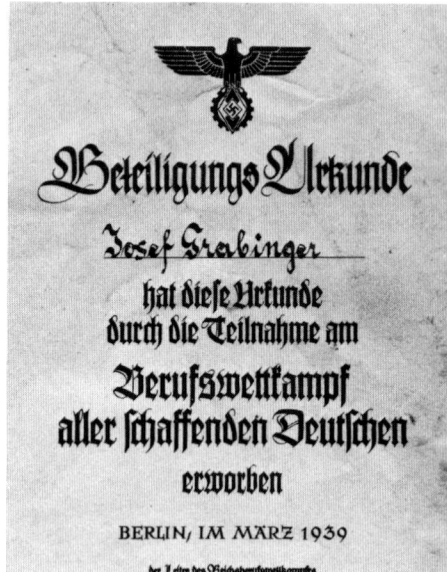

Right: 1936 version of combined Reich eagle and emblems of the HJ and DAF. After this the HJ diamond was superimposed on the DAF cog wheel.

214

# Honour Badges and Awards

### HJ PROFICIENCY BADGE
(*HJ — Leistungsabzeichen*)

In June 1934 von Schirach instituted an Achievement, or Proficiency, Badge for the HJ. Working towards winning this badge was to form the basis of all training. Every boy was issued with a *Leistungsbuch* in which his progress was recorded.

The badge is in the form of a *Tyr-rune* (or runic *T*), upon which is a swastika in a circle with, in sham runic script, "*Für Leistung in der HJ* (For Achievement in the Hitler Youth)." This badge could be in "iron" (actually white metal painted black with the swastika and lettering left "natural"), or bronze or "silver" (again, simply white metal). The colour depended on the age of the contestant: fifteen-year-olds could enter for the "iron," sixteen-year-olds for the bronze, and seventeen-year-olds for the "silver." Cloth versions of each of these were available for wearing on sports kit — black on white for the "iron" badge, brown on white for the bronze, and a whitish-grey on black for the "silver." A half-size metal miniature could be worn on the left lapel of civilian clothes.

"Silver" badge

*Hitlerjugend* with "iron" *Leistungsabzeichen*.

JILL HALCOMB

Front cover of a *Leistungsbuch* in which progress was recorded.

Cloth version of "silver" badge.

Originally boys of the DJ could enter for the "iron" badge but when, a year later, a special DJ Achievement Badge was created, the practice ceased. The badge was supposed to be worn on the right breast pocket, but possibly due to the fact that many lads wore it mistakenly on the left (the usual side for "decorations"), wearing on the left was adopted as official.

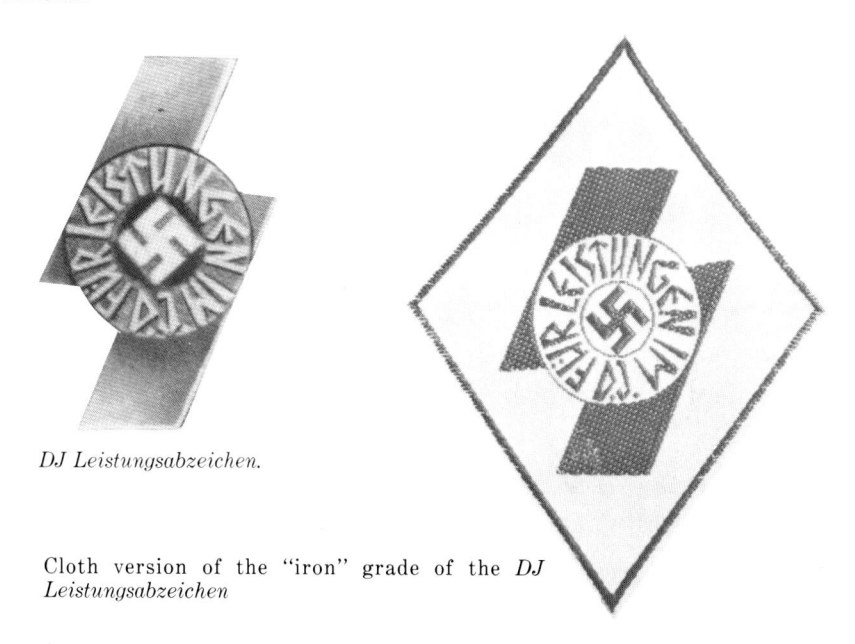

*DJ Leistungsabzeichen.*

Cloth version of the "iron" grade of the *DJ Leistungsabzeichen*

The tests leading to an award of the badge clearly show how all HJ training was militarily oriented. Only the first part, sport and athletics, was "civilian." The two other sections were wholly military: shooting (with air rifles), grenade throwing (with dummies), route-marching in full kit and *Geländesport* (field exercises) consisting of map-reading, distance judging, effective use of terrain, camouflage, etc. The *Motor-HJ* and *Marine-HJ* had additional tests appropriate to their specialty.

The actual tests were the same for all three age groups but the scoring varied. Thus the 100 metre sprint had to be completed by the seventeen-year-olds in 14 seconds, by sixteen-year-olds in 14½ seconds, and by fifteen-year-olds in 15 seconds. Similarly the seventeen-year-olds had to swim for fifteen minutes, the sixteen-year-olds for ten minutes, the fifteen-year-olds for only five minutes (the regulations state that where swimming facilities were not available, speed cycling may be substituted).

In the military-style section, fifteen-year-olds had to march, in full pack, ten kilometers, sixteen-year-olds twenty kilometers, seventeen-year-olds — twenty-five kilometers (there were time limits within which these distances had to be covered — again these varied with age). Originally there had been a fourth test, "Political Knowledge," but this was dropped during the war when the emphasis was on physical fitness and paramilitary training.

The tests leading to an award of any to the three types of badge were, in their turn, subdivided into three levels of proficiency, characterized as an *A, B* or *C* grade. In some cases this grading letter appears in place of the more customary issue number on the reverse of the arrow head (left side).

War brought not only a great expansion of numbers conferred, but also an extension of eligibility to non-German contestants (boys from the pro-Nazi movements of occupied Europe).

In 1934 issue figures were:

Silver: 76,100
Bronze: 35,900

but by the end of 1943, when the last accurate statistics were available, this had risen to:

Silver: 217,093
Bronze: 103,061.

## DJ PROFICIENCY BADGE
(*DJ Leistungsabzeichen*)

As mentioned above, boys of the DJ were for a short time, eligible for the "iron" grade of the HJ Proficiency Badge, but in September 1935 a special *Leistungsabzeichen* was created for the DJ. This takes the form of a *Sigrune* (or runic *S*) with, in the centre, a swastika in a circle with, in sham runic script, *Für Leistung im DJ* (For Achievement, or Proficiency, in the DJ).

Although boys joined the DJ at ten years old, they were not allowed to enter for the badge until they were twelve. It was in two grades: "iron" (white metal painted black with the swastika and lettering left "natural"), and "silver" (whitish-grey metal). The "iron" was for boys of twelve and thirteen, the "silver" for those of fourteen. Cloth versions of both were produced for wearing with the sport kit. A half-sized metal miniature could be worn on the left lapel of civilian clothes.

Some 152,600 awards of this badge were made by 1943.

## GOLDEN LEADERS SPORTS BADGE
(*Goldenes Führer-Sportabzeichen*)

On January 18, 1937 von Schirach decreed that all HJ and DJ leaders from the rank of *Fahnlein* to *Gefolgschaftsführer* (i.e., approximately Warrant Officer to subaltern rank) should annually pass a ten-part test to be known as the Leader's Test Exercises. There were, in fact, much the same as those in the first part of the *HJ₇Leistungsabzeichen* test (athletics, marching and small-calibre rifle shooting), but requiring a much higher standard of performance.

Since there might be some disparity in age as between contestants, two different levels of achievement were permitted. In the first, a score of 75,000 points was required, in the second only 6,500 — these were known as the *A* and *B* grades.

For those who achieved the appropriate grade, a special version of the *HJ-Leistungsabzeichen* was created on May 15, 1938. It is similar to the normal type, except that it has the addition of a wreath of oakleaves with blue enamel between these and the rest of the badge. Although described as "gold," it was in fact copper gilt. Issued examples had either a large *A* or *B* (the two gradings) on the reverse, or in large numerals, an issue number. A miniature could be worn on the left lapel of civilian clothes. By 1943 over 11,000 had been awarded. It is said that a cloth version of this badge exists, but this is unconfirmed.

DECORATION OF THE HIGH COMMAND OF THE HJ FOR DISTINGUISHED FOREIGNERS
(*Ehrenzeichen der Reichsjugendführung der HJ für Verdiente Ausländer*)

This small badge measures 34mm vertically and 33mm horizontally (across the eagle's wings). It was instituted in 1941 to reward service to the Hitler Youth on the part of foreign nationals. The badge is in full-coloured enamel. The eagle and oakleaves are silver, the HJ diamond is white/red/black and the outer edge, which has the words, *Hitler Jugend* is normally brown, but examples in which the outer edge is green (as illustrated) or red also exist. It is fairly certain that these latter types were only projected or "pilot" types never actually issued.

## GOLDEN HJ BADGE OF HONOUR

On June 23, 1934 Baldur von Schirach instituted a golden version of the diamond-shaped badge worn by all HJ on the left breast pocket. This golden badge is of the same dimensions (29mm by 17mm), but the parts which are silver on the standard-issue badge (the border, the lines dividing the segments and the background to the swastika) are gilt on the "gold" version. Known variously as the *Golden Hitler Youth Badge of Honour*, the *Golden Hitler Youth Badge* and the *Golden Decoration (Ehrenzeichen) of the Hitler Youth*, it was awarded to all members of the HJ and BDM who had joined prior to October 2, 1932 (Potsdam Day), and who had to their credit not less than five years unbroken service either with the HJ, or if they had since "outgrown" this, with some other Nazi Party organization.

It could be awarded also for a special act of merit within the HJ, irrespective of the length of service. It was worn on the left breast pocket in place of the normal HJ membership badge. With civilian clothes a half-size miniature could be worn on the left lapel. Prior to the institution of this award, the former round enamel HJ badge was worn as a "tradition" badge by those who had enrolled before June 1, 1932. More than 13,170 were issued.

As from March 26, 1936 the badge could be worn on military uniform.

## GOLDEN HJ BADGE OF HONOUR WITH OAKLEAVES

This badge, which counted as an official Party decoration, was instituted in 1935. It could be conferred on foreigners as well as Germans, and could be worn on any uniform. It was similar to the above but was in genuine silver gilt with a much higher grade of enamel work and the addition of a surround of golden oakleaves. Because the gilt border was much narrower than on the Golden HJ Badge, the addition of the oakleaves does not result in its being overall much larger. It is, in fact, only 32.5 mm by 19.5 mm as against 29 mm by 17 mm for the above. It was given for exceptional service in, or to, the Hitler Youth and since only 250 were ever issued it must rank as a very rare decoration. The recipients (apart from members of the HJ itself) were often highly placed persons — Himmler, Robert Ley of the Labour Front, Albert Speer — are some examples.

A Special Grade (*Sonderstufe*) of this badge was created for Baldur von Schirach on the occasion of his 35th birthday on March 9, 1942. In this "Special Grade" (which is unique), the red parts of the HJ diamond are replaced by rubies, the silver parts by diamonds and the golden parts are of genuine high quality gold. It was made up by Munich's leading jeweller, Peter Rath. The actual size is not known, it may possibly have been larger than the normal Golden HJ badge with Oakleaves. The accompanying coloured sketch is based on a black and white photo (not to scale) which appeared in the German press at the time of the award.

Special Grade (a tentative sketch only)

## HJ EXPERT SKIER'S BADGE

This badge, is the largest of the HJ awards, measures 60mm in diameter and is matt silver all over apart from the coloured enamel HJ emblem in the centre. On the circle was *HJ Skiführer*. On the reverse are two horizontal pins for (presumably) affixing the badge to the left, or possibly right, breast pocket. The date of institution is not known. It is shown in an HJ manual for 1934 which describes it as being for "... the HJ, BDM, JM...." It would seem more likely that what is meant is that it was for *instructors* in these branches of the youth movement rather than for the young members themselves — it is hard, for example, to imagine that it could be gained by the little girls of the JM. It may, therefore, come more into the category of a qualification badge rather than an actual award.

## DECORATION OF THE NATIONAL SOCIALIST GERMAN STUDENTS UNION

The NSDSt.B equivalent of the HJ Golden Badge for membership before January 30, 1933 takes the form of the black/white/red membership badge of the NSDSt.B upon a wreath of silver oakleaves. It is a small pin badge (the above illustration is actual size). It was instituted by the Reich Student Leader, possibly in 1933 or 1934, but the exact date is unknown.

## MEDALLION "FOR THE FURTHERING OF THE HJ HOSTEL BUILDING PROGRAMME"

In 1937 a special award was instituted for those "... who had energetically assisted in the Hitler Youth hostel building action (*Heimbauaktion*)...." This award takes the form of an aluminum non-portable medallion, 70mm in diameter. On the obverse is the HJ emblem surmounted by a scroll, on which is *Heim der Hitlerjugend* (Home of the Hitler Youth). On the reverse, above a sprig of oakleaves, is *Für die Förderung der Heimbeschaffung der Hitler-Jugend* (For the furthering, or sponsoring, of Hitler Youth hostel building).

Shooting Awards (Schiessauszeichnungen)

## SHOOTING AWARDS
(*Schiessauszeichnungen*)

In 1936 von Schirach instituted a badge for rifle-shooting skill by members of the Hitler Youth. In 1938 a further, higher grade was added, and a special type for boys of the DJ created:

*HJ Rifleman's Badge (HJ Schützen-Abzeichen):* A 21mm round silver and black target with coloured HJ emblem in the centre, behind which are two silver crossed rifles. The test was firing five shots from a lying position with rifle supported on a sandbag, five from lying positioned with rifle unsupported, and five from a kneeling position with unsupported rifle.

*HJ Marksman's (or Sniper's) Badge (HJ Scharfschützen-Abzeichen):* Similar to the above, but with the addition of an outer wreath of silver oakleaves. Ten shots had to be fired from the same positions as above with, in addition, a further ten "rapid fire" from a standing, rifle unsupported, position.

*HJ Champion Shot (HJ Meisterschützen-Abzeichen):* This top class badge was added in December 1941. It is identical to the previous one, except that the oakleaves are gold, not silver. The firing positions were as before, but a much higher score was required.

*DJ Rifleman's Badge (Schiessauszeichnung des DJ):* This Rifleman's Badge or Shooting Award of the Jungvolk is a silver and black target with silver crossed rifles. In the centre is a white *Sigrune* with, on either side, *DJ* (also in white).

Conditions for the award of this DJ badge are not known, but they may have been the same tests as for the HJ Rifleman's badge, but requiring a lower standard of performance.

Pre-war issues are well made, with good enamel work, but wartime examples are often of a much lower standard of execution with paint replacing the enamel and plastic the metal. Thus, ironically, although the Champion Shot's Badge is the highest grade, it was (being a wartime creation) less well made than the pre-war lower classes.

Accurate figure for numbers awarded are available up to the end of 1943 and are as follows:

| | |
|---|---:|
| HJ Rifleman | 273,545 |
| HJ Marksman | 31,904 |
| HJ Champion Shot | 852 |
| DJ Rifleman | 580,872 |

POTSDAM BADGE (POTSDAM-ABZEICHEN)

On the 1st and 2nd October 1932 approximately 100,000[†] members of the Hitler Youth (some 15,000 of them girls) took part in a great Nazi rally at Potsdam. The "day" badge issued in connection with this event is bronze and shows a downward-pointing sword with a wreathed swastika on its hilt, around this the words, *NS 1 Reichsjugendtag 1932* (First National Youth Day 1932). Later this "day" badge was elevated to the status of a commemorative award. It is, in this version, silver. The wearing of the bronze badge as a commemorative piece was thereafter forbidden. Worn on the left breast pocket, the badge measures 23mm by 48.5mm. A miniature could be worn with civilian clothes.

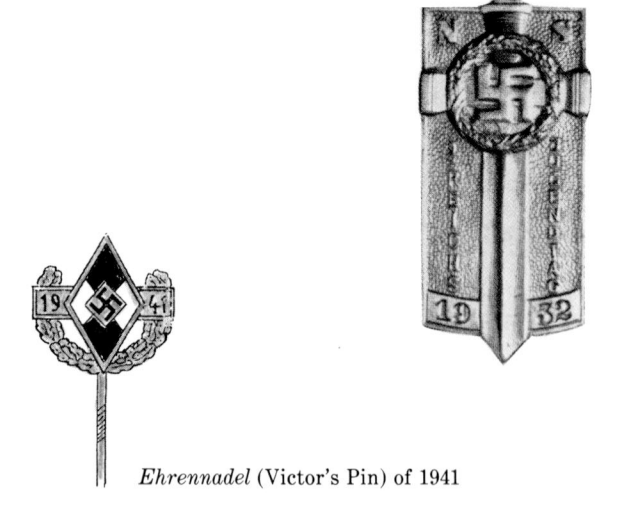

*Ehrennadel* (Victor's Pin) of 1941

VICTORS' BADGES IN NATIONAL SPORTS COMPETITION

In 1942 the RJF instituted a Victor's Pin (*Siegernadel*) for winners in the National Sports Competition. It takes the form of a golden HJ badge behind which is a bar with the date *1941* and an open oak leaf wreath (both bar and wreath are gold). There is not "background" between the wreath and the HJ diamond.

---

[†] This was the figure quoted by the Nazis themselves, but it may have been an exaggeration.

National Champion
(gold)

German Youth Champion
(gold)

The following year (1942) the design of the badge was modified and new grades added. The modified design retains the HJ badge, date bar and open oak leaf wreath, but the background is now "solid," and the word *Reichssieger* (National Champion) appears at the base. It was awarded in three grades: gold, silver or bronze for first, second or third place. On the first two the background is in blue enamel, but the third is all bronze, apart from the coloured HJ diamond.

The version of the badge, in its three grades, was awarded either to competitors below the age of sixteen, or the victors in branches of sport with few participants.

For older youths a German Youth Champion's Badge (or Pin) of Honour (*Ehrennadel des deutschen Jugend-meisters*) was created. It is a round badge, 30mm in diameter with, as before, the HJ badge in full colour in the centre. The background to the silver and gold class is blue enamel (whether this is also the case with the bronze badge is uncertain). The bronze and silver classes differ from the gold class in that they have at the base the word, *Kampfspiele* (Competitive Games), whereas the gold grade has *Jugend-meister* (Youth Champion). These badges could be worn permanently on the left breast pocket.

## JUNGSTURM HITLER COMMEMORATIVE BADGE

A commemorative badge for former members of the *Jungsturm Adolf Hitler* was instituted after the Nazis accession to power, but the precise date is unknown. This badge exists in two forms. One shows a swastika and barley ears from which rays of sunlight emanate, and upon which is the date *9. Nov.* (referring to the unsuccessful *Putsch* of November 9, 1923 in Munich). At the top is a scroll with *Jungsturm Hitler, 1921-1923*. The dates are, in fact, inaccurate, since the *Jungsturm* existed only during 1922-1923!

Jungsturm Hitler Commem. Badge.

Alternative version.

225

The alternative version of this badge is round with a large swastika in the centre on a sun burst with, in Gothic script, *Jungsturm Adolf Hitler 1921-1923*. The reason for these two different designs is not known.

## BDM AND JM PROFICIENCY CLASPS

A clasp for proficiency in the BDM and JM was instituted on April 28, 1934. This achievement badge (*Leistungsabzeichen*) takes the form of the initials *BDM* inside a rectangular frame upon a piece of *plain red* ribbon, the letters and frame being either bronze or silver, according to the grade awarded. The same letters and frame in silver on a background of red/white/red ribbon was given as the achievement badge of JM until 1940 when a special JM clasp was created. This new clasp is simply the letters *JM* in silver within a silver frame with a red ribbon as the background. The red/white/red background ribbon was thereafter used only on the BDM clasp.

The tests leading to an award of either badge had to be completed within the span of twelve months and covered nursing, first aid, "political knowledge," as well as physical and athletic exercises. More than 115,000 awards of the BDM and 58,000 of the JM clasp were made by 1943.

Issued examples are usually numbered on the reverse, but some have, instead, a letter *A* or *B* (possibly an age grading like that for the Golden Leader's Sports Badge for males).

Although girls joined the JM at ten-years-old they could not enter for the JM clasp until their twelfth birthday.

BDM Clasp     JM Clasp

## "HARVEST ACTION BADGES"

Less prestigious than an award, but certainly higher than a "day" or donation badge, was the *Ernteeinsatz der Hitlerjugend* (Harvest Action of the Hitler Youth) coloured enamel badge (see illustration), which was issued for the years 1939, 1940 and 1941 (these dates appearing on the badge itself). The design proved unpopular and was not used again after 1941.

PHIL BAKER

Less prestigious than an award, but certainly higher than a "day" or donation badge, is the *Ernteeinsatz der Hitlerjugend* (Harvest Action of the Hitler Youth) coloured enamel badge (illustrated above) which was issued for the years: 1939, 1940 and 1941 (these dates appearing on the badge itself). The design proved unpopular and it was not used again after 1941.

An award certificate (*Urkunde*) issued in connection with this badge. It is to a BDM girl for "war harvest action" in Gau Styria (Austria) between 8th July and 14th August 1940. It is signed by the Gauleiter of Styria and the BDM Leader of Obergau Styria.

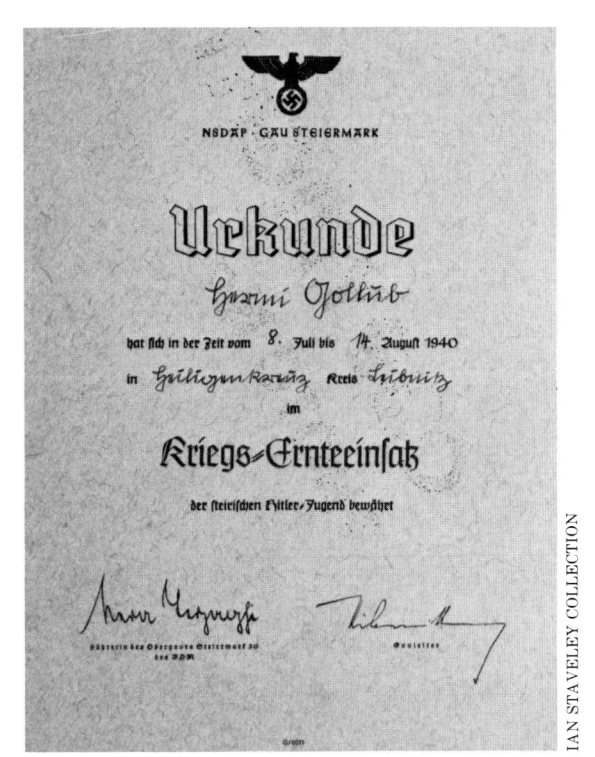

IAN STAVELEY COLLECTION

Left: a less well made badge (it is in uncoloured alloy) for "Student (literally "academic") harvest help 1939." A bronze badge exists (also with the NSDStB emblem) for "harvest action in East Prussia 1939" which has the motto *"Einsatzdienst im Osten ist Ehrendienst"* (Work service in the East is a service of honour). There may well have been other similar reward voluntary agricultural

## NSFK FLYING MODEL AIRCRAFT ACHIEVEMENT BADGE (NSFK MODELFLUGLEISTUNGSABZEICHEN)

Although not strictly a Hitler Youth award, this badge, in its various grades, was awarded almost exclusively to members of the HJ or DJ Flying Model Aircraft Groups (*HJ und DJ Modelfluggruppen*).

These groups were formed to encourage an understanding of the principles of flight through the building of power-driven or glider model aircraft; models which could be entered in competitions under the aegis of the NSFK (Nazi Flying Corps).

The lowest grade (Grade A) takes the form of a blue-grey cloth badge with two white cotton circles upon which is a white cotton glider and a line, intended to represent the edge of a cloud. The Grades *B* and *C* badges have the same type of glider and cloud, but this time within an oval wreath of oakleaves with a swastika at the base. In the Grade *B* badge this is yellow thread on blue-grey cloth, in the *C* Grade it is silver bullion on blue-grey. There was, in addition, what would appear to be a metal version of the Grade *C* badge. It has an outer wreath of oakleaves and the cloud is "solid" (i.e. there is no space left between the edge and the wreath). The date of institution is not known.

Whereas the younger members of the HJ and DJ had to content themselves with flying model gliders, boys in the higher age groups were permitted to train on actual gliders and enter for the tests leading to an award of a grade of the Glider Pilot Certificate. This international test is in three grades: A, B and C, each with an appropriate qualification badge (again international in design). The A Grade was represented by one stylized "bird" in a circle, the B by two "birds," the C by three. When worn on uniform, the birds and circle are white cotton or silver bullion, and the background blue-grey cloth, but an enamel badge (roughly half the size of the foregoing) could be worn on the left lapel of civilian clothing.

Grade A Badge

Grade B & C Badge

Unidentified metal Badge

Grade C Badge

HJ boy wears "B" Grade Gliding Badge and winners Badge of NSFK *Grossflugtag* Frankfurt a Main, 1939.

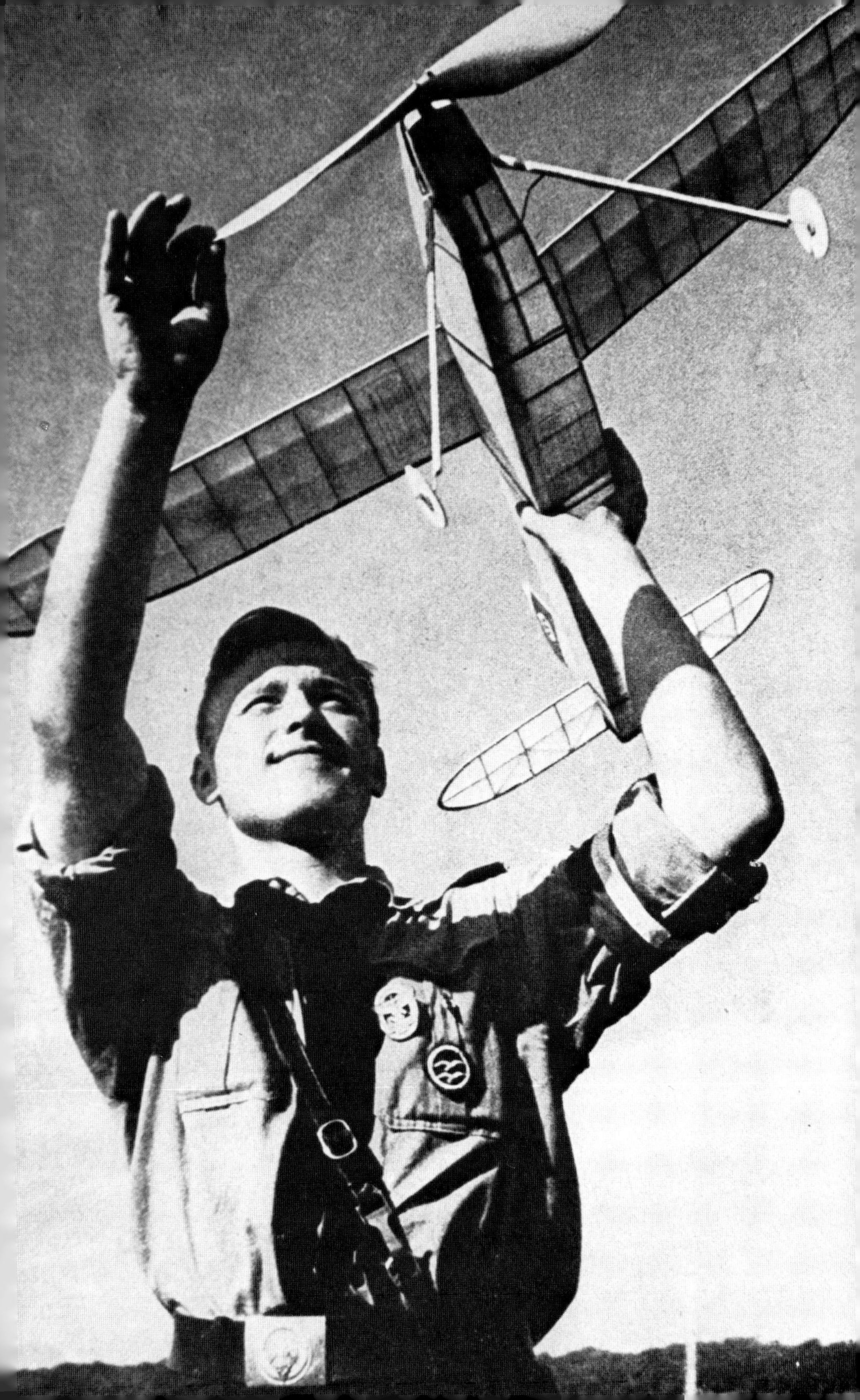

# 24

# "Day" and Donation Badges

In order to be successful, a fascist regime must discover the secret of perpetual emotion. Under the Nazis this was achieved by a seemingly endless succession of rallies, marches, parades and other public manifestations. To celebrate these events, scores of badges were produced in every conceivable design and from a great diversity of materials, from finely-executed bronze to low quality tin (more commonly the latter, which have earned them the disparaging epithet of "tinnies"). The Hitler Youth was not, of course, left out of this bonanza. No event of any significance was allowed to pass without its appropriate badge. For the sake of convenience, these badges may be divided into two categories:

(a) Badges sold in the manner of "flag day" items, solely for the purpose of raising money for the HJ;

(b) Badges issued to participants in an actual happening (a camp, rally, sports day, propaganda march, etc.).

The first category might be termed "donation" badges, the second, "day" badges, since they were intended to be worn only on the day, or days, of the event in question. In the scale of values certain "day" badges must rank higher than others, for example, those which commemorate participation in a team, entering a national, or international, competition, since membership of such a team (even though it might not eventually be successful) was in itself something of an achievement.

It would be impossible to list *all* the "donation" and "day" badges, but a selection is given here to illustrate the diversity in design. Like their adult counterparts, the HJ badges differed in quality of materials and "make," some being well executed, others poorly pressed out of cheap metal. Occasionally bronze was used, but this was rare; most common materials were tin, white metal or alloy. The event commemorated is usually clearly stated on the badge; when it is not, it is probably, a mere "donation" item.

232

(1) Competitive Games of the Swabian HJ-1938.
(2) Sports Day of Gebiet 7 North Sea Jadestadte (towns on the Jade River) 29th-30th August 1936.
(3) Bann Rally of the HJ 19th-21st May 1934, Ansbach.
(4) Sports Festival 1935.
(5) Tyrol-Vorarlberg Ski Competition, Innsbruck 1939 (has SA and HJ emblems).
(6) Schlageter Memorial Day. HJ Bann South Holstein "Fell 25. 5. 1923" (date of the execution by the French of Leo Schlageter).
(7) North Sea Gebiet Rally Bremen, 1933.
(8) "Mountain Home Games" 800 years of Burg Castle. HJ Oberbann Roemryke Berge, 17th September 1933.
(9) Bann and Untergau Sports Festival of the Hitler Youth, 1939.
(10) Hochland Camp 1936. This example has an embossed number (1003) on the front, but it also exists without a number. The number may have indicated that it was worn by an official of the camp.
(11) Oberbann Rally Honnef 1934 (Honnef is in Rhine-Westphalia).
(12) Hitler Youth Bann Rally March Halle-Merseburg. Halle, 1933.
(13) Third Kreis Rally Burgdorf, 2nd-3rd July 1938 (Burgdorf is in Hanover).
(14) Norderney 1934 "We fly."
(15) HJ Rally Eichstatt, 1934 (Eichstatt is in Franconia).
(16) Würzburg, 14th-15th July 1934.

(a) (b) (c) (d)

(e) (f) (g) (h)

(a) HJ Unterbann Rally, Brake i. O. (in Oldenburg) 1933.
(b) German Youth Festival 1936. (This is bronze, but an exactly similar one in "silver" was issued for the same event in 1937).
(c) "Ten years of Gebiet Hochland," 1928-1938. It has the motto of the Blood Order "And yet you have conquered" and the facade of the Feldherrnhalle at Munich (which also features on the Blood Order).
(d) Hitler Youth, Munich 1923-1933. Similar motto and facade as above.
(e) Youth Festival, 1935.
(f) Bann and Untergau Sports Festival, Komotau 1st-2nd July 1939 (the town of Komotau, or, in Czech Chomuto, is in NW Bohemia — at this time part of the "Protectorate" of Bohemia-Moravia).
(g) South-West German Gebiet Rally of the Hitler Youth, Karlsrühe, 6th-7th May 1933.
(h) First Festival of German Youth, 24th June 1933.

(i) (j) (k) (l)

(m) (n) (o) (p)

(i) HJ Rally of Banne Hanover and Brunswick in the Royal City of Goslar 1st May 1933 (unusual in that the HJ emblem here is first type).
(j) Rally March of Gebiet Westphalia 9.
(k) Tented camp HJ Gebiet 13, 1935.
(l) Tented camp HJ Gebiet 13, 1936.
(m) Thuringian HJ Rudolfstadt, 1933.
(n) Tented camp of the Franconian HJ, 1936.
(o) Second Gebiet Rally march North Sea (7) Bremen' 1937. "The North Sea HJ thanks the Old Guard" (HJ boy and SA man).
(p) HJ Ski Championship, Gebiet Hochland, 1933-1934.

(i) "For the Führer's Youth." (undated)
(ii) Unmarked/undated but with DLV emblem, Probably to encourage "air mindedness."
(iii) "House of the Hitler Youth" at Aschaffenburg (near Frankfurt a. M.) 13.10.35.
(iv) "Offerings Day" for the HJ Youth Hostels (undated).
(v) German Youth Hostels day, 1937.
(vi) Parade march from Hamburg for the dedication of the "Hein Godewind" (floating) Youth Hostel, 8th April 1934.
(vii) Josef Goebbels Youth Hostel (undated). Possibly to commemorate the opening of this hostel or for making a donation towards it completion.

(1) Jungbann Sports Festival 1935. Jungbann Lower Elbe 24/25th August Elmshorn
(2) Jungbann 2/59 and 2/91 Tented camp. July 1934
(3) Jungbann Sports Festival Bann 1/33 Gunzenhausen (undated)
(4) Jungvolk Rally. Bückeburg 3rd October 1933
(5) Jungbann Rally of Jungbann 2/84 on 7th-8th July 1934. Glückstadt
(6) Sports Competition of Jungbann 392 in Steinau, 7th-8th August 1937

The above are, of course, merely a selection of "day" badges issued in connection with DJ events. The total number was probably less than those issued for HJ occasions since the DJ was a smaller organization.

# *Daggers and Knives*

All HJ and DJ boys carried a "Travelling (or Camping) knife" (*Fahrtenmesser*), which they received on being inducted as full members of the DJ or HJ. There was no distinction between the HJ knife and that of the DJ. Some post-war studies have postulated the existence of a special DJ knife and characterized this an an "economy version," introduced at the start of the Second World War. Such a knife existed, but was most certainly an unofficial item.

Before, and even for some time after, the introduction of the regulation HJ/DJ *Fahrtenmesser* in 1933, privately produced knives of various kinds were carried. Although these often feature the HJ emblem, they cannot be regarded as official, since in 1934 strict regulations were brought in, banning the manufacturer of *any* item of Party equipment or insignia by anyone not specifically authorized to do so by the RZM, and decreeing that all items had to carry the RZM stamp or tab.

The honour dagger (*Ehrendolch*) of the SA was sometimes awarded to HJ leaders who could wear it with their HJ uniform. This practice ceased after the death of Röhm.

In 1937 a special "Leader's Dagger" (*Führerdolch*) for the rank of *Gefolgschaftführer* and above was introduced. Prior to this, leaders had worn the same *Fahrtenmesser* as the boys. The leader's dagger could be worn with a belt upon the tunic, suspended from leather hangers with unadorned silver oval buckles, or without a belt, *below* the tunic. When worn with a greatcoat the dagger hangers fastened to a clip sewn to a strap inside the left of the coat, with a finished opening just below and under the top flap of the left sidepocket. The hanger extended through the opening and under the flap, thus allowing the dagger to be worn suspended on the outside of the coat.

The practice of awarding daggers with suitably engraved blades as tokens of honour did not seem to have been often followed in the Hitler Youth.[**] Some of the pre-standardization knives have been described by certain writers as "honour daggers." This is almost certainly mistaken.

---

[**] Examples of the *Fahrtenmesser* with a blade inscription *do* exist, but this would seem to have been done privately.

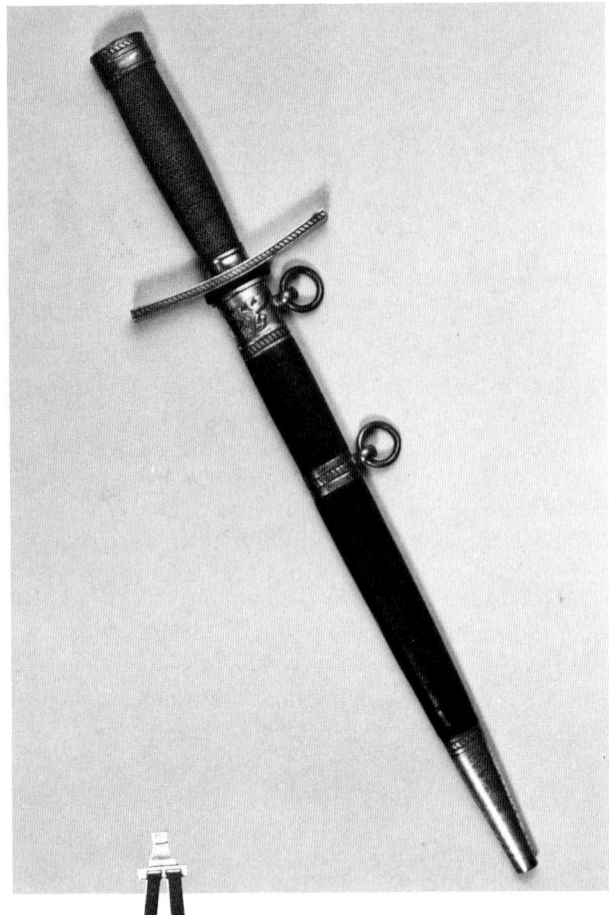

Officer's dagger (*HJ Führerdolch*)

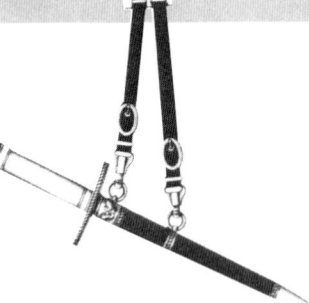

Method of wearing — black leather hanger with silver buckles etc.

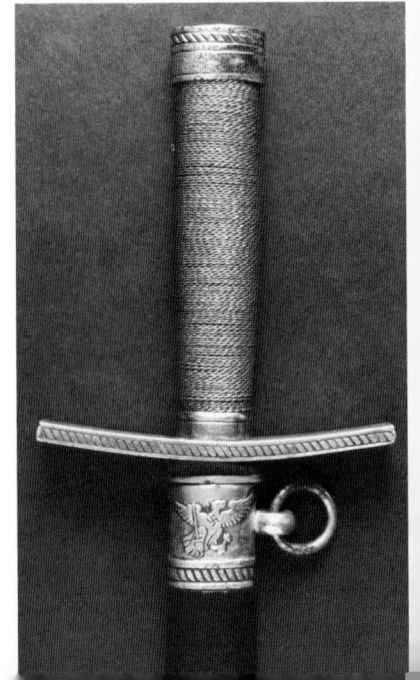

Detail of hilt and top of scabbard.

An HJ *Gebietsführer* talks to lads of a Hitler Youth unit. Note the *Führerdolch* worn *under* the tunic. The officer wears the German Horseman's Badge and the Golden Party Badge.

Staff and senior pupils at an NPEA carried a dagger similar to that of the SA/SS. This was known as the "Holbein dagger," since it was closely modelled on a sixteenth-century Swiss dagger, featured in some of the paintings by the artist, Hans Holbein. The first design of this NPEA dagger is simply the standard SA type, minus the SA monogram. Later, olive-green tended to replace the brown colour on the scabbard. The student dagger has a plain grip, i.e. no eagle-and-swastika. From 1933 to 1936 the NPEA officer's dagger was worn from a single loop suspension, but when a double chain was introduced for the SA and SS daggers, it was likewise adopted by NPEA officers. Students wore their dagger in the manner of a bayonet from an olive green, or less commonly black, leather frog. Some student's daggers *did* have the eagle-and-swastika on the grip, but these may have been intended for student leaders only. Junior pupils at an NPEA, that is to say those who were still in the DJ age group, wore the standard HJ/DJ *Fahrtenmesser*. All the

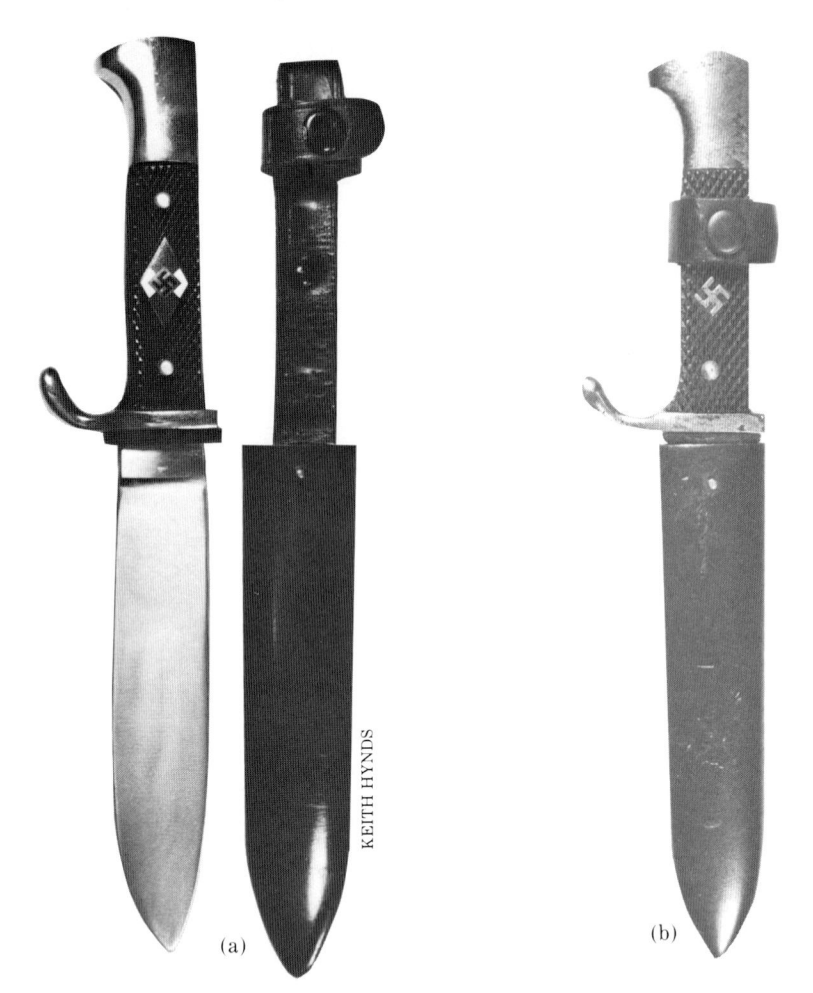

Two examples of the HJ *Fahrtenmesser*, or Camping Knife worn by all ranks up to *Oberscharführer*. (a) is the standard type, (b) is one of several variants.

NPEA "Holbein" daggers, whether officers' or students', have etched on the blade the motto, *Mehr sein als scheinen* (Be more than you seem).

The personal bodyguard (*Wachgefolgschaft*) of the HJ Chief (von Schirach, later Axmann) carried a dress bayonet or side arm. A unique feature of this was the ornamental silver knot (*Troddel*) — a characteristic of German army dress side arms, but used nowhere else in the HJ. The blade of this side weapon was *not* inscribed.

The officers' *Führerdolch* and the boys' *Fahrtenmesser* had on their blades the motto, *Blut und Ehre* (Blood and Honour), but after 1938 this motto was no longer inscribed on the *Fahrtenmesser*.

The HJ supplied daggers and knives to some of the fascist movements of Germany's allies. For example, the Bulgarian Brannik Youth dagger was simply the HJ *Fahrtemesser* with the HJ emblem replaced by a Cyrillic *B*. The Levente Youth of Hungary also received a version of the HJ *Fahrtenmesser*. Even the "Holbein" dagger of the NPEA can be found with Belgian fascist emblems (see "Foreign" section).

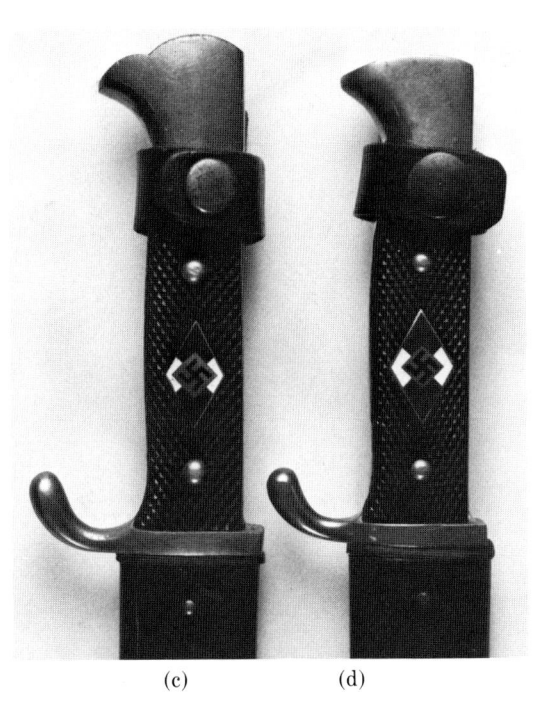

Two slightly different versions of the standard HJ. *Fahrtenmesser*. Note the different tops to the hilts. This is without significance and was almost certainly merely a maker's variant.
(c) Is the earlier of the two; (d) is the more commonly found type.

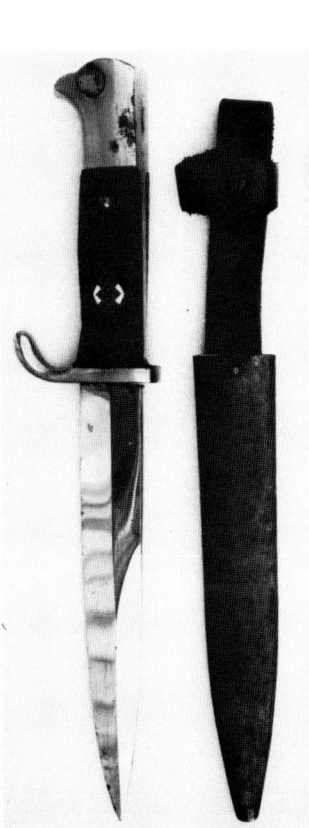

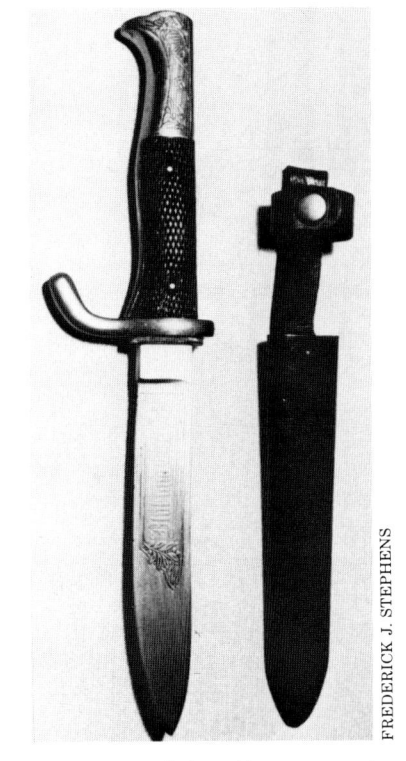

(c)   (d)

Two early unofficial HJ *Fahrtenmesser*. *Left:* Knife constructed from a World War I bayonet or fighting knife (*Kampfmesser*) Blade is not inscribed.
*Above:* Commercially produced knife with engraved pommel. There are different versions of this pommel ornamentation: as here with uncoloured HJ flag; with HJ flag in coloured enamel; with HJ diamond emblem in coloured enamel and (possibly) also with HJ diamond uncoloured. The blade is elaborately etched *Blut und Ehre*. It has to be emphasized that these are not (as is sometimes stated) special "presentation daggers" but simply pre-standardization privately purchased items. No HJ knife which is not RZM marked (as these are not) can be considered official. There may well have been *other* commercially produced variants in addition to the above.

241

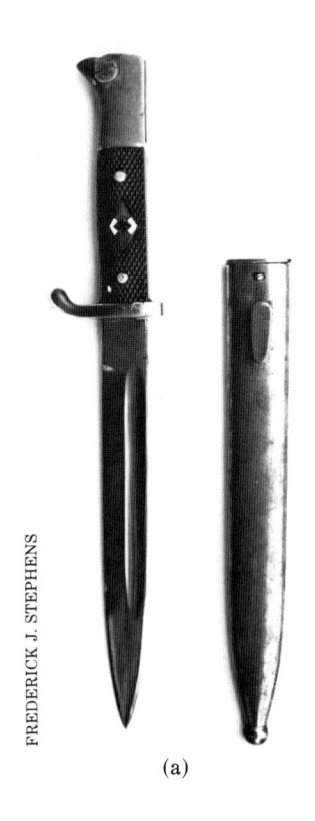

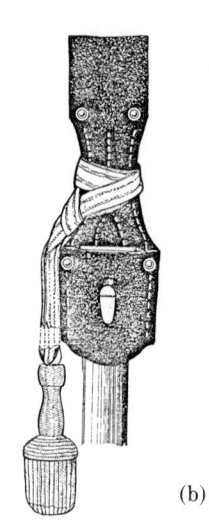

(a) An HJ dress bayonet (*Seitenwaffe*) for a member of a Guard Company (*Wachgefolgschaft*). It has a black hilt with the HJ diamond in coloured enamel. The scabbard is also black. There is no inscription on the blade.
(b) Method of attachment to the belt with ornamental knot as used with armed forces daggers and dress bayonets.

Two versions (one with, and one without, the HJ emblem) of a *Fahrtenmesser*. This unidentified knife is sometimes ascribed to the DJ, but as it is unmarked by the RZM it may well be only a commercial piece adapted for HJ use or a very early semi-official type. It is certainly *not* the DJ version of the *Fahrtenmesser*.

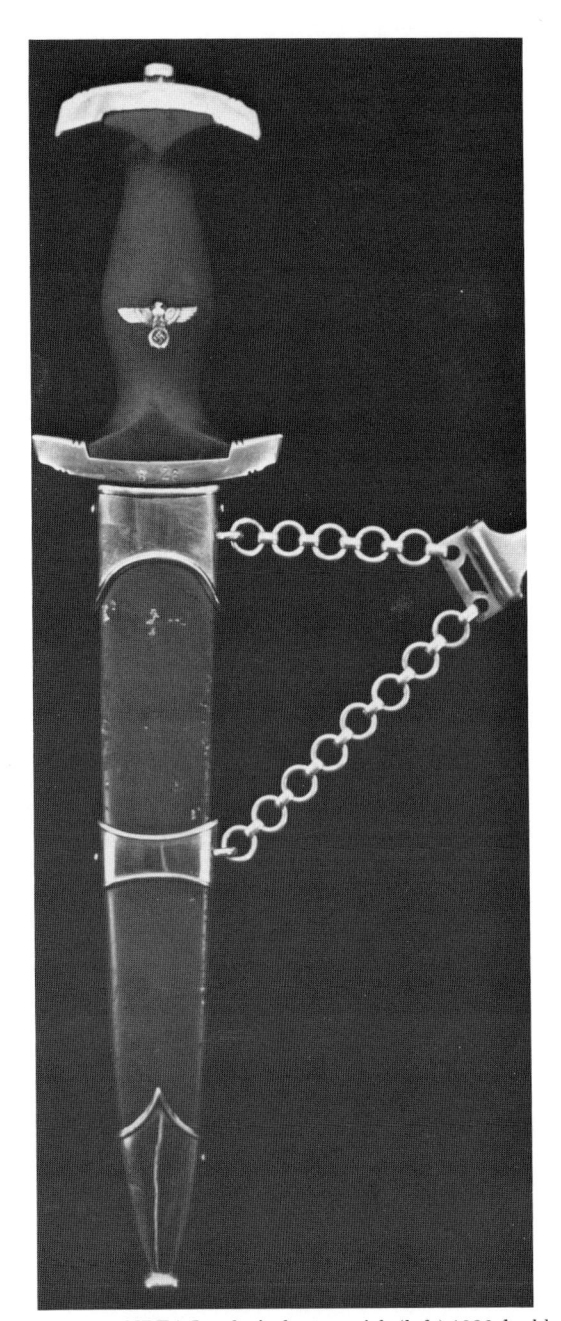

NPEA Leader's dagger with (left) 1936 double chain suspension. Right is blade with motto *Mehr sein als scheinen* ("Be more than you seem").

NPEA Student's dagger (*Kurzteilnehmer Dienstdolch*) with its bayonet-type scabbard.

F. J. STEPHENS

Example of an engraved legend on top cross guard. Here NPEA Spandau Kriegsjahr (war year) 1942

(a)

(b)

Two examples of place names and numerals on lower cross guard: (a) *SP* for Spandau (b) *N* for Naumburg. Motto on blade of both Leaders' and Students' daggers. Note the variant Ss on the lower example, this type of *S* is the less usual.

Mehr sein als scheinen.

Mehr sein als scheinen.

A very unusual, possibly unique, variant of the *Führerdolch* was carried by HJ officers during their visit to Japan in 1939. This has white, instead of black, hangers and the scabbard is also white (or possibly silver).

The *Führerdolch* was, on occasions, awarded by the RJF to leaders of foreign youth groups as a mark of honour or appreciation.

## Hitler Youth at War

The outbreak of war on September 1, 1939 must have found the youth of Germany better prepared physically and psychologically than that of any of the other combatants. Was not war the logical outcome of all that had gone before? Was it not the ultimate object of all the Hitler Youth's years of training? The response to the call for volunteers was immediate and overwhelming. The German news agency, DNB, announced that in the first four weeks of the war 1,091,000 young persons of both sexes had offered themselves for service of some kind. Boys and girls took the place of men drafted into the forces from the Postal and Telegraph services, the railways, the trams, and police, in addition to working as couriers to the armed forces. BDM girls assisted in hospitals or with welfare work connected with servicemen's families in the so-called Neighbourhood Help (*Nachbarschaftshilfe*) and Domestic Action (*Haushaltungseinsatz*). Hardly any aspect of civilian life which suffered loss of manpower to the armed forces was outside the scope of the *HJ-Kriegseinsatz*. Most prominently in this respect was the work of volunteers on the land. In truth the German agricultural economy could scarcely have survived without the assistance of the army of youthful volunteers. Here girls more than outnumbered boys. For example, in the 1942 harvest 600,000 boys participated as against 1,400,000 girls.

In the first twenty-one months of the war, especially after the fall of France in June 1940 (some German army units were actually *demobilized* in the wake of this apparently war-winning victory), there tended to be more young volunteers than were actually needed.

War has its casualties. One of those was Baldur von Schirach. In all his time as leader of the HJ von Schirach had suffered from what might be termed a credibility problem. His fellow top Nazis simply found it impossible to take the rotund, cherubic, poetry-spouting *Reichsjugendführer* seriously. By the summer of 1940 this difficulty had become a public embarrassment. It was felt that someone with greater military experience and personal authority was needed to head the Hitler Youth in time of war. True, von Schirach had served, even in a somewhat nominal capacity (achieving the phenomenally rapid promotion from Private to 1st Lieutenant in six months) in the army, but others had won higher distinction in the field, among them the Chief of the HJ Social Office, Artur Axmann.

On August 2, 1940 von Schirach was "elevated" to the post of Reichs

Leader of the NSDAP for Youth Education (a high-sounding, but basically meaningless post) and created *Gauleiter* and *Reichsstatthalter* of Vienna. It was the German equivalent of "kicking upstairs" to the Lords a bothersome Member of Parliament — a flattering way of rendering him harmless. The vacated post of *Reichsjugendführer* was given to Artur Axmann, an able and efficient organizer who had served with distinction in the Polish and French campaigns. When Germany invaded Russia ten months later Axmann again asked to be released to serve in the army. Permission was granted and he remained at the front until December 1941 when, after loosing his right arm below the elbow, he was discharged. His war disablement lent prestige to his new post.

If, in the autumn of 1940, there had been more would-be young helpers than were needed, the invasion of Russia, coupled with the increasing severity of the allied bombing offensive, markedly altered this situation. Boys in the upper age groups of the HJ had, since the start of the war, been given additional training as Air Raid Wardens. By the summer of 1942 this became a standard component of *all* training, not only for the HJ, but also for the BDM and even DJ youngsters.

A *Jungstammführer* in the DJ (rank indicated by his white lanyard) delivers a letter in his capacity as an auxiliary postman (note his *Reichspost* brassard below his DJ *Sigrune* and Berlin "District Triangle").

An army NCO instructs HJ boys in the use of a *Panzerfaust* (an anti-tank rocket). This mass-produced weapon was widely used by the *Volkssturm*.

As the war progressed the Hitler Youth was increasingly called upon to play an active combatant role. The work of the HJ Fire Brigade units and of the Flak helpers of the Luftwaffe is dealt with separately hereafter. Heavy responsibilities were now placed on the shoulders of young people. Melita Maschmann, a BDM leader, recalls in her reminiscences of the period (*vide* "Bibliography") how, without previous experience or training of any sort, she was ordered to take charge of the welfare and feeding of hundreds of German refugees fleeing before the Red Army's advance into East Prussia. Before this, again without any prior instruction, she had been required to supervise the settlement of German agricultural workers in the newly annexed Polish territories.

On October 18, 1944, in a final attempt to stave off defeat, all German males between the ages of sixteen and sixty were mobilized in the *Volkssturm* (Home Guard). In the end practically everyone from the ten-year-old *Jungvolk* boy upwards was required to bear arms in the defense of the Fatherland.

The units in which HJ and DJ lads served were often hastily-assembled scratch formations made up of miscellaneous army, Luftwaffe, *Volkssturm*, Police or Labour Service bodies under the immediate command of SS officers and NCO's, their overall control being vested in the local *Gauleiter*, who had responsibility for the defense of his *Gau*. In some sectors sufficient HJ lads could be mustered to form HJ regiments and these fought as semi-independent units. At Breslau, for example, in January 1945 *HJ-Gebietsführer* Herbert Hirsch formed a two-battalion regiment of local Hitler Youth and, armed with infantry and anti-tank weapons, it held the junction of the *Kaiser Wilhelm Strasse* and the *Augustas Strasse* against repeated attacks by the Red Army, thereby earning for the district the nickname "Hitler Youth Corner" (*Hitlerjugendeck*). The youthful defenders held out until the final collapse of Germany in May 1945.

As *Gauleiter* of Vienna von Schirach was also its *Reichsverteidigungskommissar* (Reich Defense Commissioner). He now sported the field grey greatcoat with red facings of an army general! An HJ "Werwolf" Battalion was formed from among the trainees at the various *Wehrertüchtigungslager* around Vienna (this had, however, no connection with the Wehrwolf movement envisaged by Dr. Goebbels as a sabotage formation intended to be operated *behind* enemy lines). The Austrian Werwolf comprised some 800 to 900 lads armed with anti-tank weapons and classed as *Panzer-Jagdkommando*. Later this was expanded into two battalions (each of three companies) and redesignated a *Kampfgruppe* ("Battle Group") — a very vague term which could denote anything from thousands to a few score). The battalion adopted a wolf's head as its vehicle emblem and some members even (unofficially) stitched a wolf's head on their uniforms. In the city of Vienna BDM girls served on the anti-aircraft defense and, like their male colleagues, suffered heavy losses.

In Berlin Axmann ordered the raising of HJ Regiments to defend the city in the role of "tank-busters." Even eleven-year-olds had a *Panzerfaust* trust into their hands and told to use it against Russian tanks. Hitler's last public appearance was in the grounds of the Reichs Chancellory on April 20, 1945 (his 56th birthday) when he decorated twenty boys of the Berlin Hitler Youth with the Iron Cross (the youngest recipient being only 12 years old).*

In the West HJ formations and the *Volkssturm* also engaged the enemy but with markedly less fanaticism. Many were happy to surrender to the Americans as did large numbers of the defenders of Munich in April 1945. This is not to say that examples of individuals acts of reckless courage on the part of HJ boys were not to be found on the western as well as the eastern front.

HJ Flak helpers decorated with the Iron Cross. Second Class. Note that the boy, centre, wears the tank destruction award.

JOSEF CHARITA

---

* The medals had actually been bestowed beforehand by Axmann. Hitler only emerged briefly from his Bunker to congratulate the boys for the benefit of the news cameras.

In March 1945 boys from the higher classes (sixteen and seventeen year-olds) at the Ordensburg at Sonthofen were drafted into the hurriedly constituted *38. SS Panzer-Grenadier Division Nibelungen,* along with cadets from the SS Officer Training School at Bad Tölz and a company of RAD personnel. The whole "division" amounted to only 2,719 men and boys. It surrendered to the Americans at Landshut two months later.

Neither Axmann nor von Schirach elected to die rather than surrender (as they had urged their followers to do). Both were taken prisoner, unhurt, both tried, convicted, and eventually, released. "Faithful even unto death," it would appear, was good enough for ten and eleven year-olds; it was not a philosophy which recommended itself to their leaders.

## MILITARY TOUGHENING-UP CAMPS

The HJ had, since the autumn of 1936, run week-end courses in *Geländesport* (field exercises) and small calibre rifle shooting. Initially it had relied on its own personnel to furnish the instructors, but increasingly the army, and latterly, the SS became involved in the paramilitary training of the HJ. An important step in this connection was the establishment, in 1939, of *Wehrertüchtigungslager der HJ\** in which lads between the ages of sixteen-and-half and eighteen were put through a three week course (160 hours of actual training) culminating in an award of the so-called *K-Schein* (*Kriegsausbildungsschein* — War Training Certificate) in which was recorded the boy's attainments in field exercises, rifle shooting and his "general bearing" (*allgemeine Haltung*). The Wehrmacht provided liaison officer for every *Bann* to supervise the training, but it was the Waffen-SS that came to dominate the work of the *WE Lager.*

Von Schirach (kneeling) at the *Wehrertüchtigungslager* at Exelberg (outside Vienna), 1944. He wears what is basically HJ leader's uniform but on this his insignia are those of an NSDAP *Reichsleiter.* Such mixtures of uniforms were not uncommon among top Nazis! His cuff-title is probably the Sutterlin *Hitlerjugend* type, but it is possible that it could be *Grossdeutschland* (the élite army division in which he performed his military service in 1939/40).

---

\* Known at that time as *Reichsausbildungslager* (National Training Camps). The change of name was made in March 1942.

Hitler congratulates boys of the HJ decorated with Iron Cross for bravery in the defence of Berlin. picture was taken on 12th April (or the previous Hitler's last appearance before the news cameras w a similar ceremony one week later (20th April) ju days before his death.

An interesting photo of (left to right): Dutch, Danish and Norwegian lads at a *Wehrertüchtigungslager* in Germany during the war. They wear the uniforms of their respective country's collaborationist youth movement.

By 1943 there were around 150 such camps, and these now included among their members (both as trainees and instructors) volunteers from the Nordic countries (Denmark, Holland, Flanders and Norway — there were also some Latvians). Training was geared predominantly towards ground combat but the *Flieger-HJ* and *Marine-HJ* also had camps providing training appropriate to the needs of respectively the Luftwaffe and *Kriegsmarine*. It has to be said that the *K-Schein*, prized as it was by it recipients, carried no weight at all with the military authorities. It exempted its holder from not one day of standard recruit training!

Front-line veterans, officers and NCOs, many of them former HJ leaders and often bearers of high decorations for bravery, furnished the main component of the training cadre. In overall command of the *WE Lager* programme was Gerhard (Gerd) Hein with the rank of *HJ-Gebietsführer*. Hein had served in the *Leibstandarte Adolf Hitler* Division of the Waffen-SS and had been decorated with the Knight's Cross with Oakleaves.

Gerhard ("Gerd") Hein, winner of the Knight's Cross and Oak Leaves was, with the rank of *HJ Gebietsführer*, responsible for the entire *Wehrertüchtigungslager* programme. Later, as an *SS-Hauptsturmführer*, he commanded the Panzer-Gren. Rgt. 26 of the 12. SS Panzer Division "Hitlerjugend."

There was a sound practical reason why the SS took such an interest in the *WE Lager*. It furnished them with a means of circumventing the Wehrmacht's monopoly on recruitment. The Waffen-SS possessed no powers of direct conscription (except in what it regarded as its own unique fief — the youth of the German *Volksgruppen* outside the Reich). A young man could, of course, on being called to the colours, express a preference for the Waffen-SS, just as he could for the Luftwaffe or the Navy, but his ultimate posting was entirely in the hands of the Wehrmacht. If, however, he could be persuaded to volunteer for the Waffen-SS *before* being due for military conscription, his wish was respected. The normal age for conscript service in Germany (as in most European countries) was one's twentieth year. The SS therefore strove to induce *WE Lager* lads to volunteer for service in one of its divisions after they had obtained their *K-Schein*. The legal age to do so was eighteen, but this was progressively reduced as the war situation worsened. So rich was the harvest to be garnered from the *WE Lager* that the Waffen-SS was able to raise one entire division from this source alone.

Two trainees at a WE Lager take notes from an army General with the Knight's Cross. The boys wear military style field-grey tunics wthout insignia (an alternative garb to the rush green "*Drillich*"). In the background is an HJ officer.

## 12. SS PANZER DIVISION "HITLERJUGEND"

The loss of a whole army at Stalingrad in the winter of 1943-1944 caused an already difficult manpower shortage to become so acute that in February 1943 Hitler was prevailed upon to authorize the raising of a division from volunteers of the "class" of 1926 (under normal circumstances not liable for conscription until 1946). These were to be sought from among the young persons now under training at *WE Lager* throughout the Reich. Himmler informed Axmann that Hitler wished the division to have the title "Hitlerjugend" and had suggested that one of its regiments might bear the name of the HJ's most celebrated martyr, Herbert Norkus. Volunteers were to be drawn from those born between January and June 1926 (i.e. seventeen-year-olds). The normal requirement of six months RAD (Labour) Service — the customary prelude to full military service — was to be waived and they would be accepted directly into the Waffen-SS.

Despite objections from Dr. Goebbels to the title "Hitlerjugend" ("Would not this suggest to our enemies that Germany has been reduced to calling up children?"), the name was willingly accepted by both the Waffen-SS and the HJ (proudly so in the case of the latter). The idea of a "Herbert Norkus" regiment was, however, not followed up.

It was laid down that the Division should have 830 officers and 4,000 NCOs. But where were these to be found? The answer was to be principally from the most prestigious Waffen-SS formation — the *Leibstandarte Adolf Hitler*. To command the newly raised division Himmler selected *SS-Standartenführer* (Colonel) Fritz Witt. Commander of the 1. SS Panzer Grenadier Regiment of the LAH, Witt had been with the *Leibstandarte* since its inception and who had a distinguished record as a front-line soldier having as recently as March 1st of that year been invested personally by Hitler with the Oakleaves to his Knight's Cross of the Iron Cross.

He was promoted *SS-Brigadeführer und Generalmajor der Waffen-SS* when he formally took command of the month-old division (recruiting started officially on June 1st). But the hard-pressed Waffen-SS could not alone furnish sufficient officers and NCOs. Fifty officers (mainly former HJ leaders) had to be seconded from the Army. The HJ and DJ leadership throughout the Reich was combed for "volunteers." Experienced NCOs found themselves, willingly or otherwise, dispatched to officer training establishments and many a junior officer received accelerated promotion.

But if finding staff was difficult (no problems were encountered with regard to the young volunteers themselves), the question of providing their material requirements proved very much harder. Even uniforms were in short supply. Of a theoretical complement of 186 tanks, the division had, by October 1943, only three! This had risen to ten by November and forty by January 1944. Thereafter the supply position rapidly improved (105 by February, 119 by May). But even by the time the division went into action in June 1944 it was still thirty-eight short of the authorized establishment.

The same applied to other vehicles. It had a paper allocation of 2,214 transport trucks (*Lastwagen*), but in reality possessed only 1,834. Oddly, the only exception to this picture of overall shortages lay in the realm of artillery. Here the division was up to, and actually *over*, the prescribed number of field and anti-tank guns.

Many of the personnel assigned to the new division came from the 1. SS Panzer-Division "Leibstandarte Adolf Hitler" and they continued to wear the "Adolf Hitler" cuff-title (pictured above) after the creation of the division.

Led by Hitler Youth officers and Waffen SS, NCOs lads of the embryonic Division under training in Germany.

Training at Divisional level was carried out at Beverloo in Belgium after its diverse elements had been brought together from their preparatory courses in various parts of Germany. The Hitlerjugend Division remained in Belgium until April 1944 when it was moved to France, first to the Eure *Département* then to an area a few miles to the northeast of Argentan where it was placed on stand-by, in anticipation of an allied invasion. On June 6, 1944 the long expected landing took place. The HJ Division was immediately ordered into action. It was directed to proceed to Caen and repel the British/Canadian invaders. It took almost twenty-four hours to reach its destination during which time it was subjected to constant harassment from the air and suffered heavy losses, but on reaching Caen was at once thrown into action against the enemy.

It is commonly assumed that a battle-experienced division will acquit itself better in action than an untried one. Post-war research has not tended to bear this out. The ideal mix, from a point of view of morale and courage, it has been shown consists of unblooded volunteers guided by experienced officers. The "green" troops are anxious to prove themselves. Their courage, an attribute no more inexhaustible than patience or good temper, has not been drained away in previous encounters with the foe, and the battle-hardened leaders can channel this drive along appropriate lines avoiding the pitfalls of misguided or reckless enthusiasm. A further contributory factor to high morale is pride in one's unit. The HJ Division possessed to the full all these desiderata. Its young volunteers, proud to belong to the élite of Germany's armed forces — the Waffen-SS — were keen to demonstrate their worthiness to wear its honoured runes. The commanders were, for the most part, well versed in battle. The result was that the division as all who fought against it can testify, proved to be the most doughty of all the enemy forces deployed in the Normandy campaign. Its members threw themselves into action without regard to losses — which were, in truth devastating. It would hardly be an exaggeration to say that the original HJ Division virtually destroyed itself in the course of this one battle.

Losses in Normandy were:

|  | *Officers* | *NCOs* | *Other ranks* |
|---|---|---|---|
| Killed (or died of wounds) ...... | 62 | 245 | 1,644 |
| Wounded ..................... | 128 | 613 | 3,684 |
| Missing ...................... | 56 | 192 | 2,012 |

A total of 8,636

Among the fallen was its CO, Fritz Witt, killed on a "quiet day" on June 14th. Divisional command was then assumed by *SS-Standartenführer* Kurt Meyer ("Panzermeyer" as he was nicknamed to distinguish him from other Meyers).

After the hammering sustained in Normandy, the division was all but finished off two months later when it was caught in the Falaise pocket. Kurt Meyer, badly wounded, was taken prisoner on September 6th. Command of what was still left of the division (about 600 men and not a single tank) passed to *SS-Sturmbannführer* Hubert Meyer (no relation). Now reclassified vaguely as a "battle group," it was withdrawn to Germany and hastily brought up to strength by an infusion of new recruits. It was in action again during the Ardennes Offensive of December 1944. When this, Hitler's last gamble in the west, failed the division was switched to Hungary where it formed part of the ambitiously named 1. SS Armoured Corps (along with two understrength divisions — one SS, one army and a Battle Group "Keitel"). Faced with the overwhelming strength of the Red Army, the German force fell back to Austria, there, at Linz, what remained of the 12. SS Panzer Division *Hitlerjugend* surrendered to the Americans.

September 1944 at Kaiserlautern in Germany Artur Axmann distributes "Hitlerjugend" cuff-titles to members of the division.
[Right:] Vehicle sign of the 12. SS Panzer-Division.
[Below:] An example of a "Hitlerjugend" cuff-title (white lettering and edges on black).

*WE Lager Schiffchen*, worn by trainees with the work dress.

## UNIFORMS

At the *WE Lager* the trainees wore as a working dress (*Arbeitanzug* or *Drillich*) a "rush green" uniform comprising a jacket with five detachable buttons and two flapless pockets, trousers and either jack boots or boots with anklets (a fashion which would appear to have been copied from the British forces). Headgear was a *Schiffchen,* or side cap, with the HJ diamond badge on the front. The HJ brassard continued to be worn on the left arm. Normally this was the only insignia worn. Due to shortages, various types of dress were, however, to be seen at the camps. Non-German participants (trainees or instructors) wore the uniform (or parts of it) of their native fascist youth organization. German staff wore either normal service dress (army, Waffen-SS, etc.) or HJ leaders uniform with RJF on the shoulder straps and "district triangle."

Once accepted as SS trainees, the recruits could wear the SS arm eagle, but the collar runes could not be worn until they had passed through basic training and taken the oath as full SS men. Many of the officer and NCOs of the Hitlerjugend Division were former members of the *Leibstandarte Adolf Hitler* and they continued to wear its cuff-title and retained the LAH monogram on their shoulder straps.

It was not until September 1944 that the HJ Division, in recognition of its bravery in Normandy, was awarded a cuff-title "Hitlerjugend." This was in white or silver block letters on a black band with silver edges. A handful of Flemish lads served with the HJ Division, but they did not have any special "national" emblem to distinguish them (All were from the Flemish HJ).

## HJ ASSAULT CRAFT FLOTILLA

There was, in addition to the SS Panzer Division *Hitlerjugend*, another combat formation drawn from HJ volunteers, this was the Assault Craft Flotilla "Hitlerjugend" (*Sturmbootflottille "Hitlerjugend"*) which, trained by the NSKK, was attached to the Navy as part of its *Kleinkampfmittel Verbände* (Small fighting Units).

In recognition of what Hitler called its "boldness and youthful daredevilry" (*Schneid und jugendlisches Draufgängertum*), the Flotilla was granted the right to wear a "Hitlerjugend" cuff-title. This differed from that worn by the Panzer Division both in size and colour. It was wider (33mm) and was navy blue with yellow lettering and yellow inset borders. It was worn on the left cuff.

Assault Craft Flotilla "Hitlerjugend" cuff-title.

[Left:] Another of the same ilk, this time the message is simply "You too" — today the Hitler Youth, tomorrow the Waffen-SS! Both are, of course, wartime issues.

[Right:] A recruiting poster: "German youth volunteer for the Waffen SS." It is interesting to note that the HJ boy wears the cuff-title of the *Streifendienst* since this was very much the "front door" to admission to the SS or SD.

## HJ FIRE FIGHTING UNITS

In 1938 all fire fighting units throughout the Reich were incorporated into the State Police under the control of Heinrich Himmler as SS and Police Chief. The new force was known as the *Feuerschutzpolizei* (Fire Protection Police) and was a sub-division of the *Ordnungspolizei* ("Order Police"). In cities with a population in excess of 150,000, Volunteer Fire Fighting Units (*Freiwillige Feuerschutzwehren*) were set up to act as an auxiliary to the local regulars. If the voluntary principle proved inadequate, service in these "volunteer" formations could be made compulsory. The local District Fire Chief (or *Kommandeur*) was empowered to conscript men up to the age of sixty years.

The uniform of the Volunteer Fire Fighting Units and the regular brigades was a copy of that of the Prussian Fire Service which was, predictably, Prussian blue. This consisted of a tunic with scarlet piping down the front, round the cuffs, collar and shoulder straps. The blue trousers and narrow scarlet piping down the outer seam.

In June 1939, three months *before* the outbreak of the Second World War, the respective leaders of the Hitler Youth and German Police met to discuss the participation of the HJ in the fire defences of the Reich. At this time what was referred to in official documents as the *Hitler-Jugend im Feuerlöschdienst* (Hitler Youth in the Fire Fighting Service) was established. It was stressed that this was *not* to be analogous to the other "special sections" of the HJ such as the *Flieger-HJ, Nachrichten-HJ, Marine-HJ,* etc. Despite this injunction, the term *Feuerwehr HJ* was often employed even on recruiting posters. *"Komm zur Feuerwehr HJ"* a poster at the outbreak of war in September 1939 read. It showed a group of HJ lads in normal *summer* uniform (although the regulations of this time stated that the uniform was to be the winter type with ski cap).

In December 1939 it was decreed that the HJ Fire Fighting Units would form a sub-section of the *HJ Streifendienst* and constitute part of a general "Fire Fighting Reserve Service" (*Feuerlöschdienstreserve*).

In March 1941 the official designation was altered to *HJ Feuerwehrscharen* (HJ Fire Defence Sqauds) and the HJ winter uniforms was replaced by a modified version of that of the *Feuerschutzpolizei*. The following changes were made: the collar patch and the arm badge of the *Feuerschutzpolizei* were not worn. In place of the arm badge, the HJ brassard was worn with, above this, the normal District Triangle of an HJ unit. Shoulder straps were of the HJ type with HJ ranks but in the same colour as the rest of the uniform (Prussian blue) and piped in scarlet with the HJ *Bann* numeral also in scarlet. Later, both piping and numeral were changed to white (presumably on account of the fact that this was the *Waffenfarbe* of the HJ *Streifendienst*). A special badge was introduced at this stage (March 1941) for boys who had passed the fire fighting tests. This badge is rather similar to that for HJ boys under training for the NSKK. It is the HJ segmented diamond but in *black* and white (not red and white) with upon this is the scarlet eagle-in-a-wreath emblem of the Fire Police from the top of which come scarlet and white flames. The outline of the whole is white and the backing black. It has to be said that the above badge and the authorized uniform were, in reality, the subject of considerable variations. The badge was unknown in many units (one former member of the HJ Fire units testified that he had not heard of its existence until *after* the war). The HJ brassard and HJ District triangle were often omitted and trousers and footwear were by

Prussian blue tunic of the *Feuerschutzpolizei* worn with HJ brassard and "district triangle." Piping down front of tunic and around cuffs was scarlet. Shoulder straps with HJ ranks also piped in scarlet.

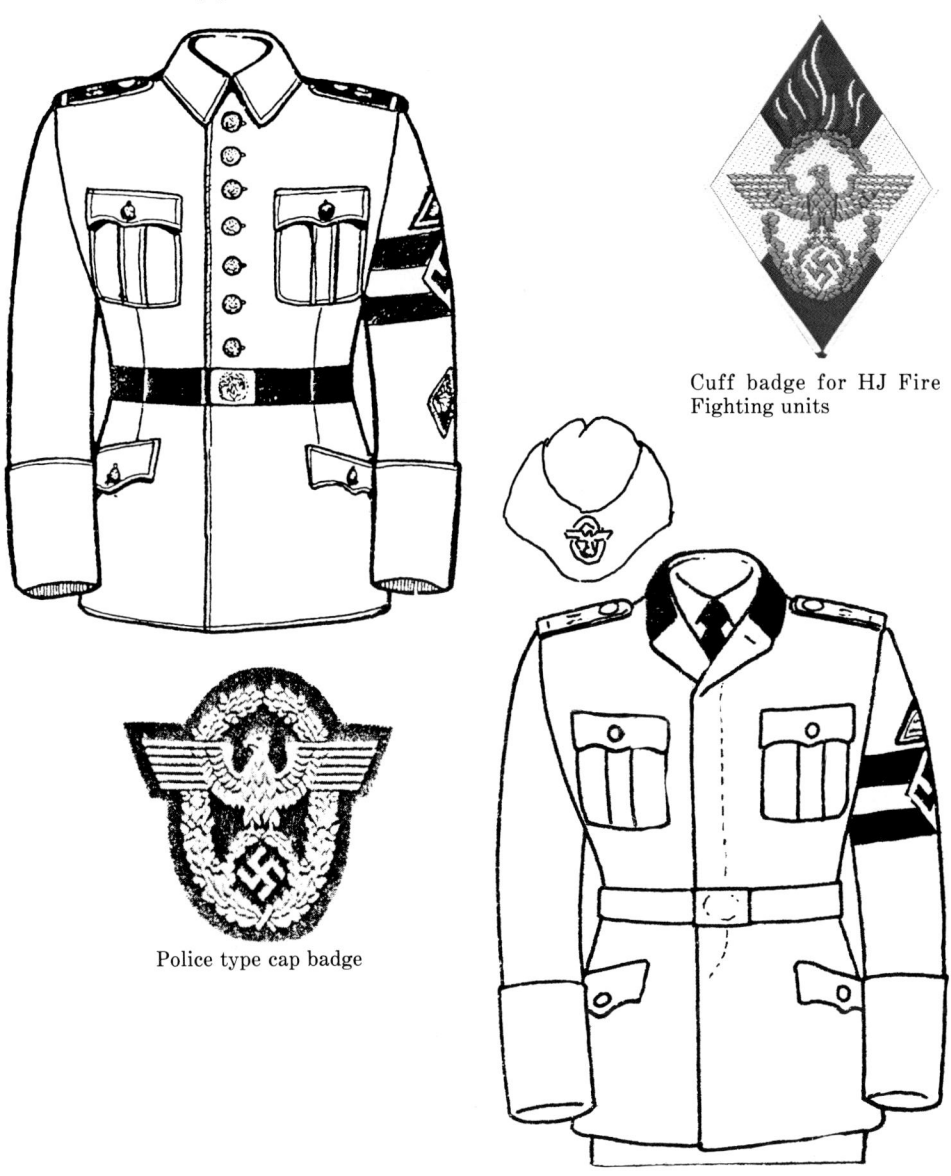

Cuff badge for HJ Fire Fighting units

Police type cap badge

[Right:] Special "olive brown" uniform introduced during 1942. Worn with a khaki shirt and black tie. Collar is dark brown. HJ brassard and "district triangle" worn on left upper arm. Shoulder straps piped in white with normal HJ rank insignia. This uniform was supposed to replace the above.

no means standard. Indeed official regulations were not even attempted in regard to the latter — where the boys were able to obtain army jack boots these were popularly worn. Units in the *Ostmark* (Austria) were allowed to wear the HJ Edelweiss on the right collar. Steel helmets were either those of the *Luftschutz* or the Police type (similar in design to those of the armed forces but slightly lighter weight). Belts were black with either the normal HJ buckle or that of the Fire Police.

A Hitler Youth group in Hamburg parade for action wearing *Feuerschutzpolizei* uniform with HJ ranks and brassard. The boy on the extreme right wears the HJ Fire Fighter's Badge on his left cuff. On the side of the steel helmet is the Police/Fire Brigade emblem (as worn on the front of the forage cap).

Fireman's helmet worn by some HJ Fire-fighting units (others wore Police-type steel helmets).

HJ decal worn on the side of fireman's steel helmet by some HJ Fire-fighting units.

HJ *Feuerschutzpolizei* tunic of the 1942 pattern.

DJ boys train as fire fighters. It is interesting to note that although these are clearly DJ boys (from their rank insignia) they wear the brassard of the HJ.

During 1942 a specially designed uniform began to be issued. It is described as "olive brown," a sort of greenish khaki, and consisted of an open neck tunic with four pockets worn with a HJ brown shirt and black tie. The collar of the tunic is dark brown — a feature then being introduced as standard for all police formations in the Reich. Shoulder straps were HJ with HJ ranks; piping was white. An HJ brassard and District Triangle was worn on the left upper arm. The HJ Fire Fighter's Badge was worn on the left cuff just above the turn-up. A black, or very dark blue, forage cap with the Police eagle on the front was the headgear. Trousers were of the same shade as the tunic, with black shoes, or boots. A black belt with the HJ buckle was worn.

In practice this uniform was by no means standard. Contemporary photos show that even in the same unit some boys retained the old Prussian blue tunic, while others had the newer "olive brown" garb.

With the ever mounting intensity of the air war, the distinction between the specially trained *HJ Feuerwehrscharen* and other HJ (even DJ) units became blurred. *All* members of the youth services acted as volunteer helpers in air raids. Age restrictions were also jettisoned at this time. Originally only boys in the top three age groups of the HJ (sixteen, seventeen and eighteen year-olds) were eligible to serve in the fire fighting units but soon even youngsters from the DJ were taking a hand in this dangerous work. By the start of 1943 there were some 700,000 lads of various ages in the *Feuerwehrscharen*. In the course of that year alone thirty-two boys were killed and 607 wounded in action during raids. For merit 134 boys were awarded the *Kriegsverdienstkreuz* (War Merit Cross) 2nd Class "without swords," and 147 invested with the same decoration "with swords" for bravery; six received the Iron Cross 2nd Class. Figures for the last years of the war are not available, but it can be assumed that the number of dead (and decorated) increased as the bombing became progressively more devastating.

## FLAK HELPERS

In the early stages of the war bombing by the RAF had been little more than a nuisance, but by late 1942 air raids were becoming a serious problem. The Americans came by day, the British by night. The role of the Flak artillery increased considerably and its personnel had to be vastly augmented. To meet the demands now being made upon it, the Luftwaffe enlisted the help of the Hitler Youth. On November 9, 1942 a regulation entitled *Kriegshilfseinsatz der deutschen Jugend bei der Luftwaffe* (Auxiliary War Action of German Youth within the Luftwaffe) was drawn up and published on January 7, 1943. Under its provisions boys (and later girls) from fifteen years upwards were called upon to serve as auxiliaries in any branch of the Luftwaffe (transport, signals, meteorological service, administration, etc.) that might require them, but most particularly in its air defenses, that is to say, the anti-aircraft gun batteries, searchlight, smoke generator, balloon barrage and sound-locator crews. At first service was on a part-time basis (usually about eighteen hours per week), but gradually it became a period of regular duty which had to be carried out between one's fifteenth birthday and call-up for military service. Those who were still at school were allowed to carry on with their education as far as this was possible. Classes were sometimes conducted on the site with blackboards erected beside the guns.

The official designation of these young people was *Luftwaffenhelfer-Hitler Jugend* abbreviated to LwH-HJ), but usually the *Hitler Jugend* was dropped and they were referred to merely as *Luftwaffenhelfer*, or perhaps more commonly, if slightly inaccurately, as *Flakhelfer* (for convenience, this latter term will be used throughout).

To begin with the boys wore their normal HJ summer or winter garb, but during the course of 1943 this was replaced by a specially designed uniform. This consisted of a battledress type of blouse in Luftwaffe blue-grey with black HJ shoulder straps piped in light blue. An HJ brassard was worn on the left upper arm. Worn above the left breast pocket was a light blue Luftwaffe eagle with a Gothic *LH* above it upon a black inverted triangle. Trousers were blue-grey and worn tucked into black boots; a blue-grey HJ type ski cap with the HJ diamond on the front completed the official uniform. In practice a number of unofficial variants crept in. The first item to be jettisoned tended to be the brassard. The black shoulder straps were sometimes left off and the HJ diamond on the cap was often replaced by the Luftwaffe eagle. Perhaps the reason for these unauthorized "modifications" was that the boys wished to discard their Hitler Youth image and be seen as "real soldiers." The special eagle and LH emblem was rarely worn but the reason, in this case, may simply have been a shortage of supply.

Badge worn by "Flak Helpers" above right breast pocket. Light blue on black.

[Right:] Blouse and cap worn by German Flak Helpers. Non-Germans had the same but without the badge worn above right breast pocket. They had their own special "national" brassard and their own version of the cap diamond. HJ boys wore *Flieger-HJ* shoulder straps (black piped in light blue) as did the non-Germans.

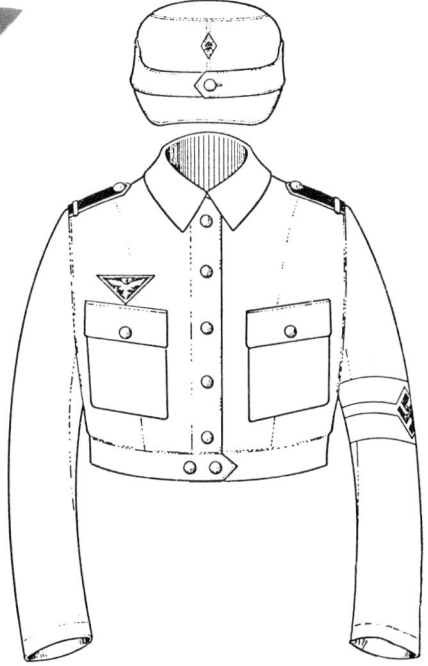

ANDREW MOLLO

A group of young HJ Flak helpers greeted by a Luftwaffe NCO. They wear the special, and unique, greatcoat. This is in Luftwaffe blue, but unlike the Luftwaffe type, it has breast pockets. The shoulder straps are black Hitler Youth type, piped with light blue.

A new design of greatcoat for the Flak Helpers was introduced in the winter of 1943-1944. This was in the Luftwaffe style but was unusual in having two breast pockets. Interestingly the forage cap worn with this winter outfit had, on the front the Luftwaffe flying eagle above the national cockade, and not the HJ diamond.

By the middle of 1943 there were some 100,000 young Germans in the Flak Helper organization, but the demands of the Reich Air Defence were insatiable. In March 1944 Göring, as head of the Luftwaffe, and Axmann, as Hitler Youth leader, approached Alfred Rosenberg, chief of the Eastern Ministry, with a request that the youth of the occupied eastern territories should also be enrolled as Flak Helpers. This would apply, as in the Reich to boys and girls from their fifteenth birthday until they were old enough to be drafted into their respective ethnic "legions." Since these legions were now under the control of the SS, this brought a third party into the transaction. Whereas the German Flak Helpers were run by the Luftwaffe and the Hitler Youth, the new auxiliaries were to be the combined responsibility of the Luftwaffe, the Hitler Youth *and* the SS. In practice it was the Hitler Youth that was the prime mover. There already existed within the Eastern Ministry an *Abteilung Jugend* (Youth Department). This Department (formed in May 1942) had offices in the *Ostland* (Estonia, Latvia, Lithuania and Belorussia) as well as the Ukraine. In all these regions except Lithuanian, youth organizations had been set up. The task of drawing them together within the framework of the Flak Helper organization was entrusted to an HJ leader, Siegfried Nickel currently serving as an officer in the army. Nickel was released from military duty and ordered

Hitler Youth boy decorated with the Iron Cross, 2nd Class for bravery during an air raid. He wears the normal HJ winter uniform (as used before the special Flak Helper uniform was issued).

Service certificate of a Flak Helper. It reads: Hitler Youth Günther Bürgel, born 28-8-27 served in the Luftwaffe between 2-4-43 and 5-10-44 as a Luftwaffe Auxiliary. On the occasion of his discharge [we] herewith extend [our] thanks and appreciation for his valuable auxiliary war service to the fatherland during the years of his youth. Signed by the Battery Commander.

to set up a new department which took his name — *Dienststelle Hauptbannführer Nickel.* This drew its personnel from the Eastern Ministry, the Waffen-SS and the Luftwaffe as well as, of course, the Hilter Youth. Nickel divided his bailiwick into five *HJ Kriegseinsatzkommandos* (HJ War Action Commandos or KEKs). They comprised:

  (i) KEK Nord (North): Estonia, Latvia and Lithuania;
  (ii) KEK Mitte (Centre): Belorussia;
  (iii) KEK Süd (South) Galicia, Slovakia and Hungary;
  (iv) KEK Adria (Adriatic): Serbia and Croatia;
  (v) KEK West: France, Belgium and Holland.

However, by the time Nickel had assumed command, the allies had liberated much of KEK West. When voluntary enlistment failed to furnish sufficient numbers, compulsion was applied. This often involved the wholesale incorporation of existing youth organizations. By these methods Nickel was able between June and September 1944 to raise the following numbers:

1,383 Greater Russians
5,933 Ukrainians
2,354 Belorussians
1,012 Lithuanians
3,000 Estonians
3,614 Latvians

"Youth in total war": a poster depicting the work of the Luftwaffe Auxiliaries of the HJ. The message, signed by Reichs Youth Leader Axmann, repeats the H.J.'s slogan for 1943 "War action of the Hitler Youth" and calls for those in areas under threat of air raids to join the Heimat Flak. It ends with an exhortation to show "the spirit of the Heroes of Stalingrad" and give one's all for Führer and Victory. The boy on right is shown as wearing the War Merit Cross 2nd Class.

The term *SS-Helfer* was first applied to them, later *Luftwaffen-Helfer* and finally *SS-Luftwaffen-Helfer*. Like their German counterparts, they were required to serve in any branch of the Luftwaffe. Of the above 18,917 young people, around 2,500 were girls. From the Estonians, 346 were later transferred to the German Navy as *Marinehelfer*.

Service in the Flak batteries was fully combatant: Forty-one of the foreign Flak helpers were killed in action and two were awarded the Iron Cross 2nd Class (these figures are from official report dated October 9, 1944).

Whereas the German Flak Helpers were issued with two uniforms (one working, the other "walking out" dress), the foreigners were given only one and, due to war-time shortages, even this was by no means standard — in some cases even ex-Italian army uniforms were issued. The foreigners were supposed to wear a "national" brassard on the left upper arm and a special "national" cap diamond. There were eight versions of these: (i) Latvian, (ii) Estonian, (iii) Lithuanian, (iv) Belorussian, (v) Greater Russian, (vi) Galizian, (vii) Ukranian, (viii) Tartar. Above the brassard the SS runes on a black triangle were also supposed to be worn. In practice the brassards were often discarded (and in some cases replaced by a national arm shield) while the SS triangle was issued to only a few foreigners. The Estonians, for example, never received it although the Greater Russians (and some others) certainly did. It is not clear if this omission was simply due to a shortage of supplies or whether it was a matter of policy.

Estonian boy as a Flak Helper. He wears (unofficially) the Luftwaffe eagle above the right breast pocket. His cap badge is the Estonian arms. Shoulder straps are black with light blue (*Flieger-HJ*) piping.

267

An indication of the very mixed nature of the personnel who manned the Flak defenses of the Reich may be gained from a study of the composition of the 14th Flak Division of the Luftwaffe which was responsible for the protection of southern Germany including several important oil refineries. It was as follows:

| | |
|---|---:|
| Regular Luftwaffe personnel | 28,000 |
| RAD (Labour Service) conscripts | 18,000 |
| "Flak helpers" (male) | 6,000 |
| "Flak helpers" (female) | 3,050 |
| Hungarian and Italian volunteers | 900 |
| Russian "Hiwis" (POW auxiliaries) | 3,600 |
| Others | 3,000 |
| Total | 62,550 |

From the above it is clear that more than half the personnel who served in these units were non-regulars, thus relieving the Luftwaffe of a very considerable burden.

Service in the Flak Helpers commenced with a four-week training period under the supervision of Luftwaffe NCOs. The boys were paid — at a rate 50 pfennig a day (just half of a soldier's pay at this time). They were entitled to the same amounts of leave as the adult servicemen and could, after nine months, be promoted to *Oberhelfer\** with a corresponding increase in pay. To offset these benefits, however, they were subject to military discipline and could be given up to ten days "confined to quarters" as a punishment.

Estonian Flak Helpers on leave in Copenhagen in 1945. Note that these boys do not have either the Luftwaffe eagle nor the HJ Flak Helper badge above right breast pocket. Belt buckle are Luftwaffe type. Boy, third left, wears a normal Luftwaffe greatcoat (not the unique HJ version) and on it (unofficially) an Estonian arm shield.

---

\* Indicated by a silver "bar" on the shoulder strap.

Latvian Flak Helper. He wears (unofficially) the Luftwaffe eagle above the right breast pocket. The badge on his left breast pocket is not the HJ diamond, but the badge of the Latvian Youth Organization. His cap badge is the Latvian army "sun burst" type.

Latvia
(red field, white stripe charged with gold,
black and red emblem)

Cap badge
(red and gold)

Estonia
(blue, black and white brassard)

Cap badge

Lithuania
(yellow, green and orange brassard)

Cap badge

White Russia
(white and red brassard)

Cap badge

Greater Russia
(white, blue, and red field)

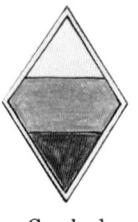

Cap badge

270

Volga Tartars (green and blue field)

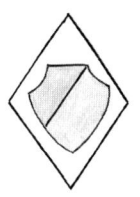

Cap badge

Ukraine (yellow and blue brassard)

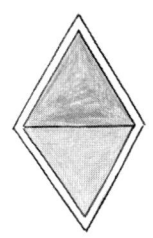

Cap badge

Galicia (yellow and blue brassard)

Cap badge

Above: S.S. runes supposed to be worn by all non-German Flak Helpers, but in fact, worn only by a minority.

Young Russian Flak helpers. Above the Russian brassard they have the S.S. runes on a black triangle.

Russian girl Flak helpers did not wear a brassard, only a diamond shaped arm badge which is a St. Andrew's cross upon a background of the old Imperial Russian colours.

## KLV (CHILDREN EVACUATION SCHEME)

Just as "evacuees" were a feature of war-time Britain, so Germany had its *Kinderlandverschickung* (literally Children-Land-Withdrawal), or KLV. Originally conceived before the war, as a means of providing under-privileged city families with a state financed holiday in the country, it was, after September 1939, adapted to take families away from those frontier regions of the Reich which might become war zones. The victories of the following year removed this possibility, and it was not until two years later, when the allied bombing had become a serious problem, that the KLV project turned into a large scale operation.

Many of the locations chosen as evacuations centres were outside Germany — Austria being particularly popular in this respect. Ironically the Warthegau and the "General Government" of Poland were also rated as "safe" areas, that is to say, until they were over-run by the Red Army.

KLV emblem

War-time poster: "Districts threatened by air attack are no place for children. Come along with [us] to the KLV camp of the Hitler Youth" (rough translation).

A teacher at a KLV camp (note his cuff-title) talks to a BDM (or JM) girl.

KLV cuff-title (white letters on black).

Lapel badge of the NSLB (Nat. Soc. Teachers League).

Country hotels, youth hostels, convalescent homes and sanitoriums were requisitioned, as well as some of the NSDAP's own properties such as the *Ordensburg* at Krössinsee and the NSFK Gliding School at Zell-am-Zee.

Girls from the KLV camp at Sellin a. Rügen wear a mixture of uniform and peasant dress. Girl on right wears a BDM tunic with *Nord Nordmark* district triangle, Medical Orderly "life rune" and a cuff-title with name of camp (this latter looks rather "home-made").

A National KLV Leaders School (*Reichsführerschule KLV*) was established at Steinau in Lower Silesia and a corresponding Girl Camp Leaders School opened in Saxony.

Although the evacuation programme was entirely voluntary, more than a million children (the youngest accompanied by their parents) were, before the end of the war, removed from threatened areas. For those of school age, education continued under the joint aegis of the Hitler Youth and the Nazi-dominated *NS Lehrerbund* (Nat. Soc. Teachers League). Each unit was intended to comprise some forty to fifty young persons. In charge was a Camp Leader (*Lagerleiter*), hopefully an HJ officer, although in practice it proved impossible to find sufficient numbers of these. Under the *Lagerleiter* was a *Lagermannschaftsführer* (Camp Leader for Males) and a *Lagermädelführerin* (Camp Leader for Girls). There was also an Administrative Officer (*Verwaltungsführer*) and a Catering Officer (*Ernährungsleiter*). Following the well-established HJ principle that "youth must be led by youth," the older children acted as monitors, leaders and even teachers. Since almost all the pupils were enrolled in the HJ, BDM, or DJ, the camps were run more like junior military academies than schools. Even the adult teachers wore uniform (dark blue short tunic and trousers and the by now almost universal ski-cap headgear).

The controlling authority was the Inspectorate of the *NS Lehrerbund*. A *Hauptlagerleiter* was in charge of each group of camps and was directly responsible to the *NS Lehrerbund* Inspector.

The KLV programme gave full play to that celebrated German genius for organization, and it proved so successful that the concept was extended, again on a purely voluntary basis, the children from the occupied countries of the west now endangered by air attack. The majority of these came from Flanders and Holland. They had their own "national" camps with their own leaders (naturally enough these were almost exclusively from the pre-Nazi youth movements of their respective homelands).

When Axmann claimed that the children in the KLV camps were 20% better fed and in better health than those in the cities he was probably speaking the truth. Many of the rural areas in which the camps were located were virtually unaffected by the war, and since accommodation was often in pre-war holiday, recreational or health centres, conditions must have seemed idyllic compared with those in the bomb-devastated cities. Being in the countryside had, from the German war economy point of view, an added advantage. It meant that in summer and autumn the children were immediately at hand to assist with the harvest.

To the Nazis the separation of children from the possibly restraining influence of their parents furnished a unique opportunity for political indoctrination which the Hitler Youth element in the camp leadership was supposed to provide. Thus scholastic, and national-socialist, education were to be made one.

# Miscellaneous Facts and Figures

HJ CALENDAR OF MAJOR EVENTS

January 24: Death of Herbert Norkus (the HJ's own special martyr, killed in 1923 aged fifteen, also the birthday of Frederick the Great of Prussia)
January 30: Anniversary of the "Seizure of Power" by the Nazis in 1933;
April 20: The Führer's birthday. Observed by the induction of 10 year olds into the HJ or JM;
May 1: Labour Day;
May 26: Death of Albert Leo Schlageter;
June 21: Summer Solstice (*Sommersonnenwende*);
September (variable dates): Annual Party rally at Nürnberg;
November 9: Anniversary of the Munich Putsch of 1923 when twenty-three Nazis were killed;
December 25: Yule Tide Feast (*Julfest*), the name the Nazis substituted for Christmas (*Weihnacht*).

ANNUAL SLOGANS OF THE HJ

From 1934 onward an annual slogan was coined by the RJF to indicate what aspect of HJ activity was to be stressed in the coming twelve months. There were also, in some instances, additional slogans (where these existed they are also included):

1934: *Jahr der Schulung* (Year of Training), also "Fighting Waste";
1935: *Jahr der Ertüchtigung* (Year of Toughening up);
1936: *Jahr des Deutschen Jungvolks* (Year of the DJ);
1937: *Jahr der Heimbeschaftung* (Year of Hostel Building);
1938: *Jahr der Verständigung* (Year of Getting Acquainted). also "Every Youth a Flier";
1939: *Jahr der Gesundheitspflicht* (Year of Health Care);
1940: *Jahr der Bewährung* (Year of Testing, or Year of Trial);
1941: *Unser Leben: ein Weg zum Führer* (Our life: a Road to Führer);
1942: *Osteinsatz und Landdienst* (Service in the East and on the Land);
1943: *Kriegseinsatz der deutschen Jugend* (War Service of the German Youth);
1944: *Jahr der Kriegsfreiwilligen* (Year of the War Volunteers).

## "HONOUR NAMES" FOR HJ BANNE

In April 1934 certain HJ *Banne* (also DJ *Jungbanne* and BDM/JM *Untergaue*) were granted individual "honour names" (*Ehrennamen*). Initially these were the names of comrades who had been killed during the *Kampfzeit*, but later names of distinguished persons from German, or NSDAP, history were allowed, and latterly even place names. These names featured on the letterheads, office plates (*Dienststellenschilder*), official rubber stamps and flag of the *Bann* (*Jungbann* etc.) so honoured.

The most celebrated martyr of the Hitler Youth, Herbert Norkus gave his name to *Bann* 201 (Berlin-Moabit). At the same time four other Berlin *Banne* received the names of fallen HJ boys. In September 1938 *Bann* 540 of *Gebiet Oberdonau* was granted the "honour name" *Bann Braunau Inn*. It is hard to imagine that this honour was unconnected with the fact that Braunau on the River Inn (Austria) was the birthplace of Adolf Hitler!

In the SA, units honoured with names were permitted to wear the name on a cuff title. This was not, however, allowed in the Hitler Youth. Any names which had been unofficially adopted by units which existed prior to January 1933 were expressly forbidden.

The name of the BDM's only martyr, Erika Jordan, was not accorded to a BDM unit. It was, however, given to the BDM Leader's School (*Führerinnenschule*) in Berlin.

## MEMBERSHIP FIGURES

| | |
|---|---:|
| End of 1929 | Less than 13,000 |
| January 1931 | 13,806 |
| April 1932 | 15,373 |
| July 1931 | 17,902 |
| November 1932 | 28,743 |
| January 1932 | 37,304 |
| June 1932 | 48,000 |
| January 30, 1933 | 55,365 |

The above figures are quoted in the book, *Das kommende Deutschland*, published in Berlin in 1940 and related to the HJ only. They do not include the BDM, DJ or JM.

The following figures, however, cover all four sections of the Hitler Youth:

| | |
|---|---:|
| End of 1933 | 7,524,000 |
| End of 1934 | 7,682,000 |
| End of 1935 | 8,172,000 |
| End of 1936 | 8,656,000 |
| End of 1937 | 9,060,000 |
| End of 1938 | 9,109,000 |
| End of 1939 | 8,870,000 |

The decline in numbers for the end of 1939 was due to the loss to the armed forces in large numbers of adult male leaders.

# HJ CASUALTIES DURING THE KAMPFZEIT

During the "year of struggle" (*Kampfzeit*), and even for some months *after* Hitler's accession to power in January 1933, the HJ suffered casualties. Twenty-two of these were fatal. They included one BDM girl.

The dead are listed below with their ages. The youngest, Josef Grün, was a twelve-year-old DJ boy; most were in their late teens; twenty-five-year-old Thewellis was a *Scharführer*, and nineteen-year-old Karl Thomas, the last to die, was an *Unterbannführer*, but the majority were mere *Hitlerjunge* or *Kamaradschaftsführer*.

It is impossible to estimate the number of those wounded or seriously injured. Most fatalities occurred in Berlin, and the worst month for deaths was October 1932, the date of the great HJ rally at Potsdam.

Of all the fallen, the most celebrated was certainly Herbert Norkus, projected by the RJF as the Horst Wessel of the Hitler Youth. Perhaps it was because the fifteen-year-old Norkus was, up to that time, the youngest HJ boy to be killed, or perhaps it was on account of the particularly horrific circumstances of his death that he was chosen for elevation to official martyrdom.

The son of an SA man, Herbert Norkus lived with his father in the notoriously pro-Communist Wedding district of Berlin, which had, two years previously, been the scene of the murder of the SA leader Horst Wessel. In the early hours of January 24, 1932 the fifteen-year-old boy set out with a small troop of fellow HJ lads to post bills announcing a forthcoming NSDAP meeting, at which some prominent HJ leaders were to speak. They had not gone far before they were set upon by a squad of *Rote Jungsturm* (their Communist counterpart). The would-be bill posters fled in disarray; only Norkus was unfortunate enough to be caught. He was stabbed twice and staggered to a nearby house to seek help, but the householder slammed the door in his face. His assailants once again fell upon him with their knives and, hideously mutilated, he was dragged into the passageway of an adjoining house and left to die. Some years later Dr. Goebbles was to canonize him in a semi-fictional film biography in which an idealized Norkus appeared as "Hitlerjunge Quex."

It was perhaps fortunate from the Nazi point of view, that January 24th, the date of Norkus' death, was also that of the birth of Frederick the Great. Thus a national patriotic occasion was capitalized on to create a Nazi memorial day.

| *Name* | *Age* | *Date of Death* |
| --- | --- | --- |
| Fritz Kröber | 17 | April 26, 1925 |
| Hans Queitsch | 16 | June 20, 1927 |
| Paul Thewellis | 25 | January 23, 1931 |
| Rudolf Schröter | 17 | February 12, 1931 |
| Gerhard Liebsch | 17 | May 26, 1931 |
| Hans Hoffmann | 17 | August 17, 1931 |
| Hans Mallon | 17 | September 3, 1931 |
| Gerhard Wittemburg | 18 | September 17, 1931 |

| | | |
|---|---|---|
| Herbert Norkus | 15 | January 24, 1932 |
| Georg Preiser | 18 | February 7, 1932 |
| Herbert Howarde | 18 | June 20, 1932 |
| Werner Gerhardt | 19 | June 30, 1932 |
| Erich Niejahr | 15 | October 5, 1932 |
| Josef Grün | 12 | October 26, 1932 |
| Erika Jordan (BDM) | 17 | October 28, 1932 |
| Walter Wagnitz | 16 | January 1, 1933 |
| Otto Blöcker | 17 | February 26, 1933 |
| Christian Grössmann | 18 | February 26, 1933 |
| Josef Neumeier | 18 | March 16, 1933 |
| Peter Friess | 16 | March 17, 1933 |
| Otto Schmelzer | 18 | April 4, 1933 |
| Karl Thomas | 19 | August 31, 1933 |

# Documents and Posters

Service book of the Hitler Youth, 1934.

Membership "paybook" of a Hitler Youth.

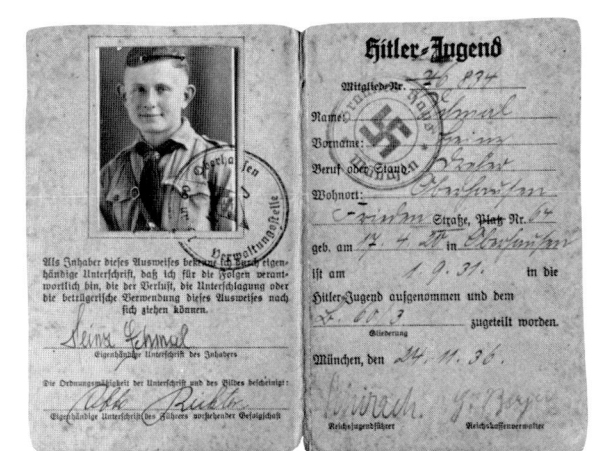

Inside of membership "paybook" of a Hitler Youth with I.D. photo.

281

Enlistment certificate (*Urkunde*) of a Hitler Youth. It reads: ... (name not filled in) "was on 20th April 1941, the birthday of the Führer, enrolled in the Hitler Youth:
Below this is a facsimile of Axmann's signature.

Another example of an enlistment certificate. In this case it reads: "I promise that in the Hitler Youth I shall do my full duty in love and loyalty to Führer and flag. Ferdinand Rath was this day admitted into the Hitler Youth and dedicated himself to the Führer. On Youth Dedication Day, 22nd March 1942."

Cover of one of the (several) songbooks of the HJ "For us the sun does not set" (rough translation of its title).

"The big book for young lads." A 1930's publication. Gives a good impression of the colour and style of HJ uniform at that time (probably 1934).

Poster advertising the work of the Greater Germany Winter Help campaign of 1939/40.

A sticker for Winter Help campaign of 24th October 1936 in Gau Hesse-Nassau. "Jungvolk collect bread" (at bottom) and around the D.J. rune "The youngest of our people help out."

# 29

# *Youth Resistance and Punishment*

Compulsory HJ service had, in theory, existed since the publication of the German Youth Law on December 1, 1936, but in practice its enforcement had been delayed until at least April 1938. Thereafter a distinction was drawn between the *Stamm* (core of volunteers) of the HJ and its *Allgemeine* (General) or *Pflicht* (duty) component.*** Even at this stage coercion to join was neither universal, nor rigourously applied. Only with the coming of war and the obligation upon the entire youth of Germany to *"serve Führer and Fatherland"* was it strictly enforced.

Conscription greatly increased the size of the HJ. It also exacerbated its problems of discipline. Unwilling or bored youngsters under the tutelage of inexperienced or very young leaders (the bulk of the *Führerschaft* having been called away to the forces) were less amenable to the idea of dedicating all their leisure hours to the Hitler Youth. Many tried to dodge parades and avoid irksome duties, while others dressed slovenly in uniform. Formerly the worst punishment that the HJ could inflict had been dishonourable discharge, somewhat more severe than it might sound as a bad record in the HJ could close the door to many future job prospects and bar one completely from state employment. Since the prospect of being excluded from service in the HJ hardly acted as a deterrent to those who had in any case no wish to belong to its ranks, it became necessary to introduce more effective measures. In September 1940 the concept of *Jugenddienstarrest* (Youth Service Arrest) allowed the police to seize any boy over the age of fourteen deemed guilty of ". . . especially severe infringements of discipline. . . ." and incarcerate him from one to three weekends (Saturday to Sunday) or, in more extreme cases, imprison him for up to eight consecutive days, during which time he was kept in solitary confinement on a bread-and-water diet.

Much stricter measures, however, were to follow. Special *Jugenderziehungslager* (Youth Education Camps) or, as they were later termed, *Jugendschutzlager* (Youth Protection Camps — in the sense here of "protective custody") were established in which those held to be incorrigible were lodged. The first of these, at Moringen in South Hano-

---

*** The physical and racial requirements of the latter were less stringent than those of the *Stamm HJ*. For example, it was possible for a boy with one Jewish grandparent to belong to the *Allgemeine-HJ*.

ver was run jointly by the SS and Hitler Youth. By 1942 it had 489 inmates. Prisoners were subjected to harsh discipline which could include up to fifteen strokes of the lash for acts of disobedience. The very existence of these camps had a sobering effect on would-be miscreants. Vague threats that "... you too could end up in one of these places if you don't mend your ways. . . ." was often sufficient to bring recalcitrant lads back into line!

Another, more subtle, way of ensuring attendance at HJ functions was the creation in 1943 of a new form of membership card, which had to be stamped every month. Food rations could be withheld from those whose cards did not contain the requisite number of stamps. The powers of the HJ *Streifendienst* were widened. They were now authorized to arrest in the street any youth whom they even suspected of evading his HJ obligations.

When the allied bombing offensive began to bring home the reality of war to the civilian population there was a marked dichotomy in the reaction of the younger generation. Most young people threw themselves into the struggle with dedication and courage, a minority of others opted out both practically and emotionally. A new phenomena now appeared in German cities. Gangs of youths garbed in deliberately provocative clothing — checked cowboy shirts or white polo-neck sweaters — affected Americanized nicknames like "Texas Jack," "Alaska Joe" or "Whiskey Bill" lounged about in cafés smoking, a disapproved activity in the HJ, listening to swing, or worse, jazz (castigated by the Nazis as "nigger music"). They jeered or insulted boys and girls in uniform. Such activities were not, on the whole, politically motivated. It was more usually the result of that not unfamiliar desire on the part of youth to flout convention.

There were, on the other hand, some who elected to follow the perilous path of active resistance. The story of one of these bodies of courageous youngster, the "White Rose" group at Munich University (Hans and Sophie Scholl, Christoph Probst and others) is perhaps the best known, but it is not unique. Others, too, when caught or betrayed, also faced the hangman. The Nazis had been so successful in equating their cause with that of German patriotism that any who resisted them were regarded as having betrayed their Fatherland and not worthy of mercy. The heroism of those who, for reasons of conscience, did resist is beyond praise, but it has to be said that they were a small minority. German youth as a whole remained loyal, however mistakenly, to the end; even to the point of sacrificing their lives in the futile defiance of the last days of Hitler's Reich.

# Unidentified or Partially Identified Items

(a) Black cuff-title with white lettering "Kriegseinsatzführer" (War action(s) Leader). There is no question that this *is* an HJ item since it was removed from an HJ tunic at the end of the war. The tunic was complete with "District triangle" and brassard, but the shoulder straps were missing so that the rank of the former wearer remains unknown. However, one may speculate that he was an officer presumably entrusted with the duty of organizing war service on the part of the youths under his charge. The motto for the year 1943 was *Kriegseinsatz der HJ*, and this item may well date from that year. Its width is 28mm and its length 185mm. In common with other HJ cuff-titles this is not intended to encircle the entire cuff but is cut short so as to be worn on the front only.

(b) Red Radio Telegraphist's badge with three red chevrons and red surround. There can be little doubt that this is for the *Marine-HJ*, although the published regulations show only a single chevron below the anchor. However, since one, two and three chevrons were used in relation to the three grades of the Sea Sport badge it may be assumed that this type of grading applied to this badge also and denotes the most advanced grade of *Marine-HJ* radio telegraphist.

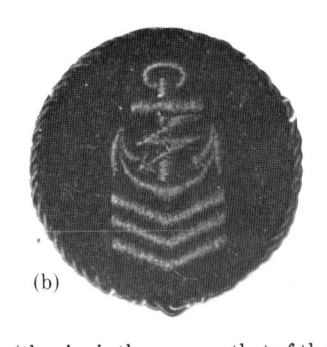

(b)

(c) Blue enamel rhombus (the size is the same as that of the normal HJ enamel badge). This has white or silver borders, segments and central square, upon which is a black swastika. An example of this badge in a private collection in Germany is marked on the reverse RZM M 1/72. The presence of the RZM *imprimateur* precludes the possibility of this being an unofficial or "early days" version of the well-known HJ emblem. It is possible that this was a trial piece never actualy adopted for use (this is not uncommon in the case of medals and badges). The use of blue rather than the more "masculine" colours, red and white, might indicate that it was intended for some female organization.

(d) Silver *Sigrune* in diamond. There is an understandable tendency to assume that anything with a *Sigrune* or a swastika *must* be Nazi. This is not the case. The *Sigrune* badge was also used by the Wolf Cubs (*Wolflinge*) of the pre-1933 German Boy Scouts (*Pfadfinderbund*) and there is a distinct possibility that the badge, often ascribed to the DJ, is, in fact, a Wolf Cub emblem.

(c)

(d)

287

(e)

(f)

WIM SARIS

(e) Black circle with white crotchet to which is attached a black flag with a red *Sigrune* on a circular white background. This was removed from a DJ shirt and would seem to indicate a DJ musician, but no documentation has been found for it (Source: Forman of Piccadilly sale catalogue).

(f) HJ diamond badge in cloth but with black replacing the normally red segments. This is sometimes attributed as "former Members of the HJ serving in the SS." This is certainly not correct. It is more likely to have been for SS personnel acting as liaison with the RJF or, alternatively, as instructors with the *HJ Streifendienst* which was under the aegis of the SS. In either case, it is really an SS, not an HJ item. The above illustration is of a cotton version of this badge, but it also exists in an aluminum wire type (presumably an officer's version).

# 31

# *The Swastika Abroad*

In this section an attempt has been made to summarize the work of the Hitler Youth among German and *Volksdeutsche* groups outside the Greater German Reich. It also deals briefly with the pro-Nazi or fascist-orientated youth movement of German-occupied Europe, many of which during the war actively cooperated with the Hitler Youth, or were trained by it.

It was an article of faith among all Nazi believers that persons of German descent, irrespective of what part of the globe they inhabited, belonged spiritually to the German Reich. To carry the work to these disparate communities, the NSDAP set up, as early as May 1931, an *Ausland Organisation.* This "Foreign Organisation," which until 1937 was quite independent of the German Foreign Ministry, catered to the interests of Reich German citizens resident abroad. Racial Germans, the so-called *Volksdeutsche,* who were, willingly or otherwise, citizens of other countries were the concern of the Nazi VDA (*Volksbund,* or *Verein für das Deutschtum in Ausland* roughly, Union of Germans in Foreign Lands). Later the SS tried (successfully) to assume control of the *Volksdeutsche.*

The Hitler Youth established its own *Gebiet Ausland,* which maintained contacts with groups in fifty-two countries. German racial communities were particularly numerous in South America and in the erstwhile German colonial empire. These domains forfeited after the First World War German East Africa, German Southwest Africa, Toga, the Cameras, German New Guinea, Samoa and Kiatchou (China). In Europe Germany had to surrender to France Alasce and Lorraine, North Schleswig to Denmark and Eupen-Malmedy to Belgium, as well as having part of East Prussia transformed into the "Polish Corridor" to the sea with the consequent isolation of Danzig (which city and surrounding area was placed under the ambiguous protection of the League of Nations).

The collapse of the Austro-Hungarian empire also meant that large German-speaking minorities were left in new countries brought into being by the Treaties of Versailles and the Trianon.

AUSTRIA
(to March 1938)
Even before 1914 there had been within the Austro-Hungarian empire a strong pan-German sentiment. With defeat in 1918 the multi-national empire disintegrated. Its ethnic components either adhered to other racially-allied countries or formed new nation states of their own, such as Czechoslovakia or Yugoslavia. Austria was now only a rump of largely, although not entirely, German-speaking people. The logic of pan-Germanism — union with her powerful northern neighbour — became more compelling. When coupled with the later financial ruin and social disruption of the Depression, it became yet more forceful. Pan-Germanism did not necessarily imply pro-Nazism, but Hitler's rise to power had, inevitably, strong repercussions in Austria.

Bavaria, that spawning ground of National Socialism, was only, figuratively speaking, "across the street" from Austria. Hitler himself was a former Austrian citizen. If the Nazi leader could banish disorder from the streets, rebuild industry, conquer unemployment and restore national self-confidence in Germany, might he not, it was argued, be able to do the same in Austria? Austrian cultural and intellectual life was permeated with Jewish influence — fertile ground for the growth of National Socialism.

A German National Socialist Workers Party (DNSAP) had been formed in Austria as early as 1919. It is interesting to note that Hitler's party had, as its title, merely a slight rearrangement of the words — the National Socialist German Workers Party (NSDAP).

In 1923 a *Nat.-Soz. Arbeiterjugend* (Nat.-Socialist Worker Youth) was formed in Vienna by Theo West. When Germany's Nazi youth took the name *Hitlerjugend*, West changed the name of his group to *Hitlerjugend Verband Nat.-Soz. Jungarbeiter* (Hitler Youth Association of National Socialist Young Workers).

At the first mass rally of the NSDAP at Nürnberg in 1929 some half of the 2,000 youths who participated came from Austria. In 1931 the Austrian police estimated that there were about 15,000 registered members of the Nazi Party in Austria, of whom around 3,000 were in the Hitler Youth.

Austria Nazism was, however, beset by internal feuding. In addition to the "official" Nazi Party, the appointment of whose *Landesleiter* was, from 1926 onward, in the hands of the NSDAP Headquarters in Munich, there was also a rival Hitler Party (*Hitler Bewegung*, or *HB*) under the leadership of Karl Schulz. In 1927 the HJ formed its own *Hitlerjugend* for boys between eight and twenty years of age, and its own BDM for girls between twelve and twenty-four. Even after the HB faded from the scene (around 1930) its youth groups continued to maintain contact with the opposite numbers in Germany.

In May 1931 the RJF officially inaugurated an *HJ Gruppe Oesterreich* (HJ Group "Austria"), whose members were entitled to wear the same uniform as their counterparts in the Reich.

After Hitler's accession to power in January 1933 agitation for union with Germany increased. There were violent clashes between pro- and anti-Nazis with the result that in June of that year the Austrian authorities outlawed the NSDAP and with it the Hitler Youth. The NSDAP in Austria disappeared from public view only to re-emerge (as so frequently happened with similar bans in other states) under a different guise, or variety of guises. Among them the most significant were:

*Deutsche Tunerbund* (1919) — German Gymnastic Association;

*Deutsche Schulverein Südmark* — German School Association Südmark;

*Deutsch-Oesterreichische Volksbund* — German-Austrian Peoples Union.

Even such innocuous-sounding bodies as the German-Austrian Alpine Association (DOeAV), with headquarters in Munich, were often merely covers for pro-Nazi operations.

Even before the ban the *Deutsche Tunerbund* had acted as a rallying point for advocated of pan-Germanism, although not all of these were votaries of Adolf Hitler. There was a wide-spread delusion among Austrians that union *with* Germany need not mean subservience *to* Germany; that Austria would enjoy the status of an equal partner, free to choose its own form of government — a sort of "union of the crowns" without a "union of the parliaments" (if one may draw a parallel with Anglo-Scottish history). It was, needless to say, a fantasy.

In a misguided attempt to counteract foreign (i.e. German) fascism, the Austrian authorities set up their own band of native Austrian fascism. A "Fatherland Front" was formed in 1935 with its *Frontmiliz* ("Front Militia") and its *Sturmkorps* (somewhat akin to the Nazi Storm Troopers). In place of the *Hackenkreuz* (swastika) the Fatherland Front adopted the so-called *Kruchenkreuz* (literally "crotchet cross"). In the Front's youth section, the *Oesterreichisches Jungvolk* (Austrian Young Folk), the now banned Hitler Youth simply formed its own secret cells.

As has already been remarked in the history of the DJ, an Austrian *Deutsches Jungvolk* had existed even before the First World War. In 1930 this had allied itself to Kurt Gruber's *Deutsche Jugendschaft* and its flag, a silver *Sigrune* on black, had been adopted as the official emblem of the German DJ.

The so-called *Kruckenkreuz* of the Austrian "Fatherland Front."

Lapel badge of the Deutsche Turnerbund (1919).

Ski award badge of the DOe.AV(*Deutscher und Oesterreichscher Alpineverein* German and Austrian Alpine Association). It is silvered metal with the HJ badge in coloured enamel at the base. "Vonier Christian" is (presumably) the name of the recipient.
(Drawn from an example in the Maitland-Titterton Collection)

Badge of 2nd Rally of the Deutsche Turnerbund Salzburg 1931. Motto at top reads "All Germany shall be one."

[Right:] Another DT rally badge. This is for "2nd Gau Youth Rally at Langenzersdorf (outside Vienna) on 22nd and 23rd May 1926." The large eagle (Germany ?) hands in the eaglet (Austria ?) the DT emblem.

The governmental proscription on the Hitler Youth in Austria did nothing to curb its activities. When uniform was forbidden, the boys adopted white shirts, black shorts and white stockings as a sort of "civilian uniform" (a practice copied by other outlawed Nazi groups outside the Reich). If anything the edict served only to stimulate pro-Hitler activity among the young by giving it the additional glamour of the forbidden. By the time of the *Anschluss* there were some 38,000 "illegal" HJ members throughout Austria.

There can be little doubt that when Hitler took over Austria in March 1938 he did so amid widespread popular approval in both countries. Any illusion that Austria would be permitted equal status within the new Greater Germany (*Grossdeutschland*) was quickly dispelled. The Austria (*Oesterreich*) was replaced by the former Carolingian appellation *Ostmark* (eastern mark or region). Upper and Lower Austria became Upper and Lower Danube (*Oberdonau* and *Niederdonau*). By 1942 even *Ostmark* had too separatist a ring to please Hitler, and the country became simply the Alpine and the Danube *Reichsgaue*. Vienna was made a *Reichsgau* in its own right.

Naturally after the *Anschluss* of March 1938 the HJ, and all other previously banned Nazi organizations, went back into uniform. The only differentiation allowed the Austrian (or *Ostmark* HJ) was the retention of an Edelweiss emblem on the left collar. Otherwise uniform was standard German.

The HJ authorities in Germany did not, of course, "recognize" the ban on its united within "German-Austria" (*Deutsch-Oesterreich*) which region it designated *HJ Gebiet 22*.

Shoulder strap of a Hitlerjunge of Oberbann 2, Bann Oe 7 (Carinthia-East Tirol). The piping and numerals are yellow since yellow was the colour of Oberbann 2.

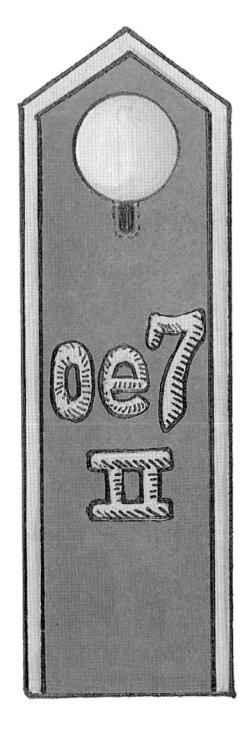

This independent *Gebiet* was subdivided as follows:

Oberbann 1
    Bann Oe 1 (Tirol-Vorarlberg);
    Bann Oe 14 (Upper Austria);
    Bann Oe 59 (Salzburg).
Oberbann 2
    Bann Oe 3 (West Styria);
    Bann Oe 7 (Carinthia-East Tirol);
    Bann Oe 27 (East Styria).
Oberbann 3
    Bann Oe 4 (Vienna, or *Wien*);
    Bann Oe 49 (Waldvierteil);
    Bann Oe 84 (Danauwacht).

Although the wearing of HJ uniform was, by law, forbidden in Austria, the HJ in Munich authorized the use of *Oe* (*Oesterreich*) on the shoulder strap followed by the Bann number with the Oberbann Roman numeral below. The colour of these and the piping around the strap was governed by the then-existing regulations relating to the use of Oberbann colours by the German-based HJ and DJ.

## BELGIUM

Two distinct racial groups made up modern Belgium: the French-speaking Walloons and the Dutch-speaking[†] Flemings, a Germanic people. The only strong nexus is their common religious faith — Roman Catholicism.

(a) Flanders

From the very start of the occupation in May 1940 the Germans attempted to exploit the differences between the two communities to their own advantage. They played upon the justified grievances of the Flemings who had long been treated as second-class citizens within their own country, even though they formed rather more than half of its total population. This resentment had, in the inter-war years, caused some sections of the Flemish community to demand the creation of a separate Flemish state, or more ambitiously, a wider *dietsche* ("Netherlandish") state, embracing Flemish Belgium *and* Holland.

The most prominent advocate of the latter solution was a lawyer and former army officer (cashiered for his nationalist agitation), Joris van Severen who, in October 1931 founded the *Verbond van Dietsche Nationaal-Solidaristen*, a cumbersome title usually abbreviated to *Verdinaso* or simply *Dinaso*. The Party had its green-shirted storm troop and its youthful *Verbond van Jongdinaso Vendels* (League of Young Dinaso Companies). The Dinaso emblem was a plough, sword and cogwheel within a circle. The *Jongdinaso* badge was a stylized sea-mew in flight above a wave in a circle.

---

[†] The language of Flanders was originally referred to as Flemish. It differed from Dutch only in minor respects and the two have now been brought into line.

A rival to Dinaso was the *Vlaasmsche Nationaal Verbond* — the Flemish National Union (VNV) formed two years after the creation of Dinaso (October 1933). Its political aspirations were even more grandiose since the new "Netherlandic" community, which it envisaged, was to embrace not only Belgium and Holland, but also French Flanders and German Friesland. Apart from this, the principal dissimilarity between Dinaso and VNV was the latter's stress on the importance of religious faith (priests were to be found among the leadership of the VNV), whereas van Severen was strongly anti-clerical.

Within the spectrum of Flemish nationalism was a seemingly minor faction, the German-Flemish Working Community (*Duitschen*, or *Deutsche-Vlaamsche Arbeidgemeenschap*), better known by its acronym of DeVlag ("The Flag"). Ostensibly dedicated to the fostering of cultural contacts between Germans and Flemings, it was, in reality, under its pro-Nazi leader, Jef van de Wiele, committed to the political fusion of Flanders with the Greater German Reich. This was not a prospect that held much appeal to the people of Flanders and DeVlag might have remained without significance, had not the coming of war altered everything.

War robbed Dinaso of its charismatic leader. Along with other suspected "fifth columnists" van Severen was rounded up in May 1940 and carried off to France. But the speed of the Germans' advance was such that their tanks almost overtook the imminent arrival of the enemy. The French shot, without trial, twenty-two of the prisoners at Abbeville on May 20th. Among the victims was Joris van Severen.

Leaderless, Dinaso began to fall apart. Some of its members chose collaboration, others resistance. The field was now open for the VNV. Its dominant position was officially established by the German authorities when, in May 1941, they announced that "all authorized political parties in Flanders "(since only collaborationist)" must merge with the VNV or be dissolved." However, an exemption was granted to "cultural" bodies which allowed DeVlag to slip through the net — something which seemed unimportant at the time but which was to have important consequences later.

The VNV Leader Staf de Clercq, delighted by his apparent elevation to political boss of Flanders, promoted himself from Leader *(Leider)* to Over-all Leader *(Algemeen Leider)*.

At the same time as the VNV gained control over political activities by adults, it was likewise granted authority over existing politically-orientated youth groups. After a year of occupation the only ones still in being were, it need hardly be said, those of a fascist or pro-German disposition. These were, in addition to the VNV's own youth section:

Jongdinaso
Rex Jeugd Vlaanderen
Vlaamsche Jeugd

To deal with these in order:

(i) Youth Section of the VNV

In 1935 the VNV formed its first youth group, the *Algemeen Verbond van National Jeugd* (General Union of National Youth) or AVNJ. After May 1940 this was renamed the AVNJ *Blauwvoetvendels* (AVNJ Stormy Petrel Companies) — a title which derived from its emblem, a stylized stormy petrel (the same bird as was used by Jongdinaso but of a slightly different design) holding in its claws the delta-in-a-circle badge of the VNV.

The AVNJ was sub-divided by sex into:

(a) DBV *(Dietsche Blauwvoet Vendels):* for boys
(b) DMS *(Dietsche Meisjes Scharen):* for girls

There was a Naval Squad *(Marineschaar)* at Antwerp and two air squads, one at Antwerp and the other in Brussels.

The wearing of uniform by political groups had been banned in Belgium since July 1934, but after the occupation this ban was lifted. The AVNJ adopted the grey shirt of the adult movement with which boys wore, black shorts, black tie, grey stockings and black shoes.

Between June 12th and 17th, 1941 some twenty AVNJ leaders attended an HJ training course at Weimar in Germany. After the takeover of the other youth groups (July 1941) the AVNJ was given a new name — *National-Socialistische Jeugd Vlaaderen* (National-Socialist Youth Flanders or NSJV). Its leader was Edward Lehembre. Its membership, at its peak, was in the region of 8,000 male and 6,000 female young persons. As a gesture of conciliation towards Dinaso, the NSJV adopted that organization's green shirt. The rest of the uniform remained as before except that for the younger boys the tie was orange. Winter uniform (worn from October 1st until the following Easter) was that of the HJ but with orange piping round the collar and shoulder straps, the piping in this case went round the end as well as the top and sides). Officers *(Hopman* and above) wore a black tunic, a khaki shirt and orange tie (higher ranks could wear a white shirt and black tie) black riding breeches and black top boots. Rank was indicated on the shoulder straps and by various coloured lanyards for non-commissioned grades and on the shoulder straps and collar for officers. Officers black collar patches, worn on both sides, were piped in orange. The shoulder strap rank scheme was virtually identical to that of the Hitler Youth.

As roughly the equivalent of the HJ's *Streifendienst*, the NSJV its *Weerkommando* (Defense Commando) which had one *Schaar* ("Squad" of about forty lads) in each of the five Flemish provinces. It was unique in being the only section of the NSJV to be armed — with daggers and, occasionally, with revolvers. Its function was to guard NSJV rallies, etc. As a tribute to the fallen Dinaso chief, its members wore a cuff-title with the name JORIS VAN SEVEREN.

DMS girls wore a dark blue skirt, white, or beige, blouse with neckerchief (orange in the case of the youngest girls). In winter dark blue short uniform jacket could be added. Leaders wore a dark blue open neck tunic over which was the collar of an open neck white shirt. Female ranks was a scheme of circles and bars worn on the left upper side of the tunic and bearing no relationship to that of the BDM. The DMS equivalent of the BDM's *Glaube und Schönheit*, known as *Adel en Schoonheid* (Nobility and Beauty), was open to girls in the eighteen to twenty-one age group. Their neckerchief was blue and they wore a blue *Odalsrune* on the left upper arm.

From 1943 onwards both sexes wore on the left cuff (some photos show left upper arm) a cloth version of the stormy petrel emblem which the NSJV had taken over, almost unaltered in design from Jongdinaso. Headgear was, on the whole, seldom worn except by male officers who sported a German-style peaked cap, but a dark blue forage cap *was* authorized for both sexes.

(ii) Jondinaso (or Dinaso Jeugd)
The youth branch of Dinaso comprised:

Klein Dinaso: boys 10-14 years
Jong Dinaso: boys 14-18 years
Jong Meisjes: girls 9-13 years
Meisjes: girls 9-13 years
Jong Vrouwen: girls 13-17 years.

Boys wore a green shirt and orange tie with black shorts, white socks and black shoes. The girls had a dark blue skirt, white blouse (with, on the left side, the Dinaso emblem), white socks and black shoes. There were, at least on paper, some fifty companies *(Vendels)*, ten in each of the five Flemish provinces. Many former senior Jongdinaso leaders achieved positions of comparable standing within the NSJV.

(iii) Rex Jeugd Vlaanderen
The Rexist Party maintained a small youth section in Flanders, although its main strength was, of course, in Wallonie. (see section on Wallonie)

(iv) Vlaamsche Jeugd
The most palpable imitation of the Hitler Youth in Flanders in 1940-1941 was the Flemish Youth. Formed almost immediately after the start of the occupation this was the junior section of the *Algemene SS Vlanderen* (General SS Flanders), the brain-child of two Flemish disciples of Hitler — René Lagrou and Ward Hermans. Like its German equivalent it was sub-divided into the following age groups:

VJ *(Vlaamsche Jeugd):* boys 14-18
JV *(Jongvolk):* boys 10-14
VJM *(Vlaamsche Jeugd Meisjes):* girls 14-18
JM *(Jongmeisjes):* girls 10-14

A VJ Kameradschaftsführer. Apart from the brassard, the uniform is entirely HJ.

It claimed a membership of around 800 with a *Ban* in each of the Flemish provinces (East and West Flanders, Antwerp, Brabant and Limburg). Its uniform was basically that of the Hitler Youth with, as its principal emblem, a black *Sigrune* (worn on a red/white/red brassard by both sexes). Officers wore the *Sigrune* on the band of an HJ leader's cap which had, on the peak, the black lion rampant of Flanders on a yellow shield. The VJ worked in close cooperation with the Hitler Youth.

As the war progressed the Germans became increasingly dissatisfied with the luke-warm attitude of the VNV, while the VNV, for their part, began to question the wisdom of putting their faith in an Adolf Hitler who refused to give any undertaking as to the future status of Flanders. DeVlag was being openly encouraged to peddle its pro-German propaganda. It even set up a rival uniformed youth organization of its own.

Even more ominous was the creation, in October 1943, of a Hitler Youth Flanders *(HJ-Vlaanderen)*. The entire youth of DeVlag in Flanders was handed over by its leader, van de Wiele, and all 350 pupils at the Flemish School at Antwerp were likewise enrolled in the HJ-V without much regard to their, or their parents', wishes.

The HJ-V set up six *Standarten*. One in each of the main Flemish towns — Antwerp, Brussels, Ghent, Brugges, Hasselt and Luik. In overall charge was a German HJ Officer, *Hauptbannführer* Gery Bennewitz, assisted by a Flemish *Landsleider* (W. Hardt). In November 15th, Flemish HJ-V leaders attended a course at the HJ Reichs Leadership School at Potsdam. In April 1944 the Walloon branch of DeVlag was absorbed into the HJ-V.

The age sub-divisions exactly paralleled those of the Hitler Youth:

HJ-JV (Jongvolk): boys 10 to 14 years
HJ-V            : boys 14 to 18 years
JM (Jong Meisjes): girls 10 to 14 years
MB (Meisjes Bond): girls 14 to 18 years

Uniforms were simply standard HJ with the addition of the black lion of Flanders on a yellow shield worn on the left cuff. This same device, surmounted by the *Standarte* place-name also appeared in the upper left corner of the HJ flags presented to each of the six HJ-V *Standarten*.

The HJ *Fahrtenmesser* was worn only by those who had attended a camp in Germany. No member of the leadership corps of the HJ-V received an HJ Leader's dagger (*Führerdolch*).

The HJ-V was seen by its German masters largely a recruiting agency for the Waffen-SS. After the creation of the 12. SS Division "Hitlerjugend" in the autumn of 1943 many HJ-V lads were persuaded to enlist in it. The SS Volunteer *Sturmbrigade* "Langemarck" also recruited young volunteers from the ranks of the HJ-V and from among Flemish trainees at the various *Wehrertüchtigungslager* in Germany.

With the liberation of Belgium in September 1944 hundreds of Flemish (and other) collaborators sought refuge in Germany. It now proved possible to upgrade the Langemarck Brigade to divisional

JOSEF CHARITA

Artur Axmann congratulates young Flemish HJ lads who have volunteered for the recently raised "Hitlerjugend" Division. July 1943.

Newsletter ("organization letter") of the Hitler Youth Flandern.

SONY BERTON

Rank insignia of the DBV (*Dietsche Blauwvoet Vendels*) of the NSJV. Apart from the use of collar patches and the unique shoulder strap of the *Jeugdleider*, the rank insignia corresponds almost exactly with that of the final design of Hitler Youth ranks.

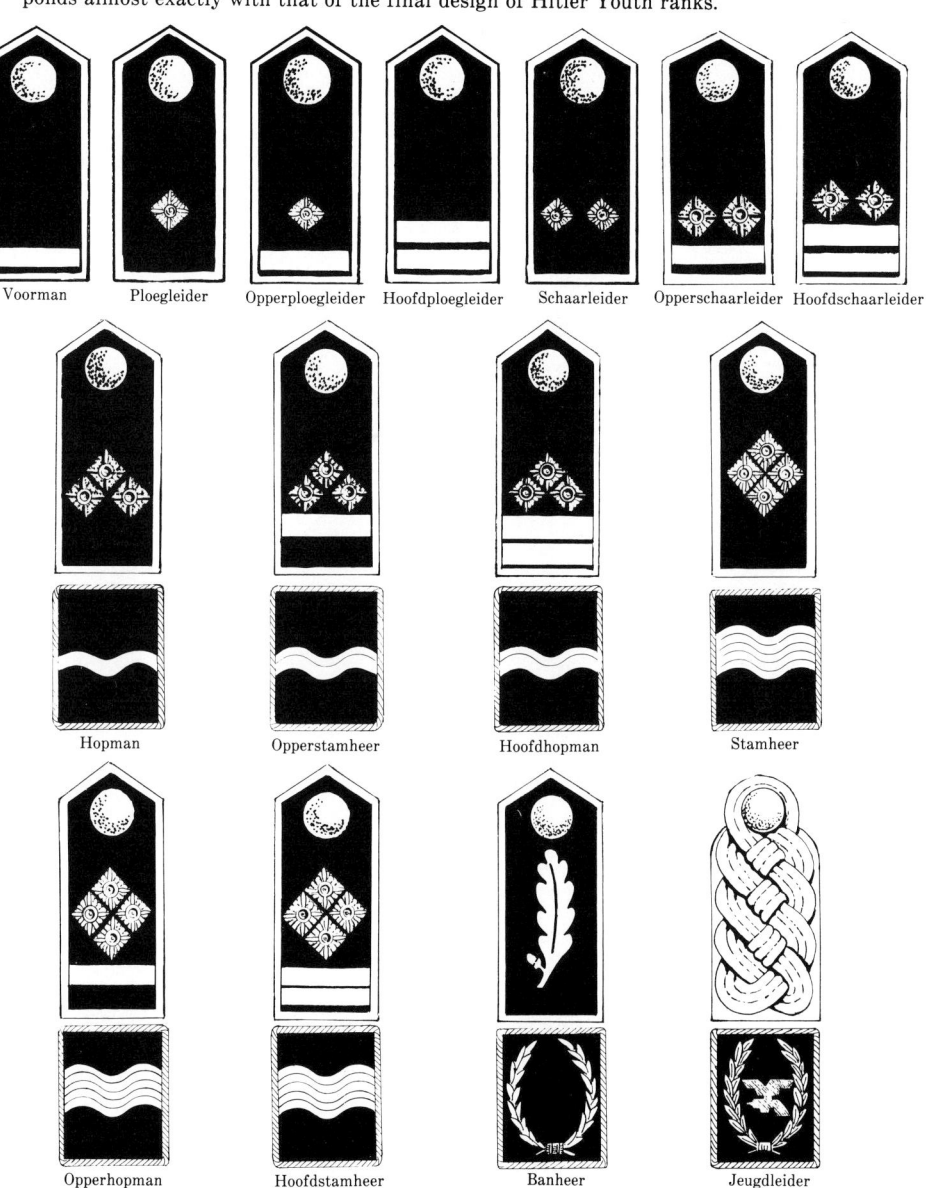

| Voorman | Ploegleider | Opperploegleider | Hoofdploegleider | Schaarleider | Opperschaarleider | Hoofdschaarleider |

| Hopman | Opperstamheer | Hoofdhopman | Stamheer |

| Opperhopman | Hoofdstamheer | Banheer | Jeugdleider |

Commissioned ranks. Shoulder straps and collar patches.

Germanic Youth cuff-title (white on black).

WIM SARIS

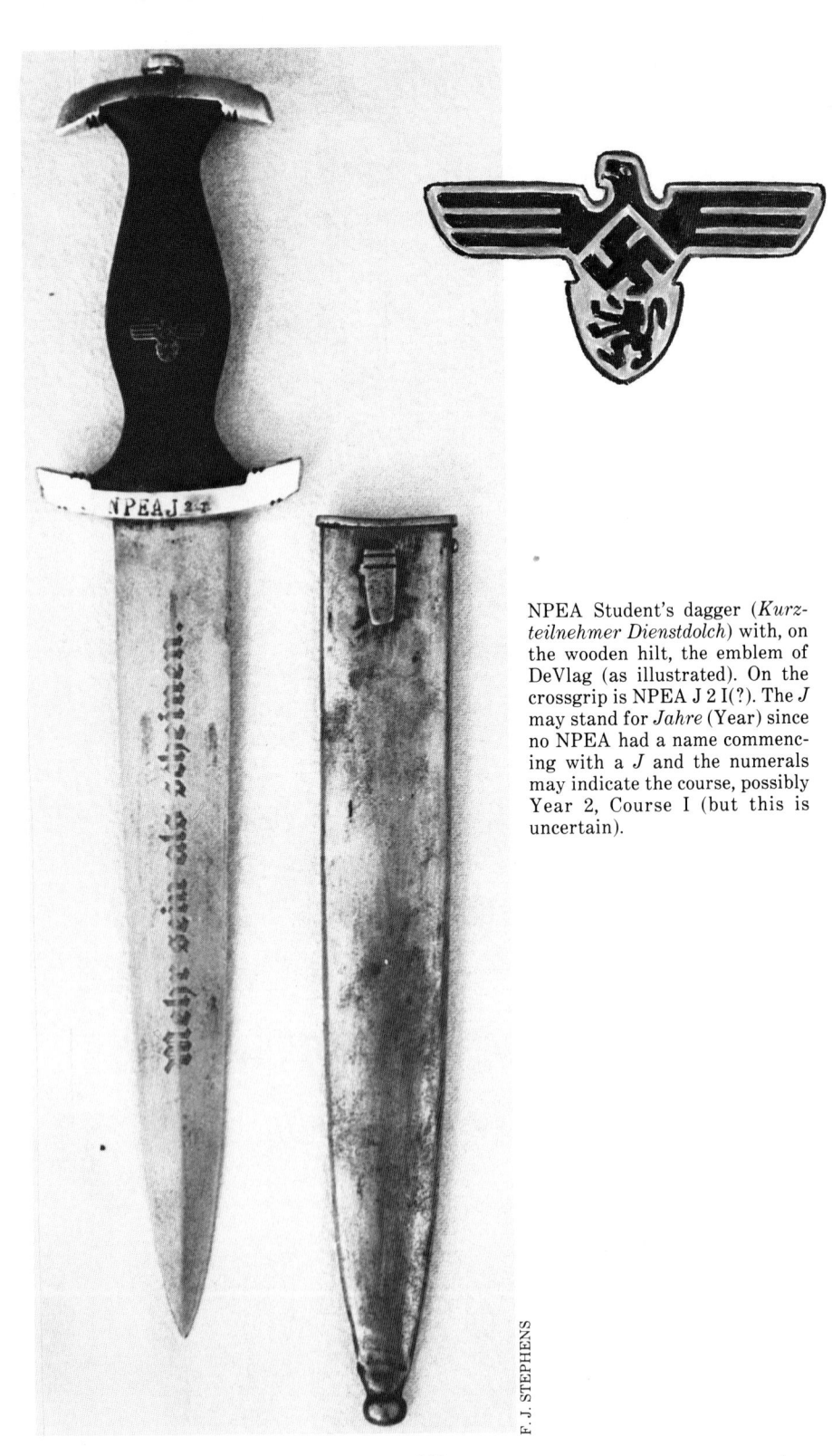

NPEA Student's dagger (*Kurzteilnehmer Dienstdolch*) with, on the wooden hilt, the emblem of DeVlag (as illustrated). On the crossgrip is NPEA J 2 I(?). The *J* may stand for *Jahre* (Year) since no NPEA had a name commencing with a *J* and the numerals may indicate the course, possibly Year 2, Course I (but this is uncertain).

JOSEF CHARITA

Axmann reviews younger boys of the Flemish HJ. They all wear the *Germanische Jugend* cuff-title. The *SS-Rottenführer* with them has the cuff-title of the *Langemarck* Brigade (or Division).

Young HJ *Flandern* lad in summer uniform.

303

HJ *Flandern* fanfare trumpeter of Gau Greater Antwerp. Heraldic lion of Flanders as worn by youth in the photo.

Youthful volunteers from Flanders for the Waffen-SS. Boy in middle wears lion of Flanders cuff badge below the NSKK trainee arm diamond. The design of this lion of Flanders badge varies considerably.

Left to right: an officer in the Vlaamsche Jeugd (VJ), two HJ officers and (in dark blue uniform with silver bugle arm badge) *Gebiedslieder* Leo Poppe of *Jongdinaso*. Poppe later became Press Chief of the NSJV.

The uniform of a VJ officer was exactly the same as that of an HJ officer except for the brassard and the cap badge. The cap badge was a silver *Sigrune* surmounted by a shield badge in metal which has the black lion of Flanders on yellow.

Flags of the Flemish Hitler Youth. They are the same as normal HJ flags but with a lion of Flanders (black on yellow as shown above) in the left upper quarter, with, above this, the *Standort* name (here Brussels).

NSJV flag. A black *Blauwvoet* (Stormy petrel) on white within a black circle on an orange field.

Boys of the NSJV parade before a sports rally in Brussels in mid-summer, 1943 carrying the NSJV flag.

Flag of the DJN and DMN. Golden "sun cross" on blue field.

Badge worn above left breast pocket by female officers of the Vlaamsche Jeugd.

strength as the 27th SS Volunteer Grenadier Division "Langemarck" (Flemish No. 1). It included a Youth Battalion made up of sixteen and seventeen year-old boys. This Battalion was virtually wiped out in a single action in April 1945 at Prenzlau on the Oder Front.

In 1944 a *Germanische Jugend Abteilung* (Germanic Youth Department) was set up under *Gefolgschaftsführer* Gollman. It may have been intended that *all* collaborating youth movements in the occupied Nordic lands would be brought under one unified command in the same way as all *Allgemeine* SS units outside the Reich had been placed under the aegis of the Germanic SS, and thus under direct German control. The rapidly deteriorating war situation seems to have prevented this from ever being translated into reality.

(b) Wallonie

Following their theory that the Nordic race was the superior, the Nazi authorities in Belgium at first favoured the Flemings. Only later were they to discover that in Wallonie they had a much more dependable and charismatic collaborator than any Flanders. This eminent individual was Léon Degrelle. In 1935 Degrelle, then only twenty-nine years of age, had made a spectacular entry into Belgian politics with his *Christus Rex* (or, Rexist) Party which, within the twelve months of its foundation, had gained twenty-one seats in the Lower House of the Belgian parliament and eight in its Senate.

However, the decline of the Rexists was as rapid as their rise and it was only the coming of war and enemy occupation that brought them back into prominence. In May 1941, at the same time as the VNV was granted a political monopoly in Flanders, the Rexists were declared the sole authorized political party in Wallonie.

Rexism was, and always had been, very much a "one man show" entirely dependent on the personality of Degrelle. It is difficult to assess its numerical strength since it never published membership figures, but it can be said with certainty that it enjoyed much less popular support than did the VNV in Flanders. Despite, or perhaps *because of*, its paucity in numbers, the Rexist Party always maintained a grandiose facade. In the beginning the party symbol had been a cross and crown with the word REX (short for Christus Rex — Christ the King), but during the occupation, significantly perhaps, this Christian imagery gave place to a new device — the ragged crossed twigs, or branches, of the Dukedom of Burgundy. This emblem (usually in red) features on the uniforms of all the Rexist political and paramilitary formations.

We are concerned here only with its youth branch. This was known as *Les Serments de la Jeuness Rexists* and was open to young persons of both sexes between the ages of six and eighteen. Males wore the black shirt of the Rexist Party with a red neckerchief (red tie for officers) and brown shirts. Girls had a white blouse and black skirt. Both sexes wore the cross of Burgundy on the left breast. Officers could wear a Belgian army khaki tunic with, on the cuffs, short bars in red or silver to indicate status. Later, all grades wore their rank insignia on the shoulder. At this stage neither scheme of insignia bore any relationship to that of the Hitler Youth (it derived, loosely, from that of the Belgian army).

Badge of the Jeunesse Légionnaire. It was worn on the left breast pocket by the boys and on the left upper arm by the girls. It is a green shield with narrow white outline. In the centre a black eagle on white against a white Burgundian cross.

Girls and boys of the Jeunesse Légionnaire at a rally in Brussels.

But in March 1943 *Les Serments* were replaced by a more broadly based youth organization, the *Jeunesse Légionnaire* (JL) which owed more to the influence of the Hitler Youth. The JL, although Rexist dominated, also encompassed two other officially tolerated youth movements — those of AGRA and the CCW.

AGRA, an acronym for *Amis du Grand Reich Allemand* (Friends of the Great German Reich) was formed in Liege in March 1941 and avoided the proscription on political parties (other than Rex) by claiming it was a "non-political society" (This despite the fact that its constitution stated that it, "recognized Adolf Hitler as the undisputed leader of the New Europe" and that its emblem was absorbed into the JL, as was the even smaller youth section of the CCW (*Communauté Culturelle Wallonne*).) This Walloon Cultural Community (founded at the same time as Agra) aimed at being the counterpart of DeVlag, but it never remotely approached the influence of its Flemish opposite number.

The JL uniform was, for boys, a green shirt with black shoulder straps (piped in green), black shorts with a black or brown belt and cross strap. A black neckerchief was worn with a HJ style open necked collar. Winter wear was the standard dark blue ski type outfit and ski cap of the winter HJ (supplied, of course, by HJ). The JL emblem, worn on the left breast pocket, was still a Burgundian cross, but this time in white on green with, in the centre, the double-headed eagle of the Holy Roman Empire. This badge, in coloured enamel, was worn on the front of the winter cap (there was, apparently, no summer headgear) and was also the civil lapel badge. The JL girls section wore white blouses and black skirts.

J.L. Badge. Worn on front of ski cap and as a civil lapel badge.

Jeunesse Légionnaire in winter uniform (as supplied by the Hitler Youth). Occasion unknown, possibly a Christmas or New Year celebration.

The Leader of the JL, Paul Mezetta, had been invalided out of the Walloon Legion after being badly wounded in Russia. The JL was voluntary, but boys, on reaching the upper age limit found themselves under pressure to "do their bit" by volunteering for the Waffen-SS or NSKK.

A youth leadership school was opened at Charleroi to train cadre personnel, the course being rounded off with a month's sojourn at an HJ camp in the Reich. JL members were also to be found at the Wehrertüchtigungslager in Germany and in the *Landdienst* in Poland.

Mention may also be made of the *Association des Etudiants Wallons* (ADEW) which was structured like the JL but was for over eighteen-years-olds at the universities of Louvain and Ghent. Its members were mainly Rexist, but there was also a sprinkling of Agra supporters among them.

ADEW Badge

Badge of "Agra" (orange and red).

## LUXEMBOURG

The Grand Duchy of Luxembourg, Belgium's small southwestern neighbour, was invaded and over-run by the Germans in May 1940 practically without loss of life on either side. On June 28, 1940 it was formally incorporated into Gau Koblenz-Trier. In February of the following year the enlarged Gau was renamed Gau Moselland.

Of Luxembourg's 299,000 inhabitants, some 17,000 were German. There had been several attempts to form a Nazi Party in the country; none had been successful. The *Auslands-Organisation* had cells among the Reich Germans as did the Hitler Youth but these were not open to non-Germans or even Volksdeutsche.

In 1934 an eighteen-year-old Luxembourger, Albert Kreins, had tried to form a Luxembourg branch of the Hitler Youth but had been told the Hitler Youth was only for the children of Reich citizens. Nonetheless he was invited to attend, the following year, a seminar held in Germany for the leaders of foreign youth movements, and in 1936 was a guest of the RJF at the Nürnberg Rally. So impressed was he by all he saw, that on his return to Luxembourg in September 1936 he founded an initiation HJ which he named the *Luxemburger Volksjugend* (LVJ) with, as its emblem, a white "life rune" on a black shield.

Girls of the LVJ on the march. Complete uniformity in dress has obviously not yet been achieved!

After the occupation a *Volksdeutsche Bewegung* (Racial German Movement, or VDB) was formed "... to bring Luxembourg back into the German Reich...." German-Nazi organizations of all types were introduced into the country. In January 1941 the LVJ was "affiliated" to the HJ; in August 1942 it was incorporated into it. At this time the total HJ membership in Luxembourg was officially quoted as 9,547. In June 1941 Artur Axmann personally presented the thirty founding fathers of the LVJ with the Golden HJ Badge.

LVJ emblem (worn on left breast pocket).

ALSACE-LORRAINE

The ethnically mixed regions of Alsace and Lorraine have been likened to the children of divorced parents — living sometimes with one parent, sometimes with another. French since the seventeenth century, the two areas were ceded to Germany after France's defeat in the war of 1870-1871. They were to remain German until 1918 when they reverted to French sovereignty. One of Hitler's first acts after the fall of France in June 1940 was to re-incorporate both territories into the Reich.

A pro-German *Elsass-Lothringisches Heimatbund* had been in existence since 1926. Its youthful counterpart, the *Elsass-Lothringische Jungmannschaft* was created the following year. Along with the *Wanderbund Erwin-von-Steinbach* (modelled on the German *Wandervogel* Movement) these two youth groups represented the pro-Nazi (as distinct from merely pro-German) influence among the German-speakers of the two regions. Not surprisingly they formed, after the reincorporation of the area into the Reich, the main basis of the national-socialist *Deutsche Volksjugend* (DV) which, in September 8, 1940 was formally incorporated into the Hitler Youth with the presentation in the Sangersaal at Strassburg of *Banne* flags. Three *Gebiet* leadership schools were established which, it was claimed, had twelve months later, turned out 820 male and 750 female leaders.

At first Alsace was linked to HJ *Gebiet* Baden, and Lorraine to HJ *Gebiet* Westmark, but with the regional reorganization of the HJ in 1943 Alsace and Lorraine each became an HJ *Gebiet* in its own right. (*Gebiet* Baden was, at this time, dissolved and *Gebiet* Westmark became *Gebiet* Moselland).

Membership of the HJ and BDM was voluntary until January 2, 1942 when it became obligatory for all young persons between the ages of ten and eighteen years. The authorities claimed that over 70% of those eligible for conscription had already joined voluntarily.

HOLLAND

Before the war there were some 52,000 Germans resident in Holland. The Hitler Youth had units there for the children of Reich-German citizens or those with one German parent or of parents who enjoyed dual nationality. But Holland had a Nazi party, or more correctly Nazi parties (there were at least four) of its own. Of these the most successful was the *National-Socialistsche Beweging* (National-Socialist Movement, or NSB) founded in December 1931 by Anton Adriaan Mussert, a civil engineer in the government's employ.

In May 1940 the Germans over-ran Holland. Thereafter the country was governed by a German civil administration headed by a *Reichskommissar* (Arthur Seyss-Inquart). On December 14, 1941, the tenth anniversary of its foundation, the NSB was granted an exclusive political monopoly in the Netherlands. All other political groups had to submit to its authority or face disbandment (most chose the latter alternative). Despite this apparent recognition, Mussert himself was not accorded a position of any sort in the apparatus of government.

The NSB claimed a membership of over 100,000 with an additional 30,000 "sympathizers." It had a variety of uniformed sub-sections, but only its youth branch, known as the *Nationale Jeugdstorm* (roughly Young Storm Troops), is of concern here. These young storm troopers were formed in May 1934 by Cornelis van Geelkerken who remained its national leader, or *Hoofdstormer*, throughout its existence.

The NSB tried to avoid too patent an imitation of Nazi-German paradigms. It never, for example, adopted the swastika as one of its emblems. Dutch Jews were even accepted into its ranks (until this practice was expressly forbidden by the occupation authorities) and there was much talk about the need for Christian faith and morality — something quite alien to Hitlerite practice. The Motto of the *Nationale Jeugdstorm* was "With faith in God, all for the Fatherland." Its constitution enjoined, "respect for religion, morality, duty and order."

It was sub-divided as follows:

Meewen (Sea Mews): boys ten-thirteen years
Meewkes (ditto female): girls ten-thirteen years
Stormers (Storm Troopers): boys fourteen-seventeen years
Stormsters (ditto, female): girls fourteen-seventeen years

All the above wore light blue shirts with, for boys, navy blue shorts, for girls, navy blue skirts. Both sexes had navy blue ties and, as their headgear, a black astrakhan cap with a red top and the *Jeugdstorm* emblem (a white sea mew in flight upon a sky blue circle). In winter a dark blue ski type garb, very similar to that of the HJ, was worn. Officers from *Vaandrig* (Ensign) and above could wear a dark blue military style tunic, dark blue riding breeches and top boots. All ranks had the sea mew emblem on their left upper arm.

Black astrakahn cap of the Nationale Jeugdstorm with metal cap badge.

ALAIN TAUGOURDEAU

Officers and other ranks of both the HJ and the Dutch Nationale Jeugdstorm await a march past by Nationale Jeugdstorm contingents in Amsterdam. Note fanfare trumpet and arm badge of young boy in foreground.

Arm badge for boys as shown in above photo. It a white sea mew and waves on a blue circle within an orange border.

Rank was originally indicated by a combination of stars (worn above the left breast pocket) and coloured lanyards or aguilettes, but in 1942 an entirely new scheme replaced this. Non-commissioned ranks now had black bars instead of stars (worn, as before, above left breast pocket) but officers wore rank insignia on the collar in a scheme which is quite clearly inspired by that of the Hitler Youth. Concurrently a new system of female ranks was introduced but, in this case, it has no German counterpart being circles of various colour combinations and complexities worn on the left upper arm.

A Motor Section and a Flying Section (both for males only) were formed in 1943 and 1944 respectively. The *Marine Jeugdstorm* wore a junior version of naval uniform.

Mussert reviews boys of the Nationale Jeugdstorm and the Marine-Jeugdstorm in Rotterdam in May 1944.

Nationale Jeugdstorm Sports Badge for Boys. Nationale Jeugdstorm Sports Badge for Girls. Both badges are bronze or white metal (there is only one class of each). Both were instituted in April 1943.

317

Dutch-Nazi students (whether at Dutch universities or attending one in Germany with a large complement of Dutch students) wore the all black uniform of the NSB with a special emblem sewn on the left breast pocket.

Mussert arriving for a mass rally of the Nationale Jeugdstorm in Amsterdam (date unknown, but possibly about 1943).

The NSB had a section for university students, known as the *NS Studentenfront*, but this was not part of the *Jeugdstorm*. Dutch-Nazi students (whether at Dutch universities or attending one in Germany with a large complement of Dutch students) wore the all black uniform of the NSB with a special emblem sewn on the left breast pocket.

The carrying of daggers or "camping knives" was not standard, although a *Jeugdstorm* dagger (or knife) with blade motto *Moed, Eer en Trouw* (Courage, Honour and Loyalty) exists and may have been intended as a mark of merit awarded only to a deserving few. Photos show *Hoofdstormer* Van Geelkirken with an HJ *Führerdolch*, but again, this is more likely to have been a special honour granted him by the Hitler Youth in Holland since *Jeugdstorm* officers did not normally carry daggers.

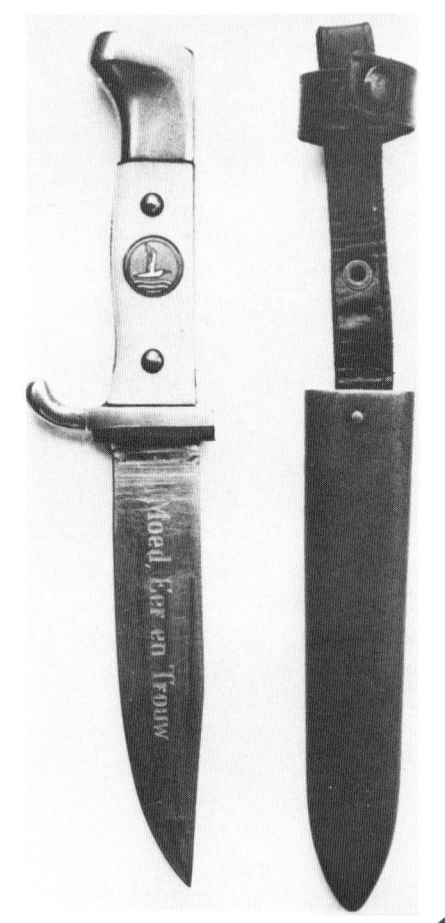

An example of a Nationale Jeugdstorm knife (F.J. Stephens Collection).

"District triangle" (here for Venlo) of the Hitler Youth in Holland *before* the German occupation (i.e. for extra-Reich units in the Netherlands).

A recruiting poster for Dutch "Hitler Youth" (probably for that of Major Kruyt's NSNAP).

There were four Jeugdstorm training schools in various parts of Holland. The normal duration of the course was three months. *Jeugdstorm* boys also attended the *Wehrertüchtigungslager* in Germany, and there were frequent exchange visits with the Hitler Youth. The Germans, however, were not greatly impressed by their Dutch comrades. Confidential HJ reports commented unfavorably on their lack of discipline and absence of true national-socialist dedication. That did not, of course, inhibit the German recruitment agencies in Holland from doing their utmost to induce young Dutch lads to join the Waffen-SS.

But, as stated earlier, the NSB was not (until December 1941) the only pro-Nazi party in the Netherlands. Apart from the Troelstra Movement and the Black Front (both fascist, rather than Nazi in tone) there was the National-Socialist Dutch Worker's Party (*Nationaal-Socialistische Nederlandsche Arbeiderspartij*, or NSNAP) which was, as its name implies, a faithful facsimile of Hitler's NSDAP. Originally created in December 1931 (more than a year before Hitler's advent to power), the NSNAP was so driven by internecine strife that it failed to make any great impact with the Dutch public and eventually split into three parties — each of which still traded under the name NSNAP and claimed for itself exclusive right to that title. One of the trio quickly sunk into oblivion leaving the NSNAPs of Major CJA Kruyt and Dr. EH Ridder van Rappard still in the field. Both had uniformed storm troopers and youth sections. Of the two, van Rappard's was the more overly pro-German. Ernst-Henri Ridder van Rappard was of Swiss-German descent (although actually born in India), a Doctor of Economics of Vienna University and married to a German. His party's policy was quite simply the incorporation of the Netherlands into the German Reich. Orders were given in German and the party structure was based almost exactly on that of the NSDAP. This applied also to its youth branch, known at first as the *Nationaal-Socialistiche Holland Jeugd*, or NSHJ, but later rechristened simply Dutch Hitler Youth (*Nederlandsche Hitlerjeugd*). It comprised:

> Jongvolk: boys of ten to fourteen years
> Jongens: boys of fourteen to eighteen years
> Jongemeisjes: girls of ten to fourteen years
> Meisjes: girls of fourteen to twenty-one years

Boys wore a brown shirt with green, not black, shoulder straps, a black tie, brown shorts, grey or white stockings and black shoes. No headgear was worn. A German HJ brassard was worn on the left upper arm but this had the addition of a blue tape sewn horizontally across the middle (thus reproducing the Dutch national colours, red/white/blue). The girls section, known as the BDM (*Bond van Duitsche Meisjes* — literal translation into Dutch of its German counterpart) wore virtually the same uniform as the German BDM except that above the left breast pocket the Dutch girls has a horizontal red/white/red bar which measures 7 cms by 3 cms.

On August 22, 1941 the van Rappard Hitler Youth was absorbed into the German Hitler Youth in the Netherlands. Van Rappard himself was at this time serving with the Waffen-SS in Russia.

Four months later Major CJA Kruty's NSNAP, along with its "Hitler Youth," was dissolved and ordered to place itself under Mussert's command. The NDB leader, however, was not keen to accept into his ranks Dutchmen who were so pro-German as to use the swastika as their emblem,* and *Nationale Jeugdstorm* leaders were, consequently, instructed to place obstacles in the way of ex-NSNAP youths who wished to join. In this way Mussert sought to demonstrate his "independence" of the German which, in reality, was as subsequent events were to demonstrate, a chimera.

Brassard of the *Nederlandsche Hitlerjeugd* (Dutch Hitler Youth) i.e. the youth section of Ridder van Rappard's NSNAP.

---

\* Both NSNAPs used the swastika as their principal emblem. The van Rappard one was black, the Kruyt type blue.

Fanfare trumpeters of the Nationale Jeugdstorm. The banners have the white sea mew on light blue above three white "waves" which was the emblem of the Jeugdstorm. The boy in the centre has on his left breast pocket the two black bars of a *Wachter* (roughly Corporal). The left hand on hip stance of these young fanfare trumpeters seems to have been copied from that of the Hitler Youth.

Red/white/blue bar (actual size) worn above left breast pocket by girls of the BDM of van Rappard's party (the rest of the uniform was identical to that of the Herman BDM).

DENMARK

At the same time as they launched their attack on Norway (May 9, 1940) Hitler's forces also invaded Denmark. The country was rapidly overrun, there being virtually no resistance on the part of the Danes.

There were already in being several pro-Nazi Danish political parties.

The largest of these was the DNSAP (*Danmarks National-Socialistiske Arbeijder Parti* — Denmark's National-Socialist Workers Party) formed in November 1930 and originally guided by a three-man committee, but in 1933 its direction was taken over by Frits (or Fritz) Clausen, a medical doctor from North Schleswig. In 1935 the DNSAP polled 16,257 in a national election. By 1939 it had almost doubled this with 31,032 votes, which secured it three seats in the Danish parliament.

The DNSAP had fifteen "Main Districts" (*Sysseler*) in Denmark and a further two abroad (one in Germany, the other in Norway). The Party emblem was a white swastika on a red circle outlined in white (Red and white being the Danish national colours). The DNSAP had its own Corps of Political Leaders, its own SA and naturally, its own youth group. This latter was known as the NSU (*National-Socialistiske Ungdom* — National-Socialist Youth) and was first brought into being in September 1934. It consisted of two age groups:

*Skjoldunge* (roughly "Youth Defence"): boys ten to fourteen years
*Vaebnere* ("Squires," in the chivalric sense): boys fourteen to eighteen years

Later the name *Hird* replaced the term *Vaebnere* as the designation of the older age group. Both age groups wore an all black uniform: shirt, trousers (or breeches), neckerchief and forage cap. Officers wore black tunics and, for ceremonial occasions, white shirts. The NSU emblem was a white closed "sun wheel." This emblem was worn, at first, on a brassard, later on a white outlined cloth shield on the left upper arm. Rank was indicated on the collar. This was, to start with, simply by means of three-cornered stars, but gradually, as the NSU expanded, rank insignia became more elaborate and was brought into line with that of the adult SA. For example, the NSU copied from the Danish SA the semicrescent of oakleaves (for highest ranks), a form of insignia which owes nothing to either Danish military, or German, practice.

Civil lapel badge of NSU. White surround and cross, edged in yellow, upon a red centre.

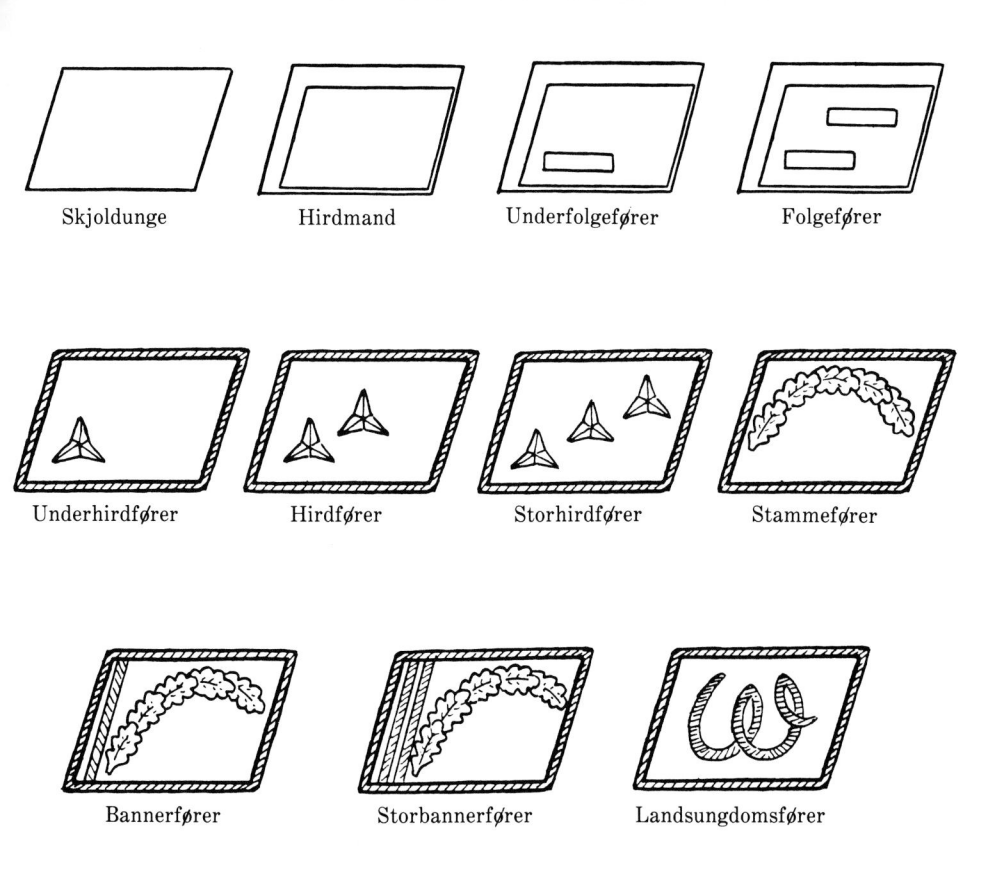

| | | | |
|---|---|---|---|
| Skjoldunge | Hirdmand | Underfolgefører | Folgefører |

| | | | |
|---|---|---|---|
| Underhirdfører | Hirdfører | Storhirdfører | Stammefører |

| | | |
|---|---|---|
| Bannerfører | Storbannerfører | Landsungdomsfører |

The tassel on the front of the forage cap and the red and white cockade, on the other hand, were taken over from Danish army usage. The Section (*Stamm*) was indicated by a white metal numeral on the collar, while the Group (*Bann*) was signified by the colour of piping around the shoulder strap. Officers wore, on the left shoulder, a lanyard of combined white and *Banne* colour. The NSU had flying (gliding), motorized and marine sub-sections as well as medical, Signals, and Music units.

The Girls Branch, the Danish Maidens (*Danske Piger*) also wore a largely black uniform, skirt, tunic (in winter), tie and forage cap, only the blouse was white. They had the same arm badge as the boys, the same forage cap with tassel and roughly the same rank insignia.

The NSU had its own sports award, but NSU youths, girls as well as boys, attended sporting meetings in Germany and were eligible for the various HJ sports badges and awards. NSU boys were to be found among the trainees at the *Wehrertüchtigungslager* in Germany. NSU boys and girls assisted in the work of the Germanic *Landdienst* in Poland.

The first National Youth Leader was Count Christian Frederick von Schalburg who was later to command the contingent of Danish Waffen-SS volunteers known as the *Freikorps Danmark* from February 1942 until his death in action four months later.

Two officers of the Danish Maidens on a visit to Germany. The girl on left wears above the left breast pocket two of the small badges of the HJ annual National Sports Competition (of the 1940-1943 type).

A Danish maiden in summer uniform.

Badge for NSU girls working as hospital auxiliaries (in Denmark or Germany).

Arm badge (1st design).

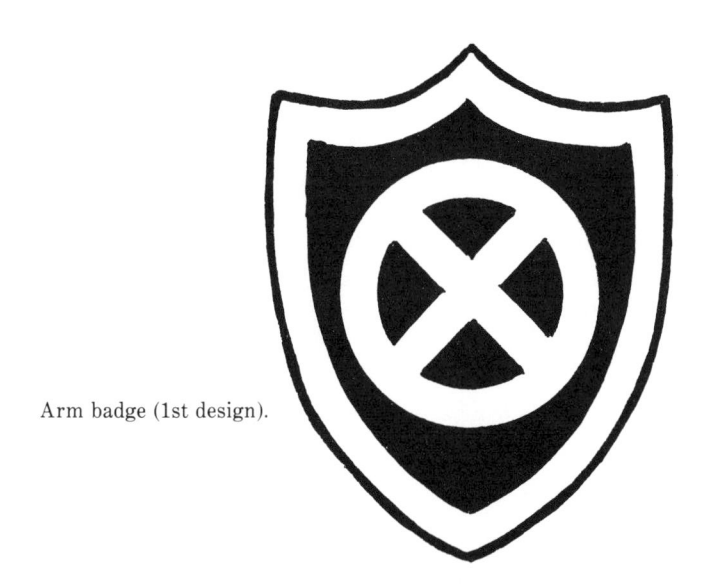

Hird youths on parade in summer uniform.

328

Skjoldunge boys set out for camp in Germany.

National flag of the NSU — white "sun wheel" on black.

329

## DENMARK NORTH SCHLESWIG

Denmark had to cede her southernmost province, Schleswig-Holstein to Prussia following her defeat by a combined Prussian-Austrian army in 1864, but after the first World War the League of Nations organized a plebiscite to determine whether the citizens of this racially mixed area wished to remain Germans or become Danish once more. The result was a compromise — North Schleswig voted three to one in favour of returning to Denmark, while South Schleswig voted four to one to remain part of Germany. This left a German minority of roughly 35,000 in North Schleswig (or, as the Danes call it, South Jutland).

With the German occupation of Denmark in May 1940, the Volksdeutsche of North Schleswig were confident that Hitler would "return North Schleswig to the Reich." This was not to be. The only significant difference that occupation made was that the previous governmental ban on the wearing of political uniforms was lifted and the NSDAPN was able to put its paramilitary bodies, which were the equivalent of those of the Reich, back into uniform. Its counterpart to the Hitler Youth was the *Deutsche Jugendschaft Nordschleswig* (DJN), first formed in July 1933. The German BDN was mirrored by its *Deutsche Mädchenschaft Nordschleswig* (DMN), formed a year later. The youth uniforms would appear to have been much the same as their equivalents in the Reich except that the swastika was replaced by a golden "sun cross," or "sun wheel" on a blue background. As already noted the "sun cross" or "sun wheel" was also the emblem of the Danish Nazi youth. The difference between the two was that the Danish one is titled on its side and is on a black background, whereas the North Schleswig Volksdeutsche version is "square" and on blue. The DJN had its own *Leistungsabzeichen* which has this type of "sun cross" upon a Roman type upward pointing sword with, in sham runic script, *"Für Leistung in der DJN."*

Achievement Badge
(Leistungsabzeichen of the DJN).

Red and white rosette worn on the front of the forage cap by all ranks.

One of several so-called "traditions flags" of the NSU (of units which existed prior to the war). It is a yellow dragon on red within a green wreath, on a black background. Many of these emblems derive from the national coat-of-arms of Denmark.

# NORWAY

The world is familiar with the name of Norway's chief collaborator. His name added a new word to the English language, but the celebrity (or notoriety) of Vidkun Quisling does not reflect his relative importance in the field of collaboration. Norway played a much lesser role in this regard, say, Holland or Flanders. Quisling's uniqueness lies in the fact that he was the only collaborator to be entrusted with an official position in the government of his country.

The National unity (*Nasjonal Samling*, or NS) party was formed by ex-Army Major Quisling in May 1933 (four months after Hitler's accession to power in Germany) and it was clearly modelled on Germany's NSDAP. Its SA was given the name *Hird*, an archaic Norxe term signifying the king's ligament. This, in turn, spawned a Young *Hird* (*Unghird*) which was loosely the counterpart of the Hitler Youth. Like its German equivalent it was sub-divided by age and sex as follows:

Guttehird: boys from ten to fourteen years
Unghird: boys from fourteen to eighteen years
Smahird: girls from ten to fourteen years
Gjentehird: girls from fourteen to eighteen years.

In 1942 a Naval Young *Hird* (*unghirdmarinen*) was created.

The NS emblem was the so-called "sun cross of St. Olaf" — a white, or yellow, cross on a red circle. All young *Hird* members wore this emblem on their left upper arm. Boys featured it on a green brassard, the adult *Hird* has the addition of two upward pointing swords. For the *Unghird*, the cross and the swords were white, for the younger *Guttehird* lads they were brown.

Swords did not feature on the girl's badge which was simply the white sun cross on red. This could be attached to a green brassard or sewn directly on the left arm.

Cap badge worn by *Unghird* (and some other NS uniformed formations).

Brassard of the *Unghird*. Green with a white "sun cross" and white swords on red.

Boys of the *Unghird* in summer uniform waiting to entrain for summer camp in Germany. The flag is red with a yellow cross.

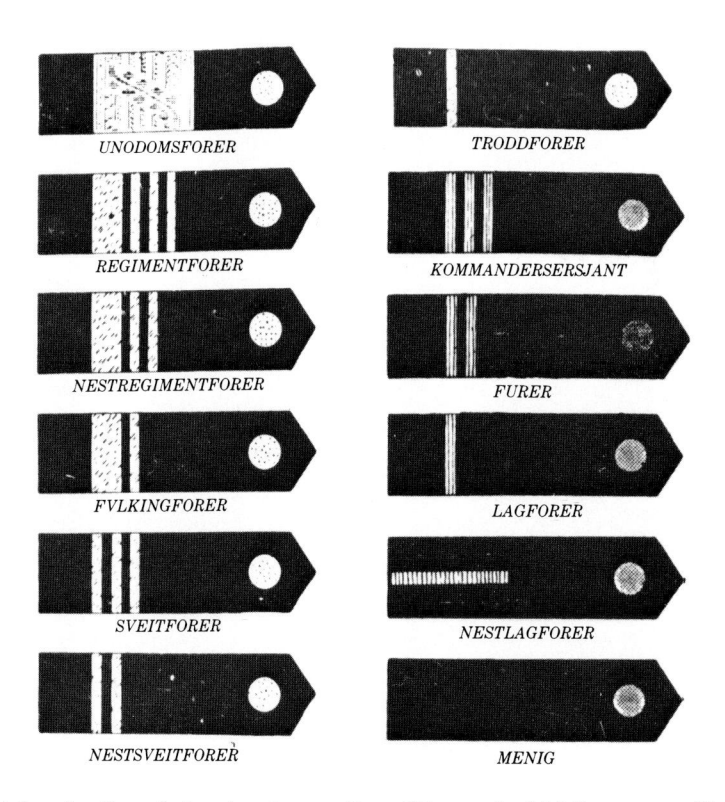

UNODOMSFORER

TRODDFORER

REGIMENTFORER

KOMMANDERSERSJANT

NESTREGIMENTFORER

FURER

FVLKINGFORER

LAGFORER

SVEITFORER

NESTLAGFORER

NESTSVEITFORER

MENIG

*Unghird* ranks. Commissioned ranks are silver. Other ranks (right) are green. Worn on both shoulders on dark blue for winter uniform and on khaki for summer dress.

Officers of the *Gjentehird*. Girl on right wears metal Gjentehird rhombus beside the German "Distinguished Foreigner" Decoration of the RJF.

In summer boys wore a khaki shirt and dark blue shorts; the tie being black for older boys, green for younger ones. In winter a dark blue short tunic and ski trousers were worn. Ranks were worn on the shoulder. These took the form of coloured bars (red for NCOs, silver for officers) in a scheme which was the same for both the adult *Hird* and the *Unghird* and which did not derive from Hitler Youth originals. The naval *Hird* boys wore a junior version of naval uniform, but rank was worn, as in the rest of the *Unghird*, on the shoulder straps.

The girls uniform was, for summer, a yellow blouse and dark blue skirt with a black tie or black neckerchief. In winter, or for formal occasions, a dark blue tunic could be added.

Both sexes wore a dark blue forage cap, although, in summer, this item of dress was omitted.

On the left breast pocket *Gjentehird* girls wore a green enamel lozenge-shaped metal badge which had, in the centre a gold-on-red sun cross on either side of which the letters *J* and *H* (*Gjente* can also be spelled *Jente)*. The *Smahird* youngsters had a similar badge except that silver replaced gold and the letters were, in their case, *S H*. Girls wore a dark blue cuff title with the name of their party district (e.g. Hedmark).

The various youth sections of the party were known collectively as the NSUF *(NS Ungdomsfylking,* roughly the NS Youth Front).

NSUF service was voluntary up to March 1, 1941 when it was made obligatory for all physically fit Norwegian children between the ages of ten and eighteen years. On February 1, 1942 Hitler appointed Quisling "Minister President" of Norway, thus the NSUF became an "official" youth organization — a status not attained by any of the other collaborating youth formation in occupied Europe.

Youth *Hird* boys took part in training at the *Wehrertüchtigungslager* in Germany, and young Norwegians of both sexes participated in the work of the Germanic *Landdienst.* There was a proposal to set up an NPEA, or *Reichsschule,* outside Bergen but this never came to fruition possibly due to the lack of suitable Norwegian pupils.

The NSUF and the Hitler Youth came together in joint sports meetings, the most popular of which was, predictably, ski competitions.

*Gjentehird* and *Smahird* girls in summer uniform.

Above: Small enamel badge worn on left breast by *Gjentehird* (red and gold on green).

Hitler greets officers of the *Unghird* (male) and *Gjentehird* (female). To the left of the Führer is von Schirach (in civilian clothes). On the extreme right in "gala" uniform (with black trousers in place of the normal black breeches and top boots) is Artur Axmann. The photo was probably taken in Vienna about the middle of the war. It would appear that all present are recipients of the "Distinguished Foreigner" Decoration of the RJF. (See section on "Awards").

# The Germanic Landdienst

The German *Landdienst* has earlier been dealt with, in 1942 the concept was extended to embrace what were known as *Ostfreiwillige der germanischen Jugend* (Eastern Volunteers of the Germanic Youth). These were young persons, of both sexes, between the ages of fourteen and sixteen (leaders could be older) who were willing to sign on for two, or a minimum of one years service in the newly created *Reichsgaue* in former Polish territories (the Warthegau and Danzig-West Prussia) or in the western Ukraine. Service was full time with one month's leave (mid-December to mid-January) to allow the young persons to spend Christmas with their families. Predictably the volunteers were drawn almost exclusively from the collaborationist youth movements in the "nordic" countries — Norway, Denmark and Holland and Flanders. Their anticipated reward — a farm in the conquered east after Hitler had won the war.

The organization was referred to as the Germanic Land Service and a cuff-title with *Germanischer Landdienst** was issued which could be worn on HJ garb or on the uniform of one's native collaborationist youth organization. By November 1943 the multifarious national uniforms had been replaced by standard HJ winter dress. Above the cuff-title a nationality badge could be worn.

Ironically the creation of the Germanic *Landdienst* coincide with a turn of the title of German military fortune in the East. After little more than two years existence, its position became untenable. It was officially wound up, so far as the western volunteers were concerned, in March 1944 and many of its male personnel were transferred into SS "volunteers" (For example, some 200 former members of the Flemish *Landdienst* were taken over by the HJ Battalion "Langemarck").

Yet at the very time that the western volunteer *Landdienst* was being closed down, a Baltic equivalent was being created. By early 1944 the exigencies of war had forced the Germans to regard the Latvians as sufficiently germanized to be admitted to the Germanic *Landdienst*.

The Latvian *Landdienst* was created to a large extent out of the LJO (the Latvian Youth Organization — see section on Latvia). The Hitler Youth supplied it with standard HJ winter uniform with which it wore,

---

\* For those not over-familiar with the niceties of the German language it may be necessary to point out that when preceded by the definite article *(Der)* this is *Germanische Landdienst*, but if the article is omitted the "r" transfers to the end of the adjective, thus making it *Germanischer Landdienst*.

on grey shoulder straps, the rank insignia of the LJO. The grey shirt and red/white *Prievite* cravat of the LJO were also retained. The *Germanischer Landdienst* cuff title was worn on the left lower arm. The Latvians did not wear HJ style District triangles, but, as an equivalent, they had a grey cloth "bar" with their district of origin (e.g. Jelgavas Aprinikis) which they wore above the left breast pocket. The LJO metal badge was worn on the left breast pocket and also on the front of the cap. In place of a brassard a Latvian national shield (diagonal red/white/red surmounted by the word Latvija) was worn on the left upper arm. Belts and belt buckles were standard HJ issue. All ranks (including officers) were allowed to carry the HJ *Fahrtenmesser*.

The Latvian *Landdienst* was used only in its homeland, mainly on agricultural work, although it also received paramilitary training. When the Red Army crossed the Latvian frontier most of the *Landdienst* boys were absorbed into the Flak Helpers and removed to Germany.

Flemish boy in the *Landdienst*. He wears, below the black lion of Flanders on yellow shield, and the cuff-title, *Germanischer Landdienst*.

Norwegian girl in the *Germanischer Landdienst*. On the upper arm she wears the badge of the *Gjentehird* (as illustrated above).

# 33

# Central and Eastern Europe

CZECHOSLOVAKIA
(a) Sudetenland

In October 1938 Czechoslovakia was obliged, under the terms of the "Munich Agreement", to hand over more than a third of its territory to Germany. This area was the predominantly German-speaking Sudetenland. Not content with this gain, Hitler seized the remainder of the Czech state in March 1939. Gau Sudetenland was incorporated into the German Reich; Bohemia and Moravia became a German "Protectorate" while Slovakia was declared an Independent State (in reality throughout its six years of existence, a German puppet).

The HJ *Obergebiet Ost* established a ten *Banne* strong *Gebiet Sudetenland* which incorporated all the former clandestine HJ units which had existed under Czech rule. These had gone under a variety of guises after the *Sudetendeutsche Volksjugend* had, along with all other Nazi organizations in Czechoslovakia, been banned by the government. The most common subterfuge used by the Nazis here (as in neighbouring Austria) to circumvent the prohibition was to reform as "Sports clubs". Thus the Turnverein, or Gymnastic Association, acted as a "cover" for the young Nazis who merely exchanged their khaki shirts for white ones which they wore with black shorts.

After the "liberation" of the Sudetenland, the *Volksjugend* leaders adopted the "provisional uniform" of the NSDAP in that part of the world — a khaki tunic, trousers and peaked cap, but in place of the elongated swastika worn on the peak of the cap by the Political Leaders they had the red/white enamel diamond badge of the HJ.

Following the incorporation of the Sudetenland into Germany in January 1939, all the standard uniforms and insignia of the Nazi organizations of the Reich replaced these "provisional" ones; this, of course, applied also to the new Hitler Youth units.

(b) Bohemia-Moravia

The Hitler Youth had its own units in the Protectorate of Bohemia and Moravia, but these were open only to German or *Volksdeutsche* youngsters. In May 1942, however, it was decided by the occupying authority in collaboration with the Protectorate's own puppet "government" that a similar organization should be set up for young Czechs. Under the general supervision of the Hitler Youth a *Kuratorium für*

A common cover for Nazi activities in the Sudetenland (and elsewhere) was the *Turnverein* (Cymnastic Association). Nominally a civilian sports society, it camouflaged a variety of illegal grouping here, quite clearly, an only thinly disguised Hitler Youth!

Emblem of the *Turnverein*. It is made up of four Fs standing for *Frisch* (Fresh), *Froh* (Happy), *Fromm* (Pious) and *Frei* (Free).

342

Before the "liberation" of the Sudetenland, the Sudeten "Hitler Youth" wore white shirts and black trousers as their "civilian uniform." Here a fife and drum band parades openly through a Sudeten town.

Hitler greets leaders of the Sudeten Germans in Prague, March 1939. The four in the centre of the picture appear to be HJ officers. They wear a plain uniform without insignia apart from the HJ diamond badge on the peak of their caps. On the extreme left is a German HJ officer, possibly an HJ *Obergebietsführer* in winter greatcoat. To the right of Hitler is German Foreign Minister von Ribbentrop.

Brassard of the *Kuratorium für Jugenderzeihung*. Red/white/red within centre the *Wenzel-Adler* (Eagle of Duke Wencelas) with the shields of Bohemia (white lion on red) and Moravia (a red and white chequered eagle on light blue).

Emanuel Moravec (second left) leader of the *Kuratorium* with an SS officer and a Hitler Youth official.

Another version of the same (from an example in a private collection in Germany).

Officer's cap badge. In metal. The rossette is in the "national" colours of Bohemia and Moravia, blue/red/white.

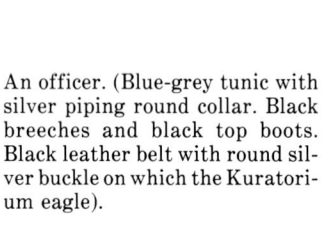

An officer. (Blue-grey tunic with silver piping round collar. Black breeches and black top boots. Black leather belt with round silver buckle on which the Kuratorium eagle).

Boy in the 16 to 21 age group.

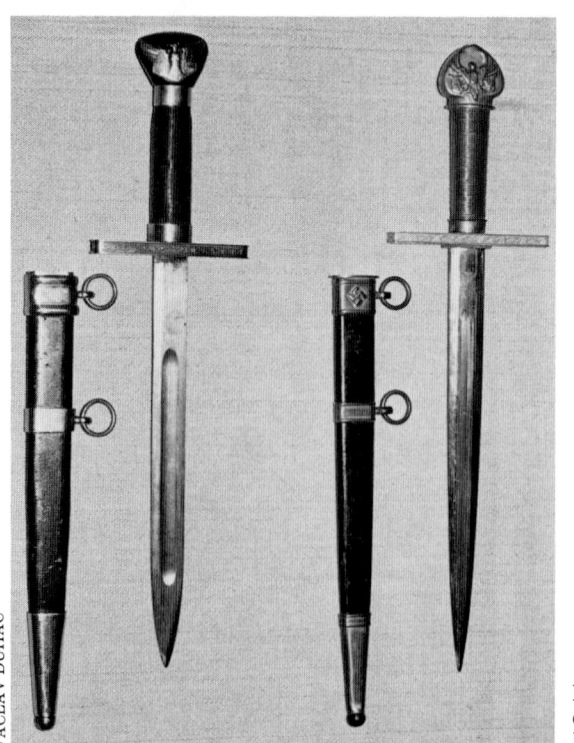

Boy in the 10 to 16 age group.

VACLAV DUHAC

Leaders daggers (left) for subordinate leaders, (right) for senior leaders.

346

*Jugenderziehung in Böhmen und Mähren* (Curatorship for Youth Training in Bohemia and Moravia) was established to which Czech boys and girls between the ages of ten and twenty-one were required by law to belong.

Membership figures (as quoted by an official source in 1944) were in excess of three hundred thousand. There is no way of knowing how accurate this estimate is.

Officers, others than those who already held HJ commissions, wore a blue-grey tunic with deep upturned cuffs and silver piping round the collar, black breeches and black top boots. On their HJ style peaked cap they had the so-called *Wenzel-Adler* (eagle of Duke Wencelas) above a white/red/blue cockade. The same eagle feature on their round belt buckle. It was also awarded (in an enamelled version) as an "honour badge" (like the Golden HJ Badge) to the fifteen best members of each *Bezirk* (District) of the *Kuratorium* in the Protectorate.

The "other ranks" were divided into two age groupings:

ten to fifteen year-olds
sixteen to twenty-one year-olds

The uniform of the younger group consisted of a blue-grey shirt (without shoulder straps) open at the neck with a neckerchief, belt and cross strap, black or brown short trousers, white stockings and black shoes. The older boys wore white shirts, black ties and black trousers with a belt which could be with or without a cross strap. Officers and older boys wore a brassard with the black *Wenzel-Adler* which has, in full colour, the heraldic shields of Bohemia (left) and Moravia (right) on its outstretched wings.

The above garb was referred to as "the emergency uniform" — presumably a more elaborate one was planned for "after final victory". But even this basic dress proved difficult to furnish with the result that a variety of uniform and civilian clothes was worn.

The leader of the *Kuratorium* was a former lecturer at the Czech Military Academy and in the Protectorate "government", Minister of Education, Emanuel Moravec who had a son serving in the Waffen-SS. Later Moravec was replaced by an even more extreme pro-German Czech, Frantisek Teuner.

How rank was indicated in the *Kuratorium* is not clear, possibly by means of coloured lanyards since officers do not appear to have worn either shoulder straps or collar patches — although Moravec himself certainly had the latter. The brassard exists in two distinct types but whether there is any significance in this difference is not known.

Girls were subject to service in the *Kuratorium*, but as no pressure was brought to bear on them to join it would appear that the female section of the *Kuratorium* remained largely, if not entirely, theoretical.

(c) Slovakia

At the time of its declared "indepedence" in 1939 the State of Slovakia had a population of around three million, of which 128,347 were registered as racially German *(Volksdeutsche)*.

The pro-Nazi movement in pre-independent Slovakia was known as the Carpathian German Party *(Karpaten-deutsche Partei)* which, October 1938 changed its name to simply German Party *(Deutsche Partei)* or DP). It had seven *Kreise* (Districts) and a Political Leadership Corps of some 3,800. The DP youth section was patterned on the Hitler Youth and was called the *Deutsche Jugend*. In January 1939 this was said to have a membership of 12,000 which, by April 1940, had (according to official sources) risen to 17,400 young persons (of both sexes) organized in three *Banne*.

The uniform of the DJ would appear to have been virtually the same as that of the HJ in the Reich except that the DJ emblem was shield shaped — red/white/red with a black swastika in the centre.

During the brief campaign against Poland in September 1939 some lads from the older section of the DJ actively assisted the armed forces. Later DJ boys were drafted to "toughening up" camps in Germany and ended up as "Volunteers" in the Waffen-SS.

Slovakia was run on authoritarian lines as a single party State by *Hlinková Slovenska L'Udová Strana* (Hlinka's Slovak Peoples Party). The name derived from Father Andrej Hlinka, a Catholic priest and champion of Slovak independence since the collapse of Austro-Hungarian rule in 1918. Hlinka died in August 1938 but the democratic slant, aping at first Italian, later German, fascism. It had its own "storm troopers", the black-uniformed Hlinka Guard and its own young persons organization, the Hlinka Youth *(Hlinková Mladez)*. This latter is described (in its official publication) as being "a voluntary organization for boys and girls of the Roman Catholic faith, of Aryan descent, in sound physical health and without a criminal record". The organization was sub-divided by age and sex in the following manner:

Emblem of the *Deutsche Jugend* in Slovakia.

Members of the Hitler Youth, DJ and BDM fraternize with boys of the Hlinka Youth.

    Vlcatá (Wolf Cubs): boys of six to ten years
    Orli (Eagles): boys of eleven to sixteen years
    Junći (Young fellows): boys of seventeen to twenty years
    Vily (Pixies): girls of six to ten years
    Tatranky (Tatrian Maidens): girls of eleven to fifteen years
    Devy (Maidens): Girls of sixteen to twenty years.

Boys wore a summer uniform similar to that of the Hitler Youth — brown shirt and black shorts, in winter they could add a brown double-breasted short tunic. Their headgear was the characteristic Czech (or Slovak) "pork pie" forage cap on which was worn a round badge featuring the Slovak eagle with the double barred cross of Saint Cyril and Saint Methodius (Patron Saints of the Slavs) on its chest and a fasces in its claws. (This badge sometimes features the letters HM = *Hlinková Mladez).* Girls wore a white shirt and black skirt. All ranks had as their principal emblem a red double-barred cross on a white circle outlined in blue (red/white/blue being the Slovak national colours). Boys wore this on the left upper arm, girls on the left side of their white blouse.

    The Hlinka Youth manual for the year 1943 makes reference to a "Dagger of Honour" and several youth medals, but does not, unfortunately, illustrate or describe any of these.

    In parts of Slovakia where only small DJ units existed, these sometimes paraded with the local Hlinka Youth or participated in joint sporting events (such as ski meetings).

Two members of the *Deutsche Jugend* of Slovakia. Note that the "district triangle" has place name only — Oberzips (Upper Zips or, in Czech, Spiš).

The stamp showing the emblem of the *Deutsche Jugend* in Slovakia is visible at the lower right of this photograph.

Record-book of a summer sports competition for the DJ held in Gilli/Römerbad on 25th to 27th June 1943. Cilli, now Celje and Römerbad, now Rimske Toplice are both in Central Slovenia (the German-seized areas of Slovenia reverted, of course, to Yugoslav sovereignty after Hitler's defeat in 1945).

Rumania

A *Verband der Deutschen in Rumänien* (Union of Germans in Rumania) had existed since 1921, but this was a cultural, rather than a political organization. The first manifestation of Nazi influence came in 1933 with the creation, by Fritz Fabritius, of a NSDR *(Nationale Selbsthilfebewegung der Deutschen in Rumänien,* National Self-Help Movement of the Germans in Rumania). The following year this was renamed the *National-Sozialistische Erneuerungsbewegung der Deutschen in Rumänien* (National-Socialist Renewal Movement of the Germans in Rumania). Its young persons branch was the *Deutsche Jugenbund in Rumänien* (DJR). This was open to males up to the age of twenty-one; there was a parallel female section known as the *Mädchenvolksdienst* (People Service for Girls) or MVD.

Fabritius was not highly regarded by his masters in Berlin, and in 1940 was replaced by Adreas Schmidt who enjoyed the not inconsiderable advantage of being the son-in-law of SS-*Brigadeführer* Gottlob Berger, head of the SS Main Office for Germans Abroad. On November 20 of that year the Rumanian government granted the Germans within its domain the status of a semi-independent "racial community". Their party was now rechristened the *NSDAP der deutschen Volksgruppe in Rumänien* (The Nazi Party of the German Racial Group in Rumania). The youthful DJR became simply the *Deutsche Jugend* (DJ).

A Hitler Youth boy from the Banat.

After the defeat of Yugoslavia in April 1941 the Yugoslav Banat was detached from the rest of the country. This multi-racial region with its mixture of Serbs, Germans and Rumanians posed something of a problem for Hitler. He had already promised it to both Hungary *and* Rumania. The question was now to which of these bitter rivals should be awarded. He resolved the dilemma in characteristic fashion by keeping it to himself. In June a German Vice-Governor was appointed. The former Jugoslav Banat was, in theory, linked to the Military Government of German occupied Servia. In practice the local *Volksdeutsche* in both the Yugoslav and the Rumanian Banat (the largest part of the Banat *is* in Rumania) ran the region in their own exclusive interests — an attitude which found approval and encouragement in Berlin.

The *Deutsche Jugend* was more-or-less an exact facsimile of the Hitler Youth. The Rumanian Nazis used the same "square" swastika as the Reich, not the mobil "sun wheel" of their Hungarian neighbours. The DJ was divided into the Regular (or Basic) Cadre *(Stamm DJ)* and the General or part-time Membership *(Allgemeine DJ)*. The 1943 *Jahrbuch* (Annual) of the Rumanian Nazis gives the following membership figures for the DJ:

```
Stamm DJ ........................................... 48,234
Allgemeine DJ (male) ................................ 17,268
Allegemeine DJ (female) ............................. 65,502
```

This, it claims, represented 90% of those eligible to join.

As in Germany, training was geared towards winning a *Leistungsabzeichen*, but the Rumanian Nazi "Achievement Badge" differs considerably from its Reich German counterpart. In place of the rune (runed T) is an upward pointing sword. The inscription around the centre piece is (in sham runic script) simply *Deutsche Jugend*. It is in three classes — "iron" (black), bronze and "silver." It could be worn on military as well as DJ dress. In September 1941 a "Hermann von Salza" Leadership School for the DJ was opened at Hermannstadt (now Sibiu), a town in Transylvania with a large German-speaking population. Would-be DJ officers had to undertake a three week course at this school. It turned out, in the first twelve months of its existence, 450 graduates (both sexes). The School also ran shorter "junior leader" *(Unterführer und Unterführerinnen)* courses for the equivalent of NCOs in the youth service. The demand for leaders was such that a second training establishment, the Prinz-Eugen-Schule, was opened the following year at Tememischburg (Timisoara).

Badge of the *Deutsche Jugendbund in Rumänien*.

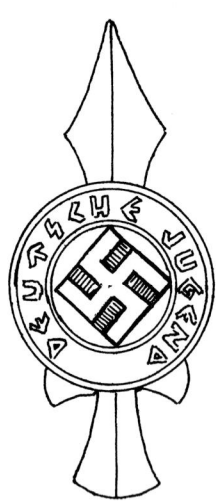

*Leistungsabzeichen* (Achievement Badge of DJ).

There was a Rumanian Nazi equivalent of the *Reichsberufswettkampf* (National Vocational Contest) known as the *bäuerlichen Berufswettkampf* (agricultural vocational contest) deemed by the RJF in Berlin to be more appropriate to the needs of the bucolic Rumanian *Volksdeutsche* than a technical examination.

Prior to the war DJR had not worn a specifically Nazi uniform, indeed it was more like the "civilian uniform" adopted by banned Nazi youth groups in Austria, Czechoslovakia and elsewhere, that is to say, a white shirt, neckerchief, black shorts, and white stockings. The only insignia was the letters DJR (possibly white on red) on an oval background on the left breast. After it became the Deutsche Jugend, Standard HJ garb would appear to have been adopted without modification.

## HUNGARY

After the First World War the Austro-Hungarian Empire collapsed. By the Treaty of Trianon (1920) Hungary lost three-fifths of its former territory and two-thirds of its former population. Thanks to Hitler, the Hungarians later regained much of their losses. Firstly, after the German occupation and dissolution of the state of Czechoslovakia, part of Slovenia and Ruthenia was granted to Hungary under a Nazi dictated settlement (which came to be known as "The First Vienna Awards"). A second "Vienna Award" (again Hitler ordained) in August 1940 removed north-eastern Transylvania from Rumanian Jurisdiction and gave it to Hungary. The defeat of Yugoslavia in April 1941 brought further acquisitions in the shape of the Backa and Baranja regions of northern Yugoslavia. The end result was that over half a million *Volksdeutsche* found themselves under Hungarian rule. Not all were necessarily pro-German, much less pro-Nazi. Some for complete Magyarization, others hoped to retain their German way of life while at the same time being loyal Hungarian citizens, but there were also those who saw themselves as expatriate Germans, physically outside the Reich but spiritually a part of it. Predictably it was this last category that the Nazis sought to encourage.

In November 1938 an Ethnic Union of Germans in Hungary (*Volksbund de deutschen in Ungarn*, or VDU) was formed by the pro-Nazi Franz Anton Basch who was granted the title of *Volksgruppenführer* (Racial Group Leader). Under strong German pressure the Hungarian government, in August 1940, accorded the *Volksdeutsche* the position of a largely selfgoverning community. The VDU consciously modelled itself on the NSDAP. In place of the "square" swastika of Hitler's Reich, the VDU adopted a mobile one, sometimes referred to as a "sun wheel" *(Sonnenrad)*. The VDU's equivalent of the German SA was the *Deutsche Mannschaft*, (DM) and of the Hitler Youth the *Deutsche Jugend* (DJ).

The DJ uniform was, at first, simply a junior version of the original DM garb, that is to say, white shirt, black trousers or shorts and black forage cap or, for officers, black breeches with top boots and grey tunic. Later, however, full HJ dress was adopted distinguished only by the fact that the "square" swastika of the Reich was replaced by a "mobile" one. The structural organization of the DJ paralleled almost exactly that of the HJ.

DJ (Deutsche Jugend): boys fourteen to eighteen years
D Jv (Deutsche Jungvolk): boys ten to fourteen years
DMB (Deutsche Mädelbund): girls fourteen to eighteen
JM (Jungmädelbund): girls ten to fourteen years.

As in the Reich, units were *Kameradschaft, Schar, Gefolgschaft Stamm* and, finally, *Bann*. There were seven *Banne* in all (including those in the newly acquired territories).

DJ cap and left breast pocket badge. Same dimensions as HJ equivalent.

DJ brassard. Similar to Hitler Youth brassard but with "mobile" swastika.

Until 1943 the DJ based its training on a programme designed to lead to an award of the HJ Achievement Badge (by this time about 300 of which had been won), but thereafter the DJ was allowed to award its own *Leistungsabzeichen*. This is virtually the same as that of the HJ except for the substitution of a "mobile" for a "square" swastika and the alteration of the wording to *Für Leistungen in der DJ* (instead of ... *in der HJ*).

The Hungarian Nazi counterpart of the NPEA of the Reich was the NSE (*National-Sozialistische Erziehungsheime*, National-Socialist training Homes) of which there were eight in various parts of Hungary.

## HUNGARIAN FASCIST YOUTH

In 1921, inspired by the Balilla youth movement of Mussolini's Italy, the Hungarians formed a nationalist youth organization known as the Levente (a name deriving from Prince Levente of Hungarian historical renown). This provided physical and paramilitary training on a compulsory basis for all fit young males between the ages of twelve and eighteen years. In 1941 compulsion was extended to females of the same age group. A year later the Levente movement was incorporated into the Hungarian armed forces. It was claimed that at this time, it had a membership of over 1,300,000.

There was occasional cooperation between the Levente lads and the DJ but mutual antagonism was, in practice, more common. This was especially so in the Backa and Banja districts where the local Germans gave the impression that they were trying to assume sole authority.

## YUGOSLAVIA

The Kingdom of Yugoslavia was created in December 1918 by the fusion of Serbia and Montenegro with the south Slav regions of the now defunct Austro-Hungarian Empire, that is to say, Slovinia, Croatia and Bosnia-Hercegovina. From the outset it was an unstable union. The Roman Catholic and Vienna-orientated Croats resented the dominance of the new state by the Greek orthodox "eastern" Serbs. Friction between the two made normal government virtually impossible — a situation not helped by Mussolini's encouragement of the rebellious Croats or the presence of a sizable German-speaking minority in the north of the country.

After Mussolini became embroiled in an unsuccessful (and unnecessary) invasion of Greece, Hitler had to step in to save his Axis partner from a humiliating defeat. This intervention involved a short "war" with Yugoslavia started (without the formality of a declaration) on April 6, 1941 and brought to a victorious conclusion little more than a week later.

Yugoslavia was then carved up by the victors in the following manner: Croatia (including Bosnia-Hercegovina and Dalmatia) was declared an "Independant State" with separate German and Italian "Zones of Influence" ("of occupation" in reality) Serbia was reduced to its pre-1912 size and placed under a German Military Governor. Slovenia was partitioned between the two Axis powers with Germany taking the

Civil lapel badges of the German *Volksgruppen* in (a) Carinthia (*Kärntner Volkbsund*) (b) Styria (*Steirischer Heimatbund*) and (c) Banat and Serbia (*Deutsche Volksgruppe im Banat u.i. Serbien*).

lion's share. Montenegro was decreed to be "independent" under Italian patronage (It was hoped an Italian Prince could be found to assume the throne — all declined the invitation). Bulgaria, which had played a less than minor part in the recent campaign, was granted most of South Serbia (Macedonia) while the northern "corner" of former Yugoslavia comprising the racially intermixed districts of Backa, Baranja and the Banat was parceled out between Germany, Hungary and Rumania. Conditions in the various territories were as follows:

An interesting DJ fanfare trumpet banner of Gebiet 30 of Steiermark (Styria).

(a) Croatia

There were some 150,000 racial Germans *(Volksdeutsche)* within the bounds of the newly established "Independent State of Croatia" — a small minority out of a total population of 6,300,000 but such was the power and prestige of the Reich, that the Germans of Croatia were granted the status of a *Voldsgruppe* and allowed to form what amounted to an autonomous state within the state. They at once set up a political organization which mirrored that of Hitler's Germany.

There had been a pro-Nazi movement among Yugoslavia's *Volksdeutsche* long before that country's defeat and occupation. A German *Kulturbund* had been in existence since 1920, its leadership passing into Nazi hands in the mid 1930s. The youth section of the *Kulturbund* was known as the *Erneuerer* (the Renewers or Rebuilders).

After the creation of a "free Croatia," the counterpart of the NSDAP among the *Volksgruppe* was the NSDGK (*Nat.-Soz deutsche Gefolgschaft in Kroatien* = the National-socialist German Community in Croatia). The youth section of which was a facsimile of the Hitler Youth with only minor alterations in the nomenclature to distinguish it. It was as follows:

Deutsche Jungvolk (DJV): boys of ten to fourteen years
Deutsche Jugend (DJ): boys of fourteen to eighteen years
Jungmädelbund (JMB): girls of ten to fourteen years
Deutsche Mädelbund (DMB): girls of fourteen to twenty-one years.

There were four *Banne* plus two independent *Stämme*, which were *Stamm Agram* (Zagreb) and *Stamm Mittelbosnien* (Central Bosnia). According to its *Jahrbuch* of 1943 the DJ had a membership of 15,000 which included special mounted, motorsport and gliding units. The *Jahrbuch* makes reference to a *JMB Leistungsabzeichen* (JMB Achievement Badge) and a *DMB Leistungsabzeichen*, but does not, unfortunately, illustrate either of these.

Pennant of a DMB *Mädelgruppe* in Zagreb. The use of the Serbo-Croat word is unusual, as the capital of Croatia is more usually referred to in Nazi documents by its German name — Agram.

Badge for "DMB Volunteer Girls' Action, Croatia." Given for harvest help.

Civil lapel badge of the German *Volksgruppe* in Croatia.

DJ emblem.

(b) Slovenia

In the German-Italian partition of Slovenia, Mussolini received an area south of the River Sava to which he gave the name Province of Ljubliana. Germany acquired Lower Styria *(Untersteiermark)* and Lower Carinthia *(Unterkärnten)* which had been part of Austria until the end of the First World War but which, due to their largely Slav populations, the victors of that war had accorded to the new state of Yugoslavia. Hitler set about reversing the racial balance. A process of "Germanization" was at once embarked upon. This culminated in October 1942 with the formal incorporation into Greater Germany of the two regions as parts of, respectively, *Reichsgau Steiermark* and *Reichsgau Kärnten*.

Prior to this enforced take-over, the *Volksdeutsche* of Lower Styria had been organized as a *Steierischer Heimatbund* with, as its youthful offshoot, a *Deutsche Jugend*. The equivalent in Lower Carinthia was, for adults, the *Kärnter Volksbund* and, for young persons, the *Kärntner Volksbund Jugend*. After the absorption of two regions into the Reich, their respective youth movements were renamed *Hitler-Jugend Anwärter Einheiten* (Hitler Youth Preparatory Units) rather than simply *Hitler-Jugend*, a modification possibly intended to indicate that boys of Slav origin might later be refused acceptance as full HJ members. However, *all* boys, between the ages of fourteen and nineteen were subject to obligatory service in its ranks.

Little information on the uniforms of the *Deutsche Jugend* in Lower Styria is available, although it would appear that they shared with the *Deutsche Jugend* of Slovakia the red/white/red shield shaped emblem with black swastika. The evidence for this is the document shown below.

(c) Serbia-Montenegro

Since either Serbia nor Montenegro had ever been part of the Austro-Hungarian Empire there were few German communities in the former and none in the latter. The small *Volksdeutsche* minority in Serbia had belonged to the *Kulturbund* but their numbers were insufficient for them to lay claim to the status of a *Volksgruppe* unlike their compatriots in Croatia. When Partisan resistance began to pose a threat to isolated communities, Himmler ordered the removal of German families to the greater safety of Croatia.

# 34

## Other Countries

The *Auslands Organisation* table of membership of June 1937 lists Brazil as having the largest number of expatriate German citizens (75,000) of whom 2,903 were registered as NSDAP adherents. Oddly, the USA comes bottom of the league with only 569 registered Nazi supporters (among the Reich-German citizens living there at this time). Argentina is given as having 1,500 Nazi Party members (out of 42,000 Germans resident there), South Africa 1,127 and Tanganyika 688 (out of its 2,140 Germans). These figures do not include racial Germans with foreign citizenship except where these enjoyed dual nationality.

The Hitler Youth had, under a variety of names, groups in a large number of countries including parts of the British Empire, e.g. South Africa and Australia. Generally speaking standard HJ uniform was worn but without the swastika. In place of the brassard a *Sigrune* was often worn on a circular background the colour of which (and the piping on the shoulder straps) indicated the continent in the following manner:

Red: Europe
Yellow: America
Green: Asia
Blue: Africa
White: Australia.

District triangles were worn with the name of the country (e.g. USA) or place (e.g. Kap Stadt — Cape Town) or both (e.g. China Schanghai). Children of Reich-German citizens resident abroad wore as their District triangle the words *Reichsdeutsche Jugend Ausland* (Reich-German Youth abroad).

The largest concourse of extra-Reich Hitler Youths took place in 1935 at Kuhlmühle in Brandenburg when some one and a half thousand young people, many of whom had never seen Germany before, took part in the so-called *Deutschlandslager* (German Camp). Later they were bussed around the Reich in a sort of mutual propaganda exercise. During the years that followed and until the outbreak of war in September 1939 visits to racial communities outside the Reich were financed by the HJ *Auslandsamt* which encouraged young Germans not merely to visit, tourist-fashion, their expatriate brethren, but also to live and work for extended periods in their midst — resident apostles of the Nazi creed.

International alarm at the increasing aggressiveness of the Nazis both at home and abroad resulted in the banning of their organizations in several countries. South-West Africa (a former German colony) led the way by outlawing the NSDAP in 1934. In February 1937, under strong pressure from the USA, Brazil prohibited Nazi activities. Chile did the same in September 1938. Japan, on the other hand, gave *Landesgruppenleiter* Rudolf Hillmann a free hand in building up HJ cells in German language schools in Tokyo and Yokohama unaware perhaps that the resident Nazis were secretly advising their young not to mingle with the "racially inferior" Japanese.

The advent of war closed some avenues of propaganda but opened others. Military victories brought large areas of Europe under Nazi control with resultant new contacts and converts. Those in Western Europe have already been dealt with, but the East also offered its harvest if on a rather more modest scale.

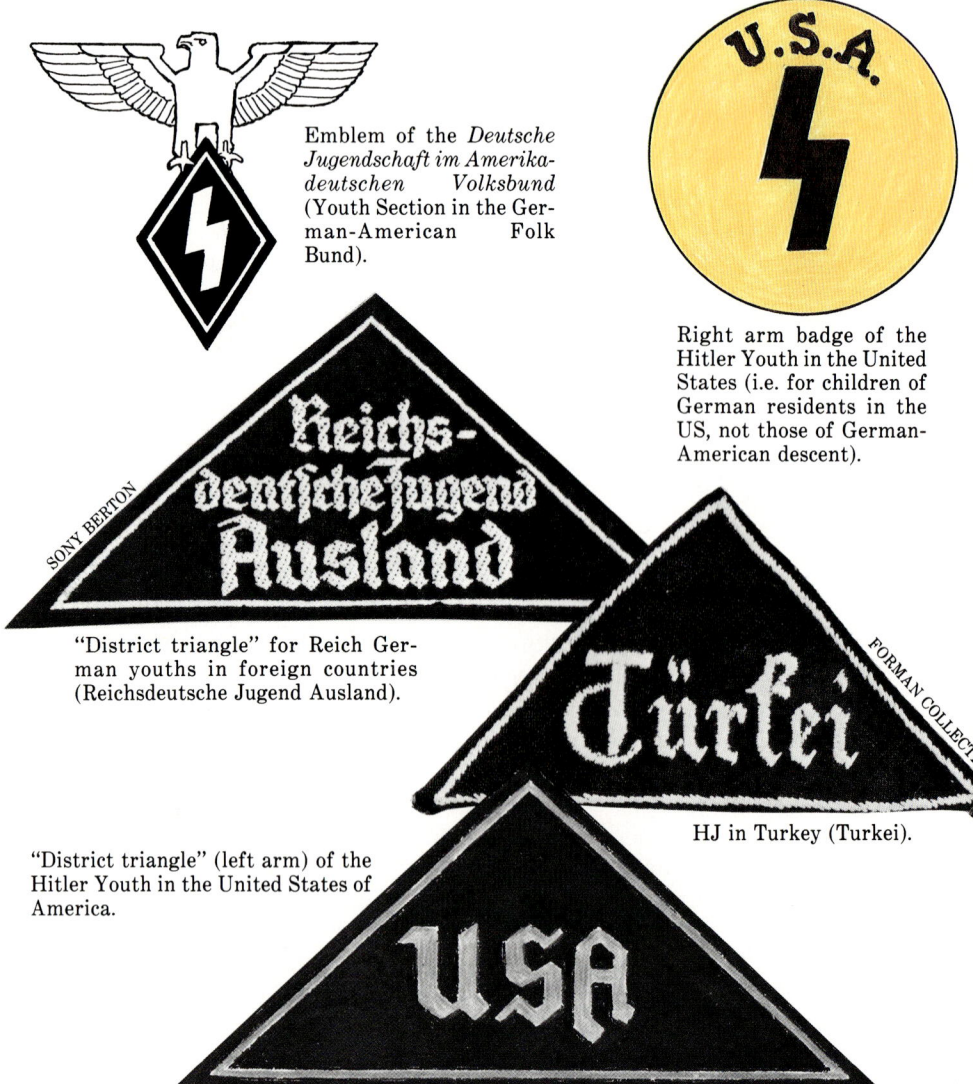

Emblem of the *Deutsche Jugendschaft im Amerikadeutschen Volksbund* (Youth Section in the German-American Folk Bund).

Right arm badge of the Hitler Youth in the United States (i.e. for children of German residents in the US, not those of German-American descent).

"District triangle" for Reich German youths in foreign countries (Reichsdeutsche Jugend Ausland).

HJ in Turkey (Türkei).

"District triangle" (left arm) of the Hitler Youth in the United States of America.

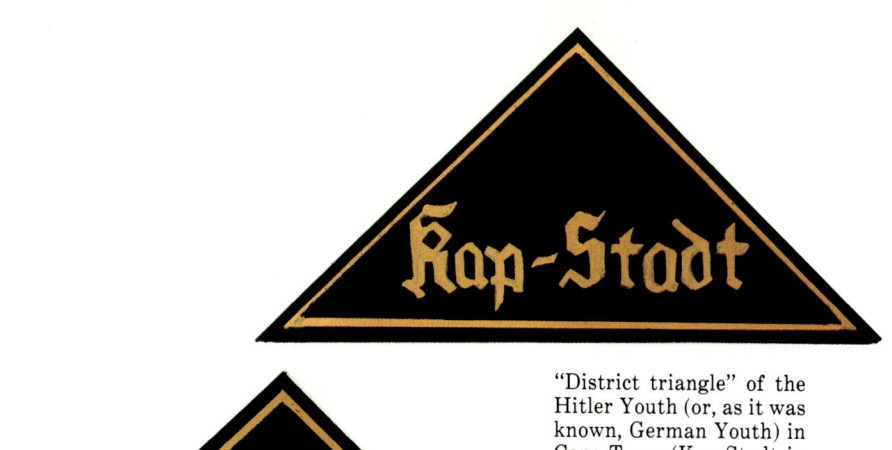

"District triangle" of the Hitler Youth (or, as it was known, German Youth) in Cape Town (Kap Stadt in German).

"District triangle" for Hitler Youth units in Schanghai, China.

Emblem of the Deutsche Jugend Südafrikas (German Youth of South Africa).

Shoulder strap (pre-1938) of HJ units in Japan.

Device of the Nazi youth in S.W. Africa. It appears on their flag and as an arm badge (S.W. Africa is now known as Namibia).

German and overseas leaders at summer camp. The two hatted youths (centre) are from German S.W. Africa. Note the very unusual brassard with map of "Afrika" in place of swastika, and also *Sigrune* belt buckle.

Boys from the former German South-West African colony attend an HJ camp in Germany in the mid '30s. On the side of their bush hats they wear a red/white/black rosette (as did the former German colonial troops). Rest of uniform, including pack, like HJ.

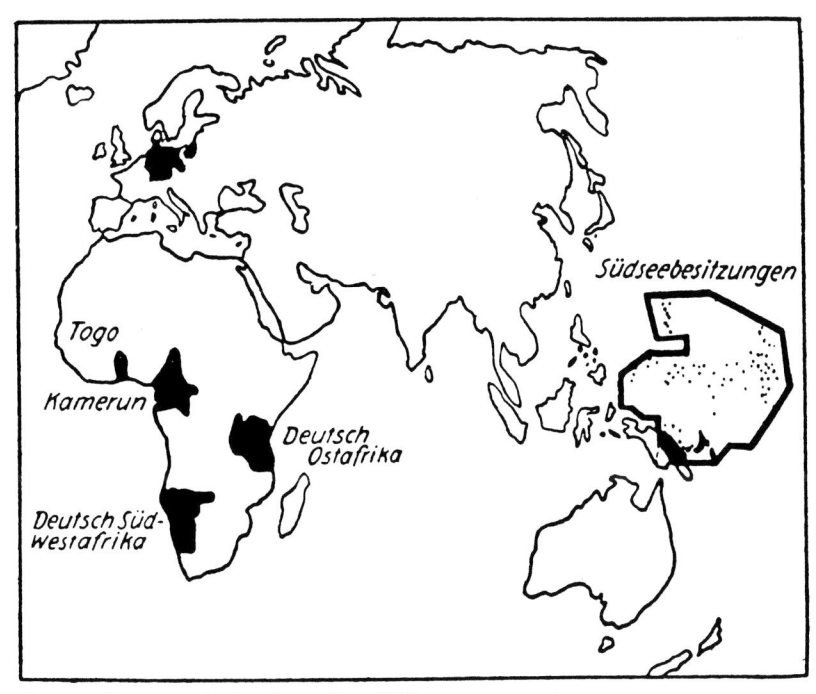

Former German colonies (lost after 1918).

[Below:] Senior LJO officer. He wears a Hitler Youth tunic and cap but a Luftwaffe belt buckle. Above his right breast pocket is *STABS* (Staff).
[Right:] Cap badge set as worn in photo. Traditional Latvian three stars and sun burst emblem over LJO enamel rhombus. This same badge also worn on left breast pocket.

Badge of the Estonian Youth.     Badge of the White Russian Youth.     Badge of the Brannik Youth.

Latvian Landdienst boys as part of a ski troop. Uniforms are standard HJ winter dress. "Bar" above right breast pocket has the name of the area of origin (the Latvian equivalent of the HJ "District triangle").

    The Danzig *Staatsjugend* (the Free City's equivalent of the HJ first formed in November 1937) was absorbed into the Hitler Youth with the re-incorporation of the Danzig region into the Reich in September 1939. *Volksdeutsche* pro-Nazi groups in the Baltic states had to wait until the summer of 1941 before Hitler's invasion of the Soviet Union brought them too within the German orbit. Latvia had a *Deutsche Jungen- und Mädchen-Bund,* Estonia a *Deutschbaltisches Pfadfinderkorps* (Baltic-German Scout Corps) which, unequal, wore a green, instead of a khaki, shirt and had, as its emblem, the "wolf hook."

    But the non-German youth of the Baltic states also attracted the interest of the HJ Leadership. Although Lithuania had to be written off

367

as being too far corrupted by Slav influence, Latvia and Estonia were held to be susceptible to future "germanization."

## LATVIA

Under German occupation Latvia formed part of the *Reichskommissariat Ostland* (under *Gauleiter* Heinrich Lohse) and had a civilian administration presided over by *Generalkommissar* Dr. Dreschsler. Youth movements (including a Latvian branch of the Boy Scouts) had flourished before the war, but most of their leaders had been deported, in many cases, killed by the Russians during the course of the brief but bloody Soviet occupation (June 1940 to June 1941). The Germans toyed with the idea of forming a "national" Latvian youth movement on the lines of the Hitler Youth, but due to Latvian unreceptiveness to the concept, it was not actually brought into being until April 1943. In that month the creation of a Latvian Youth Organization *(Latvju Jaunatnes Organizacifa* or LJO) was announced in the Latvian press and radio. Theoretically it was voluntary but in some instances headmasters simply enrolled their school membership without consulting either the pupils or their parents' wishes. By the end of the year (1943) the LJO claimed a membership of between six and seven thousand. In addition to having to fight off pressure from the German authorities the LJO leaders had also to resist attempts by native fascists (members of the prewar "Thunder Cross" association) to infiltrate its ranks. The LJO Chief, Erks Rulis, was faced by increasing German demands that the organization be used in a paramilitary capacity. By July 1944 all pretence of "consultation" between the German civil administration and the LJO leadership was abandoned and conscription was applied to all Latvian youths — girls now as well as boys. After the introduction of conscription the two main areas into which the Latvian youngsters were directed were the Germanic Landdienst and the Luftwaffe Flak Helper scheme.

It was perhaps unfortunate from the Latvian point-of-view that their national flag should be horizontal red/white/red the same as that of the Hitler Youth (although the Latvian red is of a much darker shade) or that the national emblem of Latvia is a swastika. It would seem that the Germans deliberately tried to cash in on this unfortunate similarity. The LJO badge was a rhombus, or diamond, like that of the Hitler Youth with a red swastika in the centre on a white saltire. From the start the Hitler Youth had a direct hand in the control of the LJO and supplied many of its uniforms and accessories. (The controlling body was HJ *Gebiet Ostland).* The Latvians did, however, succeed in getting one purely Latvian patriotic emblem incorporated in LJO dress. This was a sun burst and three stars which was used as the upper part of the cap badge (for officers) and as the centre piece of the red/white/red brassard — this last in defiance of German wishes that the centre piece should be the red swastika on a rhombus (like the cap badge) thus forcing an even stronger resemblance to the HJ arm band. But despite this being illustrated as both the LJO and Flak Helper some official German publications, it was not worn either by the LJO or the Latvian Flak Helpers.

In summer the LJO lads wore a grey shirt and shorts with a uniquely Latvian form of cravat known as a *Prievite* (traditionally red and white but of individual design). On the left upper arm they had a white cloth rhombus sewn to the shirt. This featured, in full colour, the sun burst and three stars emblem. Their winter garb was the standard dark blue ski outfit of the Hitler Youth. LJO officers wore HJ officer uniform with the LJO brassard as described above. The headgear was an HJ leaders peaked cap. Rank was indicated on the shoulder straps by scheme of stars and bars which bore no relationship to that of the Hitler Youth. All ranks wore the metal rhombus badge in coloured enamel on the left breast pocket. Belts and belt buckles were supplied by the HJ.

The willingness of the LJO and other Latvian organizations to work with the Germans was governed very much by the degree of proximity of the Red Army to the frontiers of the Homeland. As this menace approached so did the readiness of the Latvians to fall in with German wishes.

## ESTONIA

As in neighboring Latvia a uniformed national youth movement, the *Eesti Noored* (Estonian Youth, or EN) was set up, under the aegis of *HJ Gebiet Ostland* in the spring of 1943. At its head was an ex-regular Estonian army officer, Lt. Gustav Kalkan, who was also an Olympic sportsman — at one stage in his career he had been a ski instructor to Prince Philip of Greece (now Duke of Edinburgh). Until August 1944 membership was voluntary but thereafter conscription was applied. It was the Luftwaffe, not the HJ, that supplied the EN's grey-blue uniform. It had not originally been envisaged as a paramilitary corps, but was increasingly forced into this role by the circumstances of the war. The boys were often pressed into service as air-raid wardens, fire fighters or Home Guard *(Selbstschutz)* auxiliaries.

The EN was also employed on agricultural work although the *Landdienst* concept, as such, was never extended to Estonia. As the Red Army closed in on the Baltic states the EN was taken over in its entirety by the Luftwaffe as Flak Helpers.

The EN emblem, worn on the left breast pocket, was an enamelled metal rhombus featuring a sword and an ear of barley with, across the centre, a ribbon, or scroll, in the Estonian national colours — blue/black/white. When the EN boys were transformed into Flak helpers they wore this badge (in a cloth version) as the centre piece of their brassard (which was also in the blue/black/white national colours). Some former members of EN serving in the Waffen SS continued to wear (unofficially) their EN enamel badge on the left breast pocket of their uniform. The EN Flak helpers were assured that they would be used only in the defense of their homeland, but this promise was not honoured. When the Red Army overran Estonia the EN Flak helpers were evacuated to Germany, some ending up in Flak units in occupied Denmark.

## WHITE RUSSIA

The most westerly region of Russia, adjoining Poland and the Ukraine, is known by a variety of names — Belorussia, Ruthenia, White Ruthenia or White Russia. Being the furthest west, it was the first part of the Soviet Union to be occupied by the Germans and the last to be liberated. Its people were encouraged by the German authorities to think of themselves as being a different breed from the Russians and a moderate degree of nationalism was fostered. Some limited autonomy was permitted within, of course, an overall framework of German rule. A German *Generalkommissar* was the supreme authority but he was "assisted" by a Belorussian Advisory Council or *Rada,* which was later upgraded to a Central Council under a native "President." Until April 1944 Belorussia formed part of the *Ostland* administration along with the three Baltic states, but thereafter it was declared to be a separate entity directly subordinate to Berlin.

Two officers of the White Russian Youth (WJW). The armband is white/red/white and is as illustrated in the section on the foreign Flak helpers.

Belorussia had its own internal defense forces (against indigenous Partisans) and its own youth movement. This latter was officially inaugurated on June 20, 1943 at the Municipal Theatre in Minsk (the Belorussian "state capital"). It was known in German as the *Weissruthenische Jugendwerk* (White Ruthenian Youth Work) or WJW, but in Russian as the Union of Belorussian Youth (*Sayuz Belaruskay Moladzi,* SBM). Membership was open to boys between the ages of fourteen and nineteen and was voluntary. By the end of 1943 it had, according to its official records, 40,000 members. Leaders — ironically many of them were former *Komsomol* (Communist Youth) officials — were trained at HJ establishments in the Reich, but the main preoccupation of the WJW seems to have been practical rather than political. About 300 of the technically more adept WJW lads were appropriated by the Luftwaffe for work in its repair shops at Minsk. They were provided with blue-grey Luftwaffe "battle dress" with a brassard in the Belorussian colours —

white/red/white. In the center of this was a cloth version of the WJW emblem. The Luftwaffe seems to have been impressed by the aptitude of the boys since a further 4,500 WJW lads were selected for apprenticeships in the aircraft industry and spirited off to Germany. Others, less technically minded perhaps, were taken into the Todt Organization.

With the creation, by the joint efforts of the Hitler Youth, SS and the Luftwaffe, of the eastern European Flak Helpers, *HJ Kriegseinsatzkommando Mitte* recruited 2,354 Belorussian lads for the air defenses of the Reich. Their uniform was the same as the provided by the Luftwaffe repair workshops at Minsk.

## OTHER PARTS OF THE EAST

Recruitment by the Germans of young people in the occupied east was made easier by the fact that the war had left many fatherless. So many, indeed, that special young people's camps had to be set up to cater for the needs of what the Germans termed "the vagabond youth" of eastern Europe. *HJ Kriegseinsatzkommando Süd*, with headquarters in L'vov, recruited young people from both east and west Ukraine (the latter region being, referred to as Galicia). In Muscovite Russia the HJ attempted in May 1944 to launch a *Grossrussische Jugendwerk* (Greater Russian Youth work) which, it was claimed, succeeded in recruiting between 2,000 and 3,000 young persons. It had its own uniform and flags (details of which are, unfortunately, not available). With the Red Army's re-conquest of most of its Homeland not long after the belated creation of this "nationalist" youth movement, most of its male members doubtless found themselves drafted into the Luftwaffe as "volunteer" Flak helpers.

The Hitler Youth even tried its hand at raising a Volga Tartar youth movement (also in 1944), but as their principal concern at this late stage of the war was the procurement of paramilitary auxiliaries, the Volga Tartar youth may have been little more than a recruitment agency for the Luftwaffe or SS.

## BULGARIA

Probably the least willing of germany's "allies," Bulgaria was officially at war only with Great Britain and the United States. Pro-Russian sentiment ruled out any declaration of hostilities against the Soviet Union.

Bulgaria, like other countries had, before the war, a number of political parties based more-or-less exactly on Hitler's Nazis or Mussolini's Fascisti. A Bulgarian National-Socialist Workers' Party (NSBAP) was formed in 1932 but banned in 1934 under a government order. The Italian-orientated NZF (National Union of Fascists) was also proscribed at the same time.

But for youngsters with a taste for military style organizations the government set up a uniformed state youth known as the Brannik Youth open to all physically fit young people (of both sexes) between the ages of ten and seventeen years. Its principal emblem was a cyrillic B on a shield.

Hitler Youth boy with members of Brannik Youth. Note lion cap badges. The boy (right) has the Brannik *B* badge.

The lion rampant of Bulgaria was worn on the front of its forage cap. The boys had a brown uniform (tunic and trousers), the girls wore what would appear (from photographs) to have been a black (or dark blue) skirt with a white blouse on the left side of which was the B-in-a-shield emblem. Boys wore this emblem on the left upper arm of their tunics, or in summer when shirt-sleeves was the order of dress, similarly on the left side of the shirt.

The Hitler Youth supplied the Brannik Youth with camping knives which were simply the standard HJ *Fahrtenmesser* with the Brannik emblem on the hilt and the blade inscribed (in Bulgarian Cyrillic) "Duty and Honour."

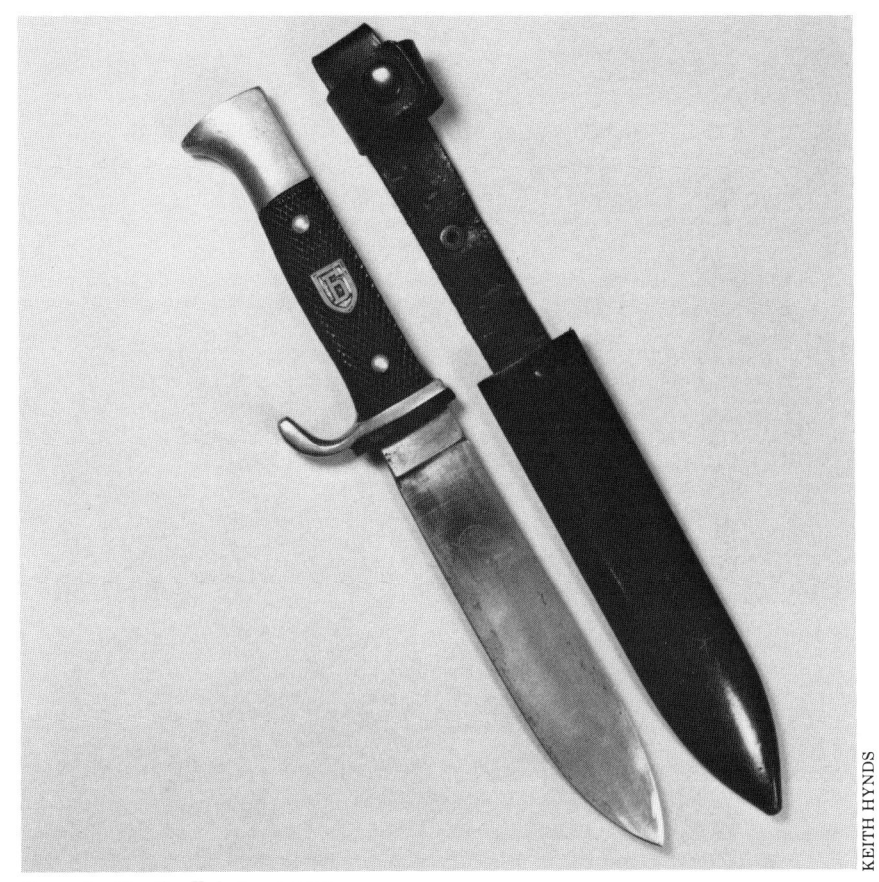

Brannik Youth *Fahrtenmesser*.

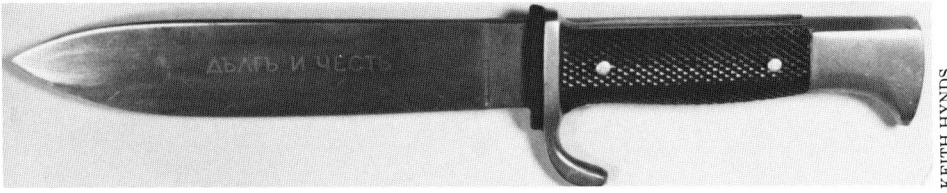

Reverse of a Brannik Youth *Fahrtenmesser*, showing the inscription on the blade.

A "foreign" branch of the Brannik Youth was formed among Bulgarian students at German universities. They wore black shoulder straps with green piping.

The Hitler Youth paid courtesy (or propaganda) visits to its counterparts in Bulgaria and leaders of the Brannik Youth were prominent among the dignitaries at the "Rally of European Youth" at Vienna in September 1942.

When the Red Army reached the Bulgarian frontier in August 1944 the Bulgarian government announced that it had "withdrawn from the war." On September 5th it declared its neutrality. But neutrality was not good enough for the Soviets who forced the Bulgarians to declare war on their erstwhile ally. Bulgarian refugees in Germany including many of the Brannik students were corralled by Himmler into a Bulgarian SS "Division" (actually the Germans could master only one small anti-tank regiment. Its contribution to the war effort is unrecorded). Some young Bulgarians may also have ended up, like so many others, as Flak helpers.

Flag of a DJ *Jungbann* in Guatemala.

# Bibliography

Ager, VerKuilen. "Reichssieger Badge Type 1: 1937-38." An article in *The Medal Collector, Vol. 32* (November 1981).
Angolia, John R. *Belt Buckles and Brocades of the Third Reich.* San Jose (California): R. James Bender, 1982.
──────────. *Edged Weaponry of the Third Reich.* San Jose (California): R. James Bender, 1974.
*Auerbachs Deutscher Kinderkalendar für 1935.* Leipzig: Fernau, 1934.
*Aufbau und Abzeichen der Hitler-Jugend.* Berlin: Deutsche Zentraldruckerei, 1940.
Bartelmas, Eugen Frieder. *Das junge Reich: Vom Leben und Wollen der neuen deutschen Jugend.* Stuttgart: Union deutsche Vorlagsgellschaft, 1935.
Beier-Lindhardt, Erich. *Ein Buch von Führer für die deutsche Jugend.* Oldenburg: Gerhard Stalling A.G., 1933.
*Bekleidung und Ausrüstung der Hitler-Jugend.* Berlin: RJF, 1934.
Bender, R. James, and Taylor, Hugh Page. *Uniforms, Organization and History of the Waffen-SS, Vol. 3.* San Jose (California): R. James Bender, 1972.
*Bild-Dokumente unsere Zeit. Mappe 2: Deutsche Jugend.* Dresden: Verlag Zigarettenfabrik Kosmos, 1934.
Bleuel, Hans Peter. *Strength through Joy.* London: Secker & Warburg, 1973.
Blohm, Erich. *Hitler-Jugend: soziale Tatgemeinschaft.* Witten: Naturpolitischer Verlag, 1977.
Boberach, Heinz. *Jugend unter Hitler.* Düsseldorf: Droste Verlag, 1982.
Brandenburg, Hans-Christian. *Die Geschichte der Hitler Jugend.* Köln: Verlag Wissenchaft und Politik, 1968.
Brennecke, Fritz. *Vom deutschen Volk und seinem lebensraum.* Munich: Zentralverlag der NSDAP, 1973.
──────────. *Vom deutschen Volk und seinem Lebensraum.* Pall Mall Press, 1967.
Cone, J. R. *One People, One Reich: Enameled Organizational Badges of Germany, 1918-1945.* Tulsa: MCN Press, 1982.
Davis, Brian Leigh. *Badges and Insignia of the Third Reich, 1933-1945.* Poole (Dorset): Blandford Press, 1983.
*Dienstvorschrift der Hitler-Jugend: Vorschrift über den Jungvolkdienst.* Berlin: RJF, 1938.
Grill, Johnpeter Horst. *The Nazi movement in Baden, 1920-1945.* Chapel Hill: University of North Carolina Press, 1983.
Halls, W. D. *The Youth of Vichy France.* Oxford: Clarendon Press, 1981.
Heering, Werner, and Hüsken, André. *Handbuch der Abzeichen deutscher Organisation, 1871-1945.* Hamburg: Werner Heering, 1984.
"Hilf mit!" *Illustriete deutsche Schülerzeitung:* Various issues between May 1934 and September 1940 (published by *NS-Lehrerbund*).
Hitler, Adolf. ed. Norman H. Baynes. *Speeches of Adolf Hitler, April 1922 to August 1939.* London: Oxford U.P., 1942.
*H.J. im Dienst: Ausbildungsvorschrift für die Ertüchtigung der deutschen Jugend.* Berlin: Verlag Bernard & Graefe, 1935.
Horn, Daniel. *Coercion and Compulsion in the Hitler Youth, 1933-1945:* An article in "The Historian" Vol. XLI No. 4 (August 1979).
──────────. *The National Socialist Schülerbund and the Hitler Youth, 1929-1933;* an article in "Central European History," Vol. I, No. 4 (December 1978).
Hüsken, André. *Dokumente deutscher Geschichte, 1933-1945.* Hamburg: Hüsken, 1985.
*Jahrbuch der deutschen Volksgruppe in Kroatien, 1943.*
*Jahrbuch der deutschen Volksgruppe in Rumanien, 1943.*
*Der Jungmädeldienst: Dienstvorschrift der Hitler-Jugend.* Berlin: RJF, 1938.

*Der Jungvolkdienst: Dienstvorschrift der Hitler-Jugend.* Berlin: RJF, 1940.
Kamenetsky, Christa. *Children's Literature in Hitler's Germany.* Athens (Ohio): Ohio U.P., 1984.
Kater, Michael H. *The Nazi Party: A Social Profile of Members and Leaders, 1919-1945.* London: Blackwell, 1983.
Kaufmann, Gunter. *Das kommende Deutschland: Erziehung der Jugend in Reich Adolf Hitlers.* Berlin: Junker & Dünnhaupt Verlag, 1940.
Klaus, Martin. *Mädchen in Dritten Reich: der Bund deutscher Mädel.* Köln: Pahl-Rugenstein Verlag, 1983.
Klose, Werner. *Generation im Gleichschritt.* Oldenburg: Gerhard Stalling Verlag, 1964.
Knötel, Herbert. *Die Uniforms der HJ.* Hamburg: Diepenbroick-Gräter & Schulz, 1933 (1934).
Koch, Hannsjoachim. *Hitler Youth: Origins and Development.* London: Macdonald & Janes, 1975.
Komjathy, Anthony, and Stockwell, Rebecca. *German Minorities and the Third Reich: Ethnic Germans of East Central Europe Between the wars.* London: Holmes & Meier, 1980.
Laqueur, Walter Z. *Young Germany: A History of the German Youth Movement.* London: Routledge & K. Paul, 1962.
McKale, Donald M. *The Swastika Outside Germany.* Kent State University Press, 1977.
McKee, Ilse. *Tomorrow the World.* London: Dent, 1960.
*Marine-Hitler-Jugend im Dienst: Lehrbuch für die M.H.J.* Berlin: Verlag E. S. Mittler, n.d.
Maschmann, Melita. *Account Rendered: Dossier on My Former Self.* London: Abelard-Schumann, 1964.
Mau, Ilse, and Oberstadt, Albert. *Fahrt: Erlebnisberichte deutscher Jungen und Mädel.* Berlin: Limpert Verlag, 1938.
*Mein Dienst: Merkbuch der Hitler-Jugend 1938/39.* Dortmund: Westfälische Landeszeitung, 1938.
*Der Merker: Jugendjahrbuch des V.D.U. 1941.* Berlin: Verlag des V.D.U., 1940.
Meyer, Hubert. *Kriegsgeschichte der 12. SS Panzerdivision "Hitlerjugend."* Osnabrück: Munin-Verlag, 1982.
Mollo, Andrew. *Daggers of the Third Reich, 1933-1945.* London: Historical Research Unit, 1967.
*Nazi Youth in the Weimar Republic.* Oxford: Clio Books, 1977.
*Organisationsbuch der NSDAP.* Munich: Zentralverlag der NSDAP (editions of 1937 and 1943).
Orlow, Dietrich. "Die Adolf-Hitler-Schulen." An article in *Vierteljahrshefte für Zeitgeschichte,* Heft 3, 1965.
Paikert, G. C. *The Danube Swabians.* The Hague: Nijhoff, 1976.
Pauley, Bruce F. *Hitler and the Forgotten Nazis.* London: Macmillan, 1981.
*Die Reichsparteitage der NSDAP, 1923-1939.* Landsberg a. Lech: Druffel-Verlag, 1981.
Reider, Frederic. *Order of the SS.* London: Foulsham, 1981.
Ringler, Ralf Roland. *Illusion einer Jugend.* St. Polten-Wien: Verlag Niederösterreichisches Presshaus, 1977.
Sautter, Reinhold. *Hitler Jugend: das Erlebnis einer großen Kameradschaft.* Munich: Carl Röhrig-Verlag, 1942.
Schätz, Ludwig. *Schüler-Soldaten: die Geschichte der Luftwaffenhelfer im zweiten Weltkrieg.* Dramstadt: Thesen Verlag, 1974.
Schmidt, Adolf. *Jugend in Reich.* Berlin: Junge Generation Verlag, 1943.
Schneider, E. A., and Seybold, Heiner. *Jugend und Heimat: ein Bildbuch der Hitlerjugend.* Munich: Vereinigte Kunstanstalten, 1938.
Seybold, Heiner. *Unser Hochlandlager.* Kaufbeuren (Bavaria): Gebiet 19 Hochland, 1936.
*The Shaping of the Nazi State.* London: Croom Helm, 1978.
Shirer, William L. *The Rise and Fall of the Third Reich.* London: Secker & Warburg, 1960.
Stachura, Peter D. *The German Youth Movement, 1900-1945.* London: Macmillan, 1981.
Steinberg, Michael Stephen. *Sabers and Brown Shirts: The German Students Path to National Socialism, 1918-1935.* Chicago: University of Chicago Press, 1977.

Stephens, Frederick J. *Hitler Youth: History, Organisation, Uniforms and Insignia.* London: Almark Publishing, 1973.

Stephenson, Jill. *The Nazi Organisation of Women.* London: Croom Helm, 1981.

*Trial of the Major War Criminals. . . . Nuremberg, 14th Nov. 1945 — 1st Oct. 1946 Vol. XIV (Case of Von Schirach).* Nuremberg: International Military Tribunal, 1948.

Ueberhorst, Horst. *Elite für die Diktatur: Die Nationalpolitischen Erziehungsanstalten, 1933-1945.* Düsseldorf: Dorste Verlag, 1969.

*Verordnungsblatt der Reichsjugendführung Aug. 1933 — Dec. 1941.*

Vincx, Jan. *Vlaanderen in Uniform, 1940-1945 Vol. 3.* Antwerp: Etnika VZW, 1982.

Weber, R. G. S. *German Student Corps in the Third Reich.* London: Macmillan, 1986.

Welch, David, ed. *Nazi Propaganda: The Power and the Limitations.* London: Croom Helm, 1983.

Wistrich, Robert. *Who's Who in Nazi Germany.* London: Weidenfeld & Nicholson, 1982.

Wykes, Alan. *The Nuremburg Rallies.* London: Macdonald, 1969.

Ziemer, Gregor. *Education for Death.* London: Constable, 1942.

Zoglmann, Siegfried. *Jugend erlebt Deutschland.* Berlin: Verlag für soziale Ethnik und Kunstpflege, 1936.